Human Rights and the Ethics of Globalization

Human Rights and the Ethics of Globalization provides a balanced, thoughtful discussion of the globalization of the economy and the ethical considerations inherent in the many changes it has prompted. The book's introduction maps out the philosophical foundations for constructing an ethic of globalization, taking into account both traditional and contemporary sources. These ideals are applied to four specific test cases: the ethics of investing in China, the case study of the Firestone company's presence in Liberia, free trade and fair trade issues pertaining to the coffee trade with Ethiopia, and the use of low-wage factories in Mexico to serve the U.S. market. The book concludes with a comprehensive discussion of how to enforce global compliance with basic human rights standards, with particular attention to prospects for stopping abuses by multinational corporations through litigation under the Alien Tort Claims Act.

Daniel E. Lee is professor of ethics and director of the Center for the Study of Ethics at Augustana College, Rock Island, Illinois. He is the author of numerous articles and books, including *Hope Is Where We Least Expect to Find It* (1993), *Generations and the Challenge of Justice* (1996), *Navigating Right and Wrong* (2002), and *Freedom vs. Intervention* (2005). He has also published op-ed pieces in *USA Today*, the *Chicago Tribune*, and other newspapers and is a published poet and author of fiction.

Elizabeth J. Lee received her J.D. from Northwestern University School of Law, where she served as a clerk at the Center for International Human Rights. After graduating from law school, she served as a judicial law clerk for Arizona Supreme Court Justice Michael D. Ryan and as Assistant Public Defender in Houston, Texas, prior to accepting her current position as Assistant Public Defender in Tucson, Arizona. Her publications include an article in the *Global Studies Journal*.

Human Rights and the Ethics of Globalization

DANIEL E. LEE
Augustana College

ELIZABETH J. LEE
Assistant Federal Public Defender, Tucson, Arizona

CAMBRIDGE
UNIVERSITY PRESS

CAMBRIDGE UNIVERSITY PRESS
Cambridge, New York, Melbourne, Madrid, Cape Town, Singapore,
São Paulo, Delhi, Dubai, Tokyo, Mexico City

Cambridge University Press
32 Avenue of the Americas, New York, NY 10013-2473, USA

www.cambridge.org
Information on this title: www.cambridge.org/9780521147996

First published 2010

Printed in the United States of America

A catalog record for this publication is available from the British Library.

Library of Congress Cataloging in Publication data
Lee, Daniel E.
  Human rights and the ethics of globalization / Daniel E. Lee, Elizabeth J. Lee.
    p. cm.
  Includes bibliographical references and index.
  ISBN 978-0-521-51933-5 (hardback)
  1. Human rights. 2. Globalization – Moral and ethical aspects.
  I. Lee, Elizabeth J., 1982– II. Title.
  JC571.L373   2010
  323–dc22   2010006572

ISBN 978-0-521-51933-5 Hardback
ISBN 978-0-521-14799-6 Paperback

Contents

Preface

In days that are now part of a distant past, work was a multigenerational experience. Younger generations grew up working with their parents – and sometimes with their grandparents as well – on family farms, in "mom and pop" grocery stores, in family restaurants, and in many other endeavors. Today, that is increasingly rare. We are diminished by these missing threads in our social experiences.

Hoping to regain some of these missing threads, the two of us – a father and a daughter – began exploring the possibility of collaborating on a book addressing issues of mutual interest pertaining to human rights and the ethics of globalization. The result is this volume. We each had particular areas of expertise to contribute to this joint enterprise – one of us from years of experience teaching business ethics and engaging in research leading to numerous books and articles, the other as a recent graduate of a top-tier law school. Both of us contributed to this volume in significant ways. Neither of us could have written this volume without the active involvement of the other. In short, it was a cooperative project in every sense of the term.

We are indebted to the following individuals, who read various portions of the manuscript and shared with us their thoughts and comments: Robert L. Anderson, Meg E. Gillette, Laura Hartman, M. Colleen Kilbride, Peter J. Kivisto, Esteban E. Loustaunau, Thomas F. Mayer, Mwenda Ntarangwi, Gail E. Ohman, Douglas Parvin, Samanta Schmelzer, Joanna Short, Van J. Symons, and Anna Xiao Dong Sun. We are further indebted to the two anonymous reviewers who evaluated the manuscript for Cambridge University Press and offered a number of useful suggestions, and to Beatrice Rehl, the editor at Cambridge with whom it has been our privilege to work. We wish to acknowledge the sabbatical support that Augustana College, Rock Island, Illinois, provided Daniel E. Lee during the 2008–2009 academic year and the support provided by the Augustana Faculty Research Fund.

Prologue

In front of the Pantheon in Rome, which is the only building from antiquity still in use today, is Piazza della Rotonda, a very pleasant plaza with a water fountain topped by one of the Egyptian obelisks stolen from their rightful owners by plundering Romans during a previous era of globalization.[1] And on the side of Piazza della Rotonda opposite the Pantheon? A McDonald's fast-food restaurant.

McDonald's golden arches have sprouted up throughout much of the world. They can be found in Argentina and Aruba, Bahrain and Bolivia, Chile and Costa Rica, Ecuador and Egypt, India and Indonesia, Jamaica and Japan, Korea and Kuwait, Malaysia and Malta, New Zealand and Nicaragua, Pakistan and Paraguay, Saudi Arabia and Singapore, Tahiti and Taiwan, and in scores of other countries, both large and small.

More than 200 McDonald's restaurants are open for business every day in Beijing, the capital of China. McDonald's, however, is not the leading fast-food restaurant in China. That honor – if indeed it is an honor – goes to KFC, with entrees such as the "Dragon Twister" specially designed for the Chinese palate. KFC, which in 1987 was the first fast-food restaurant chain to enter China, now has more than 1,600 fast-food restaurants in mainland China, spread out among

---

[1] While the Italian government is negotiating with museums throughout the world to secure the return of artifacts from antiquity that have been taken out of Italy, we are not aware of any similar negotiations with the Egyptian government to secure the return of the obelisks to their rightful owners.

350 cities. Pizza Hut, which in 1990 was the first restaurant chain to introduce pizza to China, has more than 200 restaurants located in 50 cities. Taco Bell and Long John Silver's are not far behind. KFC, Pizza Hut, Taco Bell, and Long John Silver's are all owned by Yum! Brands, Inc., based in Louisville, Kentucky.[2]

There are, however, no McDonald's, no KFCs, no Pizza Huts, no Taco Bells, and no Long John Silver's in the Forbidden City, the exclusive residence of the emperor and members of his court until his ouster in the wake of the 1911 revolution but now a tourist attraction open to the public. Starbucks got that franchise. The presence of Starbucks in the Forbidden City, however, became a matter of controversy with half a million Chinese Internet users joining television anchorman Rui Chenggang in calling for its removal. Responding to public sentiment, Starbucks closed its outlet in the Forbidden City on July 13, 2007, after seven years of operation. Starbucks, however, continues to have more than 250 other outlets in mainland China, including at the Great Wall.[3]

Globalization is, of course, a two-way street. Many of the products we buy are manufactured in other countries: RCA television sets in Thailand; Nautica shirts in Mauritius; Florsheim shoes in India; Canon cameras in Taiwan; Dansk stoneware and Epson photo scanners in Indonesia; Bose speakers, Panasonic portable telephones, Dewalt circular saws, Troy-Bilt weed trimmers, and Nortel telephones in Mexico; NorthFace jackets, Magnavox television sets, Hewlett-Packard computers, Kodak digital cameras, Cuisinart food processors, Black & Decker drills, and Char-Broil barbecue grills in China; Leica camcorders and Takamine guitars in Japan; Brooks Brothers shirts and Pioneer multichannel receivers in Malaysia; and much, much more.

---

[2] Information about Yum! Brands' China division can be accessed at http://www
.yum.com/about/china.asp.
[3] The Associated Press, "Starbucks Closes Controversial Chinese Palace Outlet," *International Herald Tribune*, July 14, 2007. It is unclear, as Mure Dickie notes in a piece that ran in the *Financial Times*, why the attention was focused on Starbucks in view of the fact that American Express has a larger brand presence in the Forbidden City with its corporate logo appearing on numerous signs providing information about various buildings. Mure Dickie, "Starbucks Faces Banishment from Forbidden City," *Financial Times* (London edition), January 19, 2007.

Globalization, however, is not just the story of where the things we buy were made or which companies have manufacturing facilities or retail outlets in what countries. Globalization is really about people – people whose lives are profoundly affected for better or for worse by the rapidly changing, highly competitive world economy in which we live. People like Yun Liu, a young woman who left the poverty-stricken rural area in China where she grew up and went to work for the Huafang Cotton Weaving Company, one of China's largest textile mills, a mill that supplies the export market.[4] People like John Ester, who worked for twenty-six years making refrigerators at the Maytag plant in Galesburg, Illinois, but saw his job disappear when the company decided to move production of refrigerators to a plant in Mexico.[5] People like Martin Zacatzi Tequextle, who worked at a textile factory in southern Mexico making Tommy Hilfiger, Calvin Klein, Levi's, and Guess jeans but was fired when he started organizing workers to demand better working conditions.[6] People like Austin Natee, who as president of Firestone Agricultural Workers Union of Liberia (FAWUL) succeeded in getting better wages and working conditions for the rubber plantation workers in Liberia the union represents.[7] People like Tadessa Meskela, the general manager of the Oromia Coffee Farmers Cooperative Union, who works tirelessly to get better prices for the coffee beans produced by the farmers he represents.[8] People like Paulette Johnson, who was one of 4,500 workers making Fieldcrest, Cannon, and Royal Velvet sheets and towels at Pillowtex Corporation's plant in Kannapolis, North Carolina, but lost her job when the company shut down the plant.[9] People like Carmen Durán, who lost her job when Sanyo shut down the

4 David Barboza, "From a Poor Village to Job Security," *New York Times*, December 6, 2004, C2.
5 Steven Greenhouse, "City Feels Early Effects of Plant Closing in 2004," *New York Times*, December 26, 2002, A26.
6 Susan Ferriss, "Workers Say Rights Denied as Firms Threaten to Pull Out," *Cox News Service*, October 30, 2003.
7 Quoted in *ibid*.
8 For an overview of the Oromia Coffee Farmers Cooperative Union, see "About Us" on their website at http://oromiacoffeeunion.org/aboutus.html.
9 Amy Gardner, "Harsh Realities Close in on Company Town's Workers; 20 Months after N.C.'s Biggest Layoff, Pillowtex Employees Grope for Security," *News & Observer*, March 13, 2005, A1.

plant at which she was working in Tijuana, Mexico, and moved production to Indonesia.[10]

Because globalization is really about people, it is ultimately about ethics. That is where things start to get complicated. In an era in which what passes for public discourse about issues of ethical significance is often nothing more than a shouting match, it is a daunting task to foster thoughtful, balanced discussion of the ethical dimensions of outsourcing and other "hot button" issues related to globalization. Yet it is a task we must take on.

And what are these issues? Issues such as the question of whether Paulette Johnson's job is more important than Yun Liu's job (or vice versa). The extent to which – if at all – it is appropriate to do business in countries with blemished human rights records. The question of whether, and to what extent, domestic guidelines intended to ensure human well-being should be extended to multinational corporations' operations in other countries. The question of what constitutes fair trade, if indeed there is such a thing as fair trade. The question of when – if at all – it is appropriate to move production facilities to low-wage countries. The question of what employment practices are appropriate (or inappropriate) in plants in low-wage countries.

Books have been written about various aspects of all of these issues, often from a one-dimensional, antibusiness perspective. There are many piecemeal discussions of cases involving issues related to globalization. What is missing, however, is a balanced, thoughtful discussion of these issues firmly grounded in ethical theory. This volume fills that gap.

In discussions of issues related to globalization, as with so many other controversies, there is a tendency for those with strongly held views to paint pictures of those who disagree with them with caricatures of the most unflattering sort. It is not unusual for those in the business world to characterize those who express concern about the social costs of globalization as "naïve do-gooders" or "trouble makers" while social critics describe business leaders as "greedy capitalists."

To be sure, as is the case with many caricatures, there is a kernel of truth that underlies these unflattering stereotypes. There *are* social

---

[10] "Maquilapolis: About the Film" at http://www.pbs.org/pov/pov2006/maquilapolis/about.html (last accessed September 26, 2008).

critics who do not have the foggiest understanding of the realities of life in the business world – realities such as the necessity of maintaining profitability if the enterprise is to be viable. And there *are* individuals in the business world who are motivated by greed, some of whom are now under indictment or doing time in prison after having been convicted of fraud and other violations of the law.

But to paint everyone with such broad brushstrokes is to do an injustice to the responsible middle – business leaders with a conscience (and there are many of them) and socially concerned individuals who recognize that market realities based on laws of supply and demand need to be taken into account (and there are many of them as well). It is to those who comprise the thoughtful middle – in the business world, in academia, and elsewhere – that this volume is addressed (as well as those on both extremes, who, it is our hope, might be persuaded to join the responsible middle).

The volume is divided into three parts. Part I, which comprises three chapters, maps out some philosophical foundations for addressing ethical issues related to the business world in an era of globalization. Part II, which comprises four chapters, examines various practical issues, drawing upon the philosophical foundations identified in Part I, while Part III examines various possibilities for bringing pressure to bear on multinational corporations that are not respectful of human rights, and the difficulties inherent in so doing.

Chapter 1 begins by observing that whenever the conversation turns to the ethics of globalization, it is not long before the language of human rights comes into play, language that unfortunately is fraught with ambiguity. If the language of human rights is to play a role in discussions of ethical issues – and we believe that it should – it is essential that it be used carefully and with precision. Drawing upon the work of John Locke and others, as well as contemporary scholars such as Mary Ann Glendon, we advocate a more limited, more carefully defined notion of rights than that reflected in documents such as the United Nations' Universal Declaration of Human Rights, while noting that the Universal Declaration of Human Rights is useful as a statement of ideals identifying goals worth striving to achieve.

At the same time, we suggest that not everything of ethical significance can be subsumed under notions of rights. Chapter 2 tackles the difficult question of what our moral responsibilities might be with respect to our distant neighbors such as coffee growers in Ethiopia, those who work on rubber plantations in Liberia, and rural villagers in China hoping for a better life. Does it make sense to talk about concentric circles of responsibility, with each of us having greater obligations to members of our families and those living near us than to those living in distant countries? Or is Yun Liu's job every bit as important as Paulette Johnson's job with no distinctions to be made about moral obligations we might or might not have with respect to the two of them? Drawing upon the basic notion of natural rights mapped out in Chapter 1 and rejecting both simple self-interest and utilitarian approaches, we argue that our obligation to refrain from harming others applies equally to our near neighbors and our distant neighbors such as coffee growers in Ethiopia, rubber plantation workers in Liberia, and textile workers in China. However, affirmative duties such as providing education and housing might plausibly be argued to be stronger with respect to our near neighbors, particularly when familial relationships, employer-employee relationships, or other social relationships are present. The caveat to this notion of concentric circles of responsibility, however, is that when multinational corporations build plants in other countries or outsource, what previously were distant neighbors become, for them, near neighbors. Indeed, in many significant respects, globalization has made distant neighbors near neighbors.

All of this sets the stage for the task we take on in Chapter 3, which maps out some ethical guidelines for business in an age of globalization. Many views of what multinational corporations ought to be doing are either too narrowly defined, focusing only on profitability, or so broadly defined that they lack coherence and practicality. We take a middle path, identifying practical guidelines conducive to human well-being, using the second formulation of Immanuel Kant's categorical imperative ("For, all rational beings stand under the *law* that each of them is to treat himself and all others *never merely as means* but always *at the same time as ends in themselves*"[11]) as a central reference point.

Chapter 4, the first of the four chapters that comprise Part II of this volume, begins with an overview of the human rights situation in

[11] Immanuel Kant, *Groundwork of the Metaphysic of Morals*, tr. Mary Gregor (Cambridge, UK: Cambridge University Press, 1998), 41 (4:433).

China, which is neither as bad as some critics would have us believe nor as good as Chinese government officials would have us believe. We argue the case for constructive engagement and advocate adopting specific, goal-oriented principles, as was done during the days of apartheid in South Africa when a number of companies with operations in South Africa signed the Sullivan Principles and underwent annual reviews to determine if they were making measurable progress with respect to the various concrete expectations specified by the principles. In the case of China, where outsourcing is widespread, we suggest that particular attention needs to be focused on supplier codes of conduct, while acknowledging that monitoring compliance can be difficult, particularly with respect to the performance of suppliers' suppliers.

In the news media and elsewhere, a good deal of attention has been focused on China, and appropriately so, for it is virtually impossible to overstate the magnitude of the role that China plays on the world economic stage. There are, however, also significant human rights issues related to globalization in Africa, Latin America, and elsewhere – issues that unfortunately are often overlooked in discussions of international economic issues. Chapter 5 takes a detailed look at a country that receives little attention in these discussions – Liberia – focusing particular attention on the role that Firestone plays in Liberia, where it is the largest employer. Chapter 6 discusses free trade and fair trade issues pertaining to coffee growers in Ethiopia. Chapter 7 examines the question of whether maquiladoras (low-wage factories in Mexico that serve the U.S. market) exploit those they employ, provide economic opportunity for Mexican workers, or some combination of both.

Part III of this volume addresses the question of enforcement, a complicated and difficult matter in an age of globalization. Though we might prefer that it were otherwise, moral persuasion alone will not ensure respect for human rights. As Reinhold Niebuhr (1892–1971) correctly observed in a book published more than eight decades ago, power must by challenged by power if there is to be any hope of securing a greater measure of social justice.[12] The practical problem

---

[12] Reinhold Niebuhr, *Moral Man and Immoral Society: A Study in Ethics and Politics* (New York: Charles Scribner's Sons, 1932), xiv–xv.

in this age of globalization is finding sources of power of sufficient magnitude to challenge the immense power of multinational corporations. Chapter 8 notes the limitations of options such as economic sanctions and treaty provisions, while the last chapter in this volume – Chapter 9 – explores the possibilities for using the Alien Tort Claims Act (ATCA) to encourage U.S. multinational companies to comply with appropriate human rights standards in their overseas operations, focusing particular attention on environmental cases involving risk to human health and well-being.

The positions we take in these nine chapters and the supporting arguments we make are in no way intended to bring to complete resolution discussions of human rights and the ethics of globalization. Indeed, what is said here is only the beginning. It is our hope, however, that this volume will contribute to thoughtful discussions of these issues in academia, in the business and professional worlds, and elsewhere. If what is said here proves to be a catalyst for thoughtful discussion, all that we have hoped to accomplish will have been accomplished.

PART I

PHILOSOPHICAL FOUNDATIONS

1

Defining Human Rights in a Coherent Manner

Whenever conversation turns to the ethics of globalization, it is not long before the language of human rights comes into play. It is, however, language fraught with ambiguity. If the language of human rights is to play a role in discussions of the ethics of globalization – and we believe that it should – it is essential that it be used in a careful manner, maintaining as much precision in definition as possible. To help set the context for this semantic discussion, we begin with a brief history of concepts of human rights.

ROOTS IN ANTIQUITY

Though the language of human rights was not widely used until after World War II, notions of what in time became known as human rights have roots in antiquity. Take, for example, the Ten Commandments, which appear in the Pentateuch (Torah) as part of the Mount Sinai story. As generations of Jewish and Christian school children who have been drilled until they can recite the Ten Commandments by heart know, they include prohibitions on killing, stealing, and coveting the property of others (Exodus 20.1–17). While they do not use the language of rights, the Ten Commandments can be interpreted as implying that people have certain basic rights, among them property rights and a right to live.

That having been said, however, it should also be noted that notwithstanding the great emphasis that many with strong religious convictions place on the Ten Commandments today, they are, at best, an incomplete statement of basic notions of human rights. For example, the list of property that should not be coveted includes wives and slaves: "You shall not covet your neighbor's house; you should not covet your neighbor's wife, or male or female slave, or ox, or donkey, or anything else that belongs to your neighbor" (Exodus 20.17 NRSV). The chapter that follows the Mount Sinai story in Exodus maps out some rules for the way slaves should be treated without in any way questioning the practice of slavery, including the practice of selling daughters as slaves (Exodus 21.1–11). Moreover, viewing wives as property is not in any way questioned.[1] In short, the Ten Commandments, though venerated by many, do not fit comfortably with contemporary notions of equal rights even though they can be viewed as containing implicit claims about certain rights.

Other ancient roots of modern notions of rights include the Roman notion of *ius gentium*, the law, often unwritten, by which those who were not Roman citizens were judged. This was based, in part, on what the magistrate believed to be right or wrong. It was not, however, viewed by Romans as arbitrary justice.[2] In *De Legibus*, the distinguished Roman statesman and philosopher Marcus Tullius Cicero (106–43 BCE), states, "For Justice is one; it binds all human society, and is based on one Law, which is right reason applied to command and prohibition."[3] He further argues that "we can perceive

---

[1] The ancient Hebrew practice of viewing the wife as property, albeit a very special form of property, is also reflected in the story of Jacob and Rachel. When Laban, who was Rachel's father, asked Jacob what his wages should be, Jacob offered to work for Laban for seven years in return for Rachel. The Genesis text states, "So Jacob served seven years for Rachel, and they seemed to him but a few days because of the love he had for her." When the time came for the property transfer to be celebrated by a feast, Laban, who had not taken a course in business ethics, gave Jacob Rachel's older sister Leah instead, a switch that Jacob did not notice until the next morning, by which time the marriage had been consummated. When Jacob confronted Laban about the switch, he equivocated by saying that in his country, the oldest daughter was always given first in marriage but offered to give Jacob Rachel as well if he would work for another seven years, which Jacob did because "he loved Rachel more than Leah" notwithstanding the fact that "Leah's eyes were lovely" (Genesis 29.15–30 NRSV).

[2] For an insightful discussion of the classical roots of international law published nearly a century ago, see Gordon E. Sherman, "Jus Gentium and International Law," *The American Journal of International Law*, Vol. 12, No.1 (January 1918), 56–63.

[3] Marcus Tullius Cicero, *De Legibus*, trans. Clinton Walker Keyes, The Loeb Classical Library (Cambridge, MA: Harvard University Press, 1928), 345 (I, xv, 43).

the difference between good laws and bad by referring them to no other standard than Nature" and adds that "it is not merely Justice and Injustice which are distinguished by Nature, but also and without exception things which are honourable and dishonourable." He concludes, "For since an intelligence common to all of us makes things known to us and formulates them in our minds, honourable actions are ascribed by us to virtue, and dishonourable actions to vice; and only a madman would conclude that these judgments are matters of opinion and not fixed by nature."[4]

FROM NATURAL LAW TO NATURAL RIGHTS

These passages from Cicero's *De Legibus* give expression to two basic claims that came to be central to the natural law tradition. One is the ontological claim that there is a moral order imbedded in nature. The second is the epistemological claim that "an intelligence common to all of us" enables us to identify at least a portion of this moral order. The medieval theologian and philosopher Thomas Aquinas (1224/25–1274), viewed by many as the most influential natural law theorist of all time, speaks of "the light of natural reason, whereby we discern what is good and what is evil, which is the function of natural law...."[5] Turning to more specific precepts, Aquinas suggests that "inasmuch as every substance seeks the preservation of its own being ... whatever is a means of preserving human life, and of warding off its obstacles, belongs to the natural law."[6] And commenting on the Ten Commandments, he asserts, "For there are certain things which the natural reason of every man, of its own accord and at once, judges to be done or not to be done: e.g., 'Honor thy father and thy mother,' and 'Thou shalt not kill, Thou shalt not steal': and these belong to the law of nature absolutely."[7]

The natural law tradition provided the backdrop for the discussion of natural right by Hugo Grotius (1583–1645) in *De Jure Belli ac Pacis*, which was to become a seminal work in the field of international law.

---

[4] *Ibid.*, 347 (I, xvi, 44–45).
[5] Thomas Aquinas, *Summa Theologica*, trans. Fathers of the English Dominican Province (New York: Benziger, 1947), I-II, Q.91, A.2.
[6] *Ibid.*, I-II, Q.94, A.2.
[7] *Ibid.*, I-II, Q.100, A.1.

He states, "Natural right is the dictate of right reason.... The actions, upon which such a dictate is given, are either binding or unlawful in themselves...."[8] (Grotius is here using the term "natural right" in a more limited sense than John Locke [1632–1704] and others were to subsequently use it; he suggests that "right signifies nothing more than what is just...."[9] Hence, as he uses the term, "natural right" is simply what is right as defined by the law of nature.) Writing at a time when the Protestant movement had fragmented the church and warring states had fragmented the political landscape of Western Europe, he could not appeal to church or emperor as a source of authority transcending regional and national differences, many of which had resulted in wars both large and small. Hence, his appeal to the nature of humanity itself as he sought a basis for a law of nations that might govern conduct in war and peace alike.

As with Grotius's *De Jure Belli ac Pacis*, the natural law tradition helped set the stage for John Locke's *Second Treatise of Government*, published in 1690, less than a half century after the death of Grotius and just two years after the Glorious Revolution, which placed William of Orange on the throne of England with limitations to his power specified by the English Bill of Rights. Locke speaks of a law of nature "which obliges every one; and reason, which is that law, teaches all mankind who will but consult it that, being all equal and independent, no one ought to harm another in his life, health, liberty, or possessions."[10] Like Grotius, Locke sees this law of nature as existing independent of anything that any government might say or do.

There is, however, a subtle shift in emphasis, a shift that was to be of great historical significance. In *De Jure Belli ac Pacis*, the emphasis is on *natural right* – that is, what it is naturally right to do. In Locke's *Second Treatise of Government*, the emphasis is on *natural rights* – that is, on rights that each individual naturally possesses. Grotius's objective was to encourage restraint in warfare, both in going to war and in the conduct of war. Locke's objective was to champion the rights of

---

[8] Hugo Grotius, *The Rights of War and Peace, Including the Law of Nature and of Nations*, trans. A.C. Campbell (Washington, DC: M. Walter Dunne, Publisher, 1901), 21 (I, 1, x).

[9] *Ibid.*, 18 (I,1, iii).

[10] John Locke, *The Second Treatise of Government*, ed. Thomas P. Peardon, Library of Liberal Arts Edition (Indianapolis: Bobbs-Merrill Company, Inc., 1952), 5 (II, 6).

the individual and challenge the traditional view of the divine right of kings.

Such being the case, it is no accident that it was Locke, not Grotius, who provided the inspiration for the ringing words that Thomas Jefferson penned when he drafted the U.S. Declaration of Independence: "We hold these truths to be self-evident, that all men are created equal, that they are endowed by their Creator with certain unalienable Rights, that among these are Life, Liberty and the pursuit of Happiness."[11]

The U.S. Declaration of Independence was to reverberate through the corridors of history, challenging those who opposed liberty and sustaining those struggling for liberty. The document, along with the Virginia Bill of Rights (adopted the same year), were formative for the Marquis de Lafayette, who played a lead role in drafting the Declaration of the Rights of Man, approved by the National Assembly of France in 1789.[12] Lafayette was familiar with both the U.S. Declaration of Independence and the Virginia Bill of Rights, having served without pay in the American War for Independence during the darkest days of the war at Valley Forge and during the siege of Yorktown, which led to American victory with the surrender of the army commanded by Lord Charles Cornwallis (who as a member of the House of Lords had, in one of history's greatest ironies, opposed nearly all of the policies that led to revolt in the American colonies.[13]) The Declaration of the Rights of Man states, "Men are born and remain free and equal in rights.... The aim of all political association is the preservation of the

---

[11] While drawing heavily on the work of Locke, Jefferson replaces Locke's repeated reference to property as a basic right with the phrase "the pursuit of Happiness." In contrast to what might initially seem to be the case, however, Jefferson's rephrasing of Locke is more stylistic than substantive. Though we customarily think of real estate and other things that can bought and sold when we see references made to property, Locke included far more when he used the term. For example, in his chapter on the ends of political society and government, Locke suggests that people unite with others to form a government "for the mutual preservation of their lives, liberties, and estates, which I call by the general name 'property'" (71 [IX,123]).

[12] Layfayette was also influenced by the writings of eighteenth-century French *philosophes*, among them François Marie Aroet, who was better known as Voltaire (1694–1778), Charles Louis de Secondat, Baron of Montesquieu (1689–1755), and Denis Diderot (1713–1784).

[13] "The American Revolution" at http://www.americanrevolution.com/LordCharles Cornwallis.htm (last accessed November 12, 2007).

natural and imprescriptible rights of man. These rights are liberty, property, security, and resistance to oppression."[14]

In time, the notion of natural rights transcended differences in political philosophy. A century-and-a-half after the U.S. Declaration of Independence, the Declaration of Independence of the Democratic Republic of Viet-Nam, drafted by Ho Chi Minh with American assistance (but ignored by American officials when it became politically expedient to do so), quoted the passage noted above from the U.S Declaration of Independence and added, "In a broader sense, this means: All peoples on the earth are equal from birth, all the peoples have a right to live, to be happy and free."[15]

In the years that have passed since John Hancock, Thomas Jefferson, and fifty four other courageous individuals signed the U.S. Declaration of Independence, it has been quoted in documents and speeches, both official and unofficial, on occasions far too numerous to be counted, as has the French Declaration of the Rights of Man.

ONTOLOGICAL AND EPISTEMOLOGICAL CHALLENGES

Though widely quoted, the natural rights claims given expression in the U.S. Declaration of Independence and the French Declaration of the Rights of Man have not gone unchallenged. Among the harshest critics was British philosopher Jeremy Bentham (1748–1832), one of the earliest and most articulate proponents of utilitarianism. In *Anarchical Fallacies*, Bentham delivered a broadside against the claim in the Declaration of the Rights of Man that there are "natural and imprescriptible rights." He declares, "How stands the truth of things? That there are not such things as natural rights – no such things as

---

[14] Declaration of the Rights of Man at http://www.yale.edu/lawweb/avalon/rightsof. htm (last accessed October 4, 2007).

[15] Declaration of Independence of the Democratic Republic of Viet-Nam at http:// www.mtholyoke.edu/acad/intrel/vietdec.htm (last accessed October 4, 2007). The document also quotes the passage noted above from the French Declaration of the Rights of Man and says of the statements on rights quoted from both documents, "Those are undeniable truths." The quotations from the U.S. Declaration of Independence and the French Declaration of the Rights of Man should not necessarily be interpreted as implying affirmation of Western notions of individual rights. Rather, Ho Chi Minh's emphasis was on securing independence from foreign domination.

rights anterior to the establishment of government – no such things as natural rights opposed to, in contradistinction, to legal [rights]. . . . *Natural rights* is simple nonsense: natural and imprescriptible rights, rhetorical nonsense – nonsense on stilts."[16]

Bentham's broadside, which was probably motivated as much by political reasons as by philosophical reasons, is directed toward the ontological claim of natural rights theorists, namely, the claim that there is an existing moral order in nature (a matter to which we will return later in this chapter). Far more problematic is the epistemological claim made by natural rights theorists and the natural law theorists who preceded them, namely the claim that "an intelligence common to all of us" enables identifying at least part of what this moral order is. Indeed, it is far easier to say that our cognitive abilities enable discerning what these basic norms might or might not be than it is to demonstrate in any sort of persuasive manner how this might be done.

As noted previously, the U.S. Declaration of Independence asserts, "We hold these truths to be self-evident. . . ." Simply saying that certain things are self-evident, however, does not automatically mean that such is the case. Granted, to those of us who firmly believe that what the U.S. Declaration of Independence says is right, the value claims made in the document might seem self-evident. But, as the eighteenth-century English theologian and philosopher Joseph Butler (1692–1752) recognized, certainty of belief is not the same as something being self-evident. Butler observes, "Indeed the truth of revealed religion, peculiarly so called, is not self-evident. . . ."[17]

A similar point is made by twentieth-century British philosopher W.D. Hudson, who poses the hypothetical example of an anguished mother whose son has been reported as having been killed in action but who firmly believes that he is still alive. If it turns out that the report was incorrect and that instead of being killed in action he is a prisoner of war, the mother, upon hearing the corrected report would undoubtedly say, "I knew it all along." But what of the other

[16] Jeremy Bentham, *Anarchical Fallacies* (200, 230) at https://www.college.columbia. edu/core/students/cc/settexts/bentanar.pdf (last accessed October 4, 2007).

[17] Joseph Butler, *The Analogy of Religion Natural and Revealed to the Constitution and Course of Nature* (London: George Routledge and Sons, 1887), 275–76 (II, conc.).

alternative – irrefutable evidence such as the recovery of his remains
that made it very clear that he indeed had died on the battlefield?
Would she still say, "I knew it all along"? Probably not. Rather, Hudson
suggests, she would be far more likely to say, "'I felt sure that he was
alive, but now I know that he is dead.'" Hudson observes, "There are
numerous examples of people feeling absolutely sure of something
and being right; and apparently equally numerous examples of them
so feeling and being wrong. But, as far as any evidence that is available
to us may go, there does not seem to be anything necessarily different
about the intuition, i.e., the feeling of certainty, in the two kinds of
examples."[18]

And so certainty of belief is not the same as something being
self-evident. The *Oxford English Dictionary* defines "self-evident" as
"evident of itself without proof."[19] But how can something be "evident
of itself without proof"? Locke wrestles with this question in *An Essay
Concerning Human Understanding*, published shortly before his *Second
Treatise on Government*. There are some things, he allows, that are self-
evident – for example, the similarity or dissimilarity of such things
as colors or geometrical forms or the fact that a man is not a horse
and a horse is not a man. Locke also observes that there are certain
mathematical relationships that are self-evident, such as the axiom
that says that if equals are subtracted from equals, the remainders
will be equal.[20]

---

[18] W.D. Hudson, *Modern Moral Philosophy* (Garden City, NY: Doubleday & Company, Inc., 1970), 101–104.
[19] *The Oxford English Dictionary*, 2nd ed. (Oxford: Clarendon Press, 1989), 14:920.
[20] John Locke, *An Essay Concerning Human Understanding*, ed. Peter H. Nidditch (Oxford, UK: Clarendon Press, 1975), 591–94 (iv, vii, 1–7). The prevailing episte-mological theme in Locke's *An Essay Concerning Human Understanding* is the asser-tion that knowledge is gained via experience. He argues, "Let us then suppose the Mind to be, as we say, white Paper, void of all Characters, without any *Ideas*, How comes it to be furnished …? To this I answer, in one word. From *Experience*: In that, all our Knowledge is founded; and from that it ultimately derives its self (104; ii, i, 2). In discussing self-evident truths, Locke, in effect, is contending that even if there are self-evident truths (which he was willing to concede), that does not stand in the way of saying that all knowledge comes from experience. In response to those who contended that (a) maxims and other self-evident truths are known to the mind prior to and quite apart from experience and (b) other parts of knowl-edge can be derived from these maxims, Locke insists, *"First,* That they are not the *Truths first known* to the Mind, is evident to Experience.… *Secondly,* From what has been said, it plainly follows, that these magnified *Maxims*, are not the Principles and *Foundations* of all our other *Knowledge"* (595–96; iv, vii, 9–10).

And indeed, it is quite apparent that regardless of the words that are used to give expression to the differences, a circle is not a square, a man is not a horse, and red is not blue. But does saying "It is self-evident that all human beings are created equal" have the same degree of certitude as saying "It is self-evident that red and blue are different colors" or "It is self-evident that a square and a circle have different shapes"? While many different words in many different languages are used to identify various colors, once linguistic variations are taken into account one is hard-pressed to find anyone anywhere (at least anyone who is not color blind) who sincerely believes that red and blue are really the same color. Similarly, it does not take extensive study to determine that squares and circles have different shapes because squares have corners and circles do not and that there are observable differences between human beings and horses. Locke was right. It is self-evident that red and blue are different colors, that squares and circles have different shapes and that a man is not a horse.

But can the same be said with respect to the claim that all human beings are created equal or any other ethical claim? Even though many of us sincerely believe that all people are born with the same basic rights, the notion that everyone has the same basic rights is by no means a universally held view. One need not look far, either historically or in the world today, to find examples of tyrants and despots who despise the notion of equality and respect for all persons. Rejection of the notion of equal rights, it might be added, is not limited to tyrants and despots. A number of the signers of the U.S. Declaration of Independence, including Jefferson himself, owned slaves. The equality of all persons, it seems, was not self-evident even to them, notwithstanding the resounding endorsement of equality given expression in the ringing words of that much-quoted and revered document.[21] The view that there are self-evident basic

---

[21] In the "original Rough draught" of the U.S. Declaration of Independence, Jefferson took a strong position against the slave trade, alleging that the British sovereign had "waged cruel war against human nature itself, violating it's (sic) most sacred rights of life & liberty in the persons of a distant people who never offended him, captivating & carrying them into slavery in another hemisphere...." and that the British sovereign was "determined to keep open a market where MEN should be bought & sold" ("Jefferson's 'original Rough draught' of the U.S. Declaration of Independence" in *The Papers of Thomas Jefferson*, Vol. I, ed. Julian P. Boyd [Princeton, NJ: Princeton University Press, 1950], 426.) However, this passage was deleted prior to approval of the document by the Second Continental Congress.

rights undoubtedly played a significant political role in the struggle
to secure more democratic forms of government. But as an ethical
theory, the claim that there are self-evident moral truths leaves us
with a lot of unanswered questions.[22]

Attempting to identify ethical values by observing nature is similarly
problematic. Many species of animals exhibit behavior that we might
not want to use as a model for human behavior. Hippopotamuses,
which spend as much as sixteen hours a day submerged in rivers and
lakes with only their nostrils above water, are not known for their
industriousness.[23] Chimpanzees – the species most like us in its
genetic characteristics – have been observed engaging in kidnapping,
cannibalism, and promiscuity.[24] Some hawks and owls reduce the size
of their broods by eating the chicks they decide not to keep.[25] Giant
pandas, who frequently give birth to twins, almost always abandon
one of them, raising only the one they do not abandon while allowing the other twin to perish.[26] Egrets have been observed standing
by and doing nothing while their larger chicks peck the smaller ones
to death, a pattern of behavior that has been witnessed in other species as well, among them pelicans and cranes.[27] The female praying
mantis will sometimes eat her mate after mating, at times even during
mating – a pattern of behavior that inexplicably seems not to deter
males from mating.[28]

The laws of nature are far from clear. Disharmony is as apparent
as harmony, chaos as order, and destruction as preservation.
Earthquakes kill thousands of people, destroying cities in the process.
Droughts lead to hunger and starvation. Deadly viruses kill millions.
Writing more than a century ago, British philosopher John Stuart Mill

[22] These matters are discussed in greater detail in Daniel E. Lee, *Navigating Right
and Wrong: Ethical Decision Making in a Pluralistic Age* (Lanham, MD: Rowman &
Littlefield Publishers, Inc., 2002), 47–76.

[23] National Geographic, "Hippopotamus" at http://animals.nationalgeographic.
com/animals/mammals/hippopotamus.html (last accessed September 23, 2008).

[24] Jane Goodall, "Life and Death at Gombe," *National Geographic* (May, 1979): 593–
621. See also Natalie Angier, "One Thing They Aren't: Maternal," *New York Times*,
May 9, 2006.

[25] Angier, "One Thing They Aren't: Maternal."

[26] *Ibid.*

[27] *Ibid.*

[28] National Geographic, "Praying Mantis" at http://animals.nationalgeographic.
com/animals/bugs/praying-mantis.html (last accessed September 20, 2008).

(1806–1872) observed, "In sober truth, nearly all the things which men are hanged or imprisoned for doing to one another, are nature's every day performances.... Everything in short, which the worst men commit either against life or property is perpetrated on a larger scale by natural agents."[29]

In the final analysis, those who claim to derive ethical values from nature are in reality making certain value assumptions about nature – value assumptions that provide a screen to sort out what they like from what they do not like. They pick and choose what they like and ignore examples such as those noted previously that do not fit comfortably with their values. Instead of deriving ethical values from nature, they are bringing their own ethical values to nature, interpreting nature in light of these values, and then claiming validation for their values by saying that they are grounded in nature.

Moreover, even if those purporting to find moral guidelines in nature are accurately describing what they observe, that does not establish whether what they observe is good or bad. The fact that things exist or occur in a certain way leaves open the question of whether they should be that way. Thus, following the lead of the British philosopher G.E. Moore (1873–1958), critics of naturalism have often decried the "naturalistic fallacy" by arguing that to attempt to define value terms in factual terms is to overlook the difference between the "is" and the "ought," between facts and values.[30]

While the epistemological challenges to the natural law tradition out of which the belief in natural rights grew have been particularly devastating, the ontological claim that there are moral norms imbedded in nature has also been met with skepticism. Bentham was by no means the only one who expressed doubt about this claim. In a widely quoted passage, the twentieth-century French philosopher Jean-Paul Sartre (1905–1980) asserts, "Man is nothing else but that which he

---

[29] John Stuart Mill, "Nature," in *Three Essays on Religion: Nature, the Utility of Religion and Theism* (London: Longmans, Green and Co., 1923), 28–30.

[30] Moore's critique of naturalism can be found in *Principia Ethica* (Cambridge: Cambridge University Press, 1960), see esp. pp. 9–17 and 37–58. William K. Frankena provides a very readable discussion of the open question argument in *Ethics*, 2nd ed. (Englewood Cliffs, NJ: Prentice-Hall, Inc., 1963), 80–83. See also R.M. Hare's discussion of definist theories in *The Language of Morals* (New York: Oxford University Press, 1964), 79–93.

makes of himself." Sartre recalls an incident in which a student came
to him during the Nazi occupation of France asking for advice about a
very difficult matter. The student's father was somewhat of a Nazi col-
laborator. His older brother had been killed during the 1940 German
offensive. His grieving mother's one consolation was her remaining
son, who was torn between a sense of duty to his mother and a desire
to avenge the death of his older brother by going to England to join
the Free French. Sartre, who himself was active in the resistance movement, makes no judgment about the father's suspected collaboration
with the Nazis. For the student seeking advice, Sartre recounts, "I
had but one reply to make. You are free, therefore choose – that is to
say, invent. No rule of general morality can show you what you ought
to do; no signs are vouchsafed in this world."[31] And so Sartre was not
only a *value noncognitivist* on the epistemological level taking exception to the claim that "an intelligence common to all of us" enables
determining that certain things are right and other things are wrong;
he was also a *subjectivist* on the ontological level, asserting that values
are simply human inventions just as subjectivists in the world of art
suggest that "beauty is in the eye of the beholder." (In contrast, natural law theorists are *objectivists* on the ontological level, asserting that
there is a moral order imbedded in nature quite apart from anything
that we might say or do, and *value cognitivists* on the epistemological
level, asserting that our cognitive abilities enable identifying at least
part of this existing moral order.)

[31] Jean-Paul Sartre, "Existentialism Is a Humanism," trans. Philip Mairet, in
Existentialism from Dostoevsky to Sartre, ed. Walter Kaufmann (Cleveland: The World
Publishing Company, 1956), 290–91. While Sartre's "Existentialism Is a Humanism"
is widely quoted, some philosophers believe that it is, in some ways, an inaccurate
representation of some of the central themes of existentialism. In the introduction
to *Existentialism from Dostoevsky to Sartre*, Kaufman, while acknowledging the popularity of the essay, states, "This is rather unfortunate because it is after all only an
occasional lecture which, though brilliant and vivid in places and unquestionably
worthy of attention, bears the stamp of the moment. It contains unnecessary mis-
statements of fact as well as careless and untenable arguments and a definition of
existentialism which has been repudiated by Jaspers and Heidegger, and ought to
be repudiated by Sartre, too, because it is no less unfair to his own thought" (45).
While this is not the place to get into a debate about the correct interpretation of
Sartre's version of existentialism, it should be noted that passages that point in the
direction of subjectivism are not limited to "Existentialism Is a Humanism." See,
for example, Sartre's *Being and Nothingness: An Essay on Phenomenological Ontology*,
trans. Hazel E. Barnes (New York: Washington Square Press, 1966), 113–114.

THE NUREMBERG TRIALS

We can only speculate about whether the subjectivism of Sartre would have in time supplanted Grotius's belief in natural right and Locke's belief in natural rights had the horrors of the death camps in Nazi Germany not occurred. We do know, however, that as people of conscience in the United States and elsewhere became aware of these horrific atrocities and responded with revulsion, the notion of crimes against humanity started to make a lot of sense.

At the Teheran Conference in 1943, Soviet Premier Joseph Stalin proposed that at the end of the war the German General Staff, its officers, and technicians – some 50,000 individuals in all – be liquidated. British Prime Minister Winston Churchill was aghast. "The British Parliament and public will never tolerate mass executions," he emphatically stated. When Stalin persisted, Churchill angrily responded, "I would rather be taken out into the garden here and now and be shot myself than sully my own and my country's honor by such infamy."[32]

Churchill preferred a judicial proceeding of some sort. There was, however, no existing international court of law that could try those accused of crimes against humanity. Such a court needed to be created if there were to be judicial proceedings.

That was accomplished. After the surrender of Nazi Germany and as the war in the Pacific neared its conclusion, representatives of the governments of the United States, the United Kingdom, the Soviet Union, and the provisional government of France signed an agreement establishing an International Military Tribunal "for the just and prompt trial and punishment of the major war criminals of the European Axis." The charter of the tribunal lists three general categories of crimes falling under the jurisdiction of the tribunal: (a) crimes against peace, (b) war crimes, and (c) crimes against humanity. The charter defines the latter as follows:

namely, murder, extermination, enslavement, deportation, and other inhumane acts committed against any civilian population, before or during the war; or persecutions on political, racial or religious grounds in

---

[32] Quoted by Whitney R. Harris in *Tyranny on Trial: The Evidence at Nuremberg* (Dallas: Southern Methodist University Press, 1954), 496–497.

execution of or in connection with any crime within the jurisdiction of the Tribunal, whether or not in violation of domestic law of the country where perpetrated.[33]

The last phrase was included because many of the atrocities perpetrated by the Nazis were legal in the sense that they were allowed by German laws, many of which, of course, had been crafted by Adolf Hitler and his accomplices.

President Harry S. Truman appointed Associate Justice of the U.S. Supreme Court Robert H. Jackson as the U.S. representative in the negotiations that led to adoption of the charter that established the International Military Tribunal, which served indictments to twenty-four former Nazi officials and seven Nazi organizations. At their trial in the Palace of Justice in Nuremberg, just a short distance from the stadium where huge carefully staged Nazi party rallies had been held, Justice Jackson presented the case against them on behalf of the United States. In his opening statement on November 21, 1945, he acknowledged:

It is true, of course, that we have no judicial precedent for the Charter.... Yet every custom has its origin in some single act, and every agreement has to be initiated by the action of some state. Unless we are prepared to abandon every principle of growth for International Law, we cannot deny that our own day has the right to institute customs and to conclude agreements that will themselves become sources of a newer and strengthened International Law.[34]

The proceedings pertaining to industrialist Gustav Krupp von Bohlen und Halbach were deferred because of his ill health. Robert Ley, leader of the German Labor Front, committed suicide before the proceedings had run their course. The tribunal acquitted three of the remaining defendants of the charges filed against them.[35] Twelve of the defendants were convicted of the charges filed against them and

---

[33] *Charter of the International Military Tribunal* in *The Case Against the Nazi War Criminals: Opening Statement for the United States of America by Robert H. Jackson and Other Documents* (New York: Alfred A. Knopf, 1946), 100–101.

[34] Robert H. Jackson, *Opening Statement for the United States of America* in *ibid.*, 77.

[35] Hjalmer Schacht, the Reich minister of Economics, Franz von Papen, vice chancellor under Hitler, and Hans Fritzsche, head of the radio division of the Nazi Party's propaganda department.

sentenced to death by hanging.[36] Seven of the defendants received prison sentences of varying lengths.[37]

And so, to the satisfaction of Churchill and others, justice was served and the mass executions Stalin preferred were averted.[38] In an article that originally appeared in the *Harvard Law Review* at the time of the Nuremberg Trials, Harvard Professor Sheldon Glueck observed that the victorious Allies could have "disposed of the Nazi ringleaders summarily by 'executive' or 'political' action, without any trial at all and without any consideration whatsoever of whether the acts with which the accused were charged had or had not been previously prohibited by some specific provision of international penal law." He added, however, that the victorious Allies, who could have "shot the Nazi leaders with no trial at all without violating international customary law," chose to "proceed in a more civilized way. So the victors provided for indictment and trial."[39]

HUMAN RIGHTS

If it was the spirit of Hugo Grotius that lived on when the International Military Tribunal wrote a new chapter in the history of international

---

[36] Herman Goering, commander-in-chief of the Luftwaffe (who cheated the hangman by committing suicide just hours before his scheduled execution); Joachim von Ribbentrop, Reich minister for foreign affairs; Wilhelm Keitel, chief of the High Command of the Armed Forces; Ernst Kaltenbrunner, chief of the security police and the security service; Alfred Rosenberg, Reich minister for the Occupied Eastern Territories; Hans Frank, governor general of Occupied Poland; Wilhelm Frick, Reich minister of the Interior; Julius Streicher, editor-in-chief of the viciously anti-Semitic newspaper *Der Stuermer*; Fritz Sauckel, plenipotentiary for the Employment of Labor; Alfred Jodl, chief of the Operations Staff of the High Command of the Armed Forces; Martin Bormann, head of the Party Chancery (tried in absentia); and Arthur Seyss-Inquart, Reich commissar for Occupied Netherlands.

[37] Rudolf Hess, Deputy to the Fuehrer – imprisonment for life; Walter Funk, president of the Reichsbank – imprisonment for life; Karl Doenitz, commander-in-chief of U-Boats and successor to Hitler – imprisonment for ten years; Erich Raeder, commander-in-chief of the Navy – imprisonment for life; Baldur von Schirach, leader of youth – imprisonment for twenty years; Albert Speer, Hitler's architect and plenipotentiary for Armaments – imprisonment for twenty years; and Constantin von Neurath, Reich protector for Occupied Czechoslovakia – imprisonment for fifteen years.

[38] Harris, *Tyranny on Trial*, xxv-xvi, 26, 32, 478–481, 485–486.

[39] Sheldon Glueck, *The Nuremberg Trial and Aggressive War* (New York: Alfred A. Knopf, 1946), 8–9, 12.

law, it was the spirit of John Locke that lived on when the United
Nations included a strong statement of individual rights in its charter,
signed June 26, 1945, in San Francisco at the conclusion of the United
Nations Conference on International Organization. The preamble
declares that "We the people of the United Nations [are determined
to] reaffirm faith in fundamental human rights, in the dignity and
worth of the human person, in the equal rights of men and women
and nations large and small...."[40]

The United Nations' commitment to human rights was given fuller
expression in the Universal Declaration of Human Rights, which the
General Assembly adopted without a dissenting vote on December
10, 1948. The thirty articles of the Universal Declaration of Human
Rights specify a wide range of rights, among them "the right to life,
liberty and security of the person" (Article 3) and "the right to just
and favourable remuneration ensuring for himself and his family
an existence worthy of human dignity, and supplemented, if necessary, by other means of social protection" (Article 23).[41] Harvard
Law School Professor Mary Ann Glendon, a leading scholar of international human rights law, says of the declaration:

In the years that followed [the adoption of the declaration], to the astonish-
ment of many, human rights would become a political factor that not even
the most hard-shelled realist could ignore. The Universal Declaration would
become an instrument, as well as the most prominent symbol, of changes
that would amplify the voices of the weak in the corridors of power.[42]

The Universal Declaration of Human Rights is simply a proclamation of human rights adopted by the U.N. General Assembly. The
proclamation has been augmented by treaties that nations have been
asked to sign and ratify, among them the International Covenant on
Economic, Social and Cultural Rights, which went into effect January
3, 1976,[43] and the International Covenant on Civil and Political

[40] *Preamble of the Charter of the United Nations* at http://www.un.org/aboutun/charter/ (last accessed October 13, 2007).
[41] United Nations, Universal Declaration of Human Rights at http://www.un.org/Overview/rights.html (last accessed October 13, 2007).
[42] Mary Ann Glendon, *A World Made New: Eleanor Roosevelt and the Universal Declaration of Human Rights* (New York: Random House, 2001), xvi.
[43] United Nations, *International Covenant on Economic, Social and Cultural Rights* at http://www1.umn.edu/humanrts/instree/b2esc.htm (last accessed October 15, 2007).

Rights, which went into effect March 23, 1976.[44] And so in the post-World War II years, notions of human rights, rooted in antiquity and nurtured in the Age of Enlightenment, grew into a tree with many branches – branches that not only protect individuals from mistreatment by the governments of the countries in which they live (the concern of Locke, Jefferson, and other proponents of natural rights during the Age of Enlightenment) but also, as human rights scholar Sumner B. Twiss notes, protection from mistreatment by multinational corporations in an era of globalization.[45]

But as the tree of human rights experienced vigorous growth in the last half of the twentieth century and the first decade of the current century, it became a tree with tangled branches. While the language of human rights is widely used, it is not always used with precision. Without clarity, the language of human rights is nothing more than a rhetorical device used to advance a particular position. It is incumbent on those of us who use the language of human rights to specify as precisely as possible what we mean when using the language.

NATURAL RIGHTS AND CONFERRED RIGHTS

As we turn to the definitional tasks at hand in an effort to bring a greater measure of clarity to discussions of human rights, it is useful to distinguish between *natural rights* and *conferred rights*. As Locke and other philosophers of the seventeenth and eighteenth centuries used the terms, natural rights are rights that each individual has independent of anything that government or any other social institution or individual might or might not do. Such being the case, they are, in the words of the U.S. Declaration of Independence, "unalienable rights." While they might be violated by tyrannical governments or unruly mobs, they cannot be taken away. As already noted, the U.S. Declaration of Independence lists as unalienable rights "life, liberty and the pursuit of happiness" while the French Declaration of the Rights of Man, using slightly different language, speaks of "natural

[44] United Nations, *International Covenant on Civil and Political Rights* at http://www1.umn.edu/humanrts/instree/b3ccpr.htm (last accessed October 15, 2007).

[45] Sumner B. Twiss, "History, Human Rights and Globalization," *Journal of Religious Ethics* Vol. 32, No.1 (2004): 39–70.

and imprescriptible rights," which are "liberty, property, security, and resistance to oppression."

In contrast, conferred rights are bestowed on the individual by other individuals in the form of contractual agreements or by a social institution of some sort, be it government, a business organization, or an educational institution. For example, at most colleges and universities, full-time faculty members have the right to vote at faculty meetings. Unlike natural rights, voting rights at faculty meetings are not something possessed by each individual independent of anything that particular colleges and universities might do. Rather, they are contingent on action taken by a particular college or university, first and foremost hiring the faculty member to whom the voting rights pertain. Moreover, unlike natural rights, they are not rights that exist in perpetuity. They typically end when the employment of that faculty member ends, be it by retirement, as a result of a negative tenure decision, or as a result of that faculty member accepting employment elsewhere.

When, in the passage cited previously, Bentham argues that "there are no such things as rights anterior to government – no such things as natural rights opposed to, in contradistinction to legal [rights] ...," he is, in effect, suggesting that all rights are conferred rights. The issue with Bentham is not whether there are conferred rights. There clearly are. The issue is whether all rights are conferred rights. For reasons that will be delineated later in this chapter, we believe that there are basic human rights that are not conferred rights.

Finally, as will be noted in greater detail later in this chapter, describing some rights as conferred rights, rather than natural rights, does not by implication suggest that they are of lesser significance. Violations of conferred rights, be they voting rights, the right to receive the healthcare coverage promised by a health insurance plan, or any of a number of other conferred rights, can be exceedingly detrimental to human well-being.

INHERENT RELATIONAL RIGHTS

Conferred rights are a form of relational rights because they are present only when certain types of relationships exist – for example, contractual relationships that give specified individuals voting rights, as in the case of college faculties. Not all relational rights, however, are conferred rights. Some rights are inherent in the nature of the relationship itself. For example, it is plausible to argue that in the parent-child relationship there are certain inherent rights that accrue to the benefit of the child, such as the right to sustenance and the right to care and protection. These rights are not conferred on the child by a parent (and absent if the parent chooses not to confer them). Rather, they are intrinsic to the relationship itself.

Put in slightly different words, inherent relational rights are, in a certain sense, halfway between natural rights and conferred rights. Unlike natural rights, they are not present without something being done by someone else. But unlike conferred rights, they are not present only if someone deliberately and consciously confers them on the individual to whom they pertain. Rather, they rise out of various types of relationships, such as the parent-child relationship, into which individuals, such as those choosing to become parents, enter. While this might at first glance seem to be a minor distinction, the significance of the distinction will become apparent in subsequent chapters when we argue that when multinational corporations engage in business activities in other countries, certain rights, such as the right to fair compensation, come into play simply by virtue of the relationship itself, quite apart from any rights that business entities might be inclined to confer on their employees or on others with whom they have business dealings.

NEGATIVE RIGHTS (RIGHTS OF FORBEARANCE) AND POSITIVE RIGHTS (RIGHTS OF ENTITLEMENT)

Another useful distinction contrasts *negative rights (rights of forbearance)* and *positive rights (rights of entitlement)*. Negative rights are basically rights of noninterference and are respected when those we encounter exercise restraint (forbearance) by not intervening in our lives or the lives of others. Most of the rights specified in the U.S. Bill of Rights (the first ten amendments to the Constitution of the United States) are negative rights. For example, citizens enjoy freedom of speech as long as they do not risk being imprisoned or otherwise being penalized if they express controversial views and freedom of assembly if no one, be it the government or an unruly mob, interferes with their meetings.

In contrast to negative rights, positive rights (rights of entitlement) suggest that something is owed to the possessor of the right.

For example, a faculty member employed by a college or university is entitled to compensation for teaching, as determined by whatever contracts apply. While most of the rights specified in the first ten amendments to the Constitution of the United States are negative rights, there are some positive rights as well. Among these is the "right to a speedy and public trial" specified by the Sixth Amendment.

An important additional observation is here in order. While claims of negative rights are either explicitly or implicitly accompanied by negative injunctions instructing others to stay out of the way and refrain from interfering (e.g., "Thou shalt not interfere with someone else's right to privacy by violating the privacy of that person's home"), positive rights must be accompanied by rules defining affirmative duties directed to specified individuals. If an employee is to receive a paycheck to which she or he is entitled, someone else – the payroll clerk or whoever else is responsible for making certain that those entitled to compensation get paid – must actually do something. In effect, there is an implicit rule defining an affirmative duty that says to the payroll clerk or whoever else is responsible "Thou shalt cut paychecks for employees entitled to compensation." Similarly, the Sixth Amendment carries with it an implicit rule defining an affirmative duty addressed to the district attorney and the district court (or whoever else has jurisdiction) that says, "Thou shalt ensure that the person accused of this crime receives a speedy and public trial." Claims of positive rights make little sense, if any, if those making the claims do not go on to address the question of whose responsibility it is to make good on that to which the bearer of the right is entitled. To use Bentham's picturesque phrase, albeit in a somewhat different context, to make claims about positive rights (rights of entitlement) without going on to address the question of whose job it is to make good on these rights is "rhetorical nonsense – nonsense on stilts."

LIFE, THE MOST BASIC RIGHT

It is not by chance that in many listings of rights, among them the U.S. Declaration of Independence, the French Declaration of the Rights of Man, and the Universal Declaration of Human Rights, life is the first right listed. And indeed, life is the most basic of rights because without life, no other rights are possible.

To list life as an "unalienable" or "imprescriptible" right, however, is not without its difficulties. If continuing to be alive is an absolute right of all human beings, capital punishment, which the drafters of the U.S. Declaration of Independence and the drafters of the charter that established the International Military Tribunal all supported, is precluded. So also is killing in war, be it for self-defense or for any other reason. It might be the case, of course, that all taking of human life is morally indefensible, as pacifists argue. That was not the view, however, of those who signed the U.S. Declaration of Independence, all of whom supported the American War for Independence. Nor was it the view of Justice Jackson and others who supported both the Allied war effort in the fight against Hitler and the capital sentences imposed at the Nuremberg Trials. How can life be an unalienable right if one allows killing enemy combatants and executing war criminals in some situations?

One response might be to say, along the lines of those who assert that liberty is not an unlimited right (a view discussed in greater detail later in this chapter), that life itself is not an unlimited right. In effect, that would be to say that life is an unalienable right when the right is present but that the right to live is not always present.

That, however, is a rather contorted response, one that has the potential of a good deal of abuse because it leaves the door open for government officials or others to decide who has a right to live and who does not. Moreover, it flies in the face of the claim that "all men are created equal, that they are endowed by their Creator with certain unalienable Rights, that among these are Life, Liberty and the pursuit of Happiness."

Short of becoming an absolute pacifist, is there a better way of responding to this dilemma? There is – one that draws upon the just war tradition. Stripped to its essentials, the just war tradition holds that war is always evil but that in some cases, such as a war of self-defense, it is the lesser of evils. When applied more specifically to life as a basic right, this argument acknowledges that killing someone violates his or her right to live and hence is always wrong. However, it also suggests that in limited and carefully specified circumstances, this might be the lesser of evils.[46]

---

[46] In *Contra Faustum*, Augustine states with respect to the question of what constitutes a just war, "A great deal depends on the causes for which men undertake wars, and

Another way of putting this is to say, as did British philosopher
W.D. Ross (1877–1971), that we often find ourselves with competing
prima facie obligations. If the conflicts between our competing *prima
facie* obligations cannot be resolved, we then are faced with the task
of establishing priorities, thereby determining which of our competing *prima facie* obligations is our actual obligation in a particular
situation.[47] Suppose, for example, that you are taking a critically ill
family member to the hospital and encounter a traffic light that is red
at 3:15 AM with no traffic in sight. Do you make good on your *prima
facie* obligation to get your critically ill family member to the hospital
as quickly as possible or make good on your *prima facie* obligation to
comply with traffic laws? If, as most would probably do, you choose
to ignore the red light and drive on through the intersection, you

on the authority they have for doing so; for the natural order which seeks the peace
of mankind, ordains that the monarch should have the power of undertaking war
if he thinks it advisable, and that the soldiers should perform their military duties
in behalf of the peace and safety of the community" (*Contra Faustum*, XXII, 75,
trans. Richard Stothert, in *A Select Library of the Nicene and Post-Nicene Fathers of The
Christian Church*, Vol. IV, *Writings in Connection with the Manichaean Controversy*, ed.
Philip Schaff [Grand Rapids, MI: Wm. B. Eerdmans Publishing Company, 1887],
301.) In *Summa Theologica*, Thomas Aquinas suggests that three conditions must be
met if a war is to be just: "First, the authority of the sovereign by whose command
the war is to be waged. For it is not the business of a private person to declare war....
Second, a just cause is required, namely that those who are attacked should be
attacked because they deserve it on account of some fault.... Third, it is necessary
that the belligerents should have a right intention, so that they intend the advance-
ment of good, or the avoidance of evil" (*Summa Theologica*, II-II, Q.40, A. 1, trans.
Fathers of the English Dominican Province, rev. Daniel J. Sullivan, Great Books of
the Western World, Vol. XX [Chicago: Encyclopedia Britannica, Inc., 1952], 578.)
Hugo Grotius, while deemphasizing *jus ad bellum* (justice in going to war) and placing greater emphasis on *jus in bello* (justice in the conduct of war) insisted that war
be conducted under the authority of a sovereign and that a declaration of war be
issued: "*It is essential to the nature of a public war that it should have the support of the sovereign power.... A declaration of war is also requisite*" (*The Law of War and Peace [De Jure
Belli ac Pacis Libri Tres]*, III, iv-v, trans. Francis W. Kelsey [Indianapolis: The Bobbs-
Merrill Company, Inc., 1925], 633.) Summarizing classical just war theory, James
Turner Johnson lists the major *jus ad bellum* criteria as just cause, right authority,
right intent, proportionality, the end of peace and last resort (*Can Modern War Be
Just?*, 18.) James F. Childress lists the traditional *jus ad bellum* criteria as just cause,
last resort, announcement of intentions, reasonable hope of success, proportion-
ality and just intention (James F. Childress, "Just-War Criteria" in *War or Peace?
The Search for New Answers*, ed. Thomas A. Shannon [Maryknoll, NY: Orbis Books,
1980], 46–48), while Ralph Potter adds highest lawful authority to the list (*War and
Moral Discourse* [Richmond, VA: John Knox Press, 1969], 43–44).

47 W.D. Ross, *The Right and the Good* (Oxford: Clarendon Press, 1930), 41–47.

would have, in effect, decided that your obligation to get your critically ill family member to the hospital as quickly as possible was the stronger obligation in this particular situation. Note, however, that if you decide to drive on through the intersection, you are not by implication saying that you have no obligation to comply with traffic laws. You are merely saying that your obligation to get your critically ill family member to the hospital is stronger than your obligation to comply with traffic laws in this particular situation.

Killing someone, of course, is a far more serious matter than driving through a red light at an intersection. The same type of argument, however, can be applied. We all have a *prima facie* obligation to respect the right of others to live. However, in certain wartime situations, and perhaps in other situations as well, competing *prima facie* obligations of a grave nature might be given priority. This is not to suggest in any way that there is not anything wrong with violating others' right to live by killing them. Rather it is merely to suggest that sometimes taking life is the lesser of evils – something to be done mournfully and with great regret, but nevertheless something that is sometimes justifiable on moral grounds.

IS SURVIVING A RIGHT OF ENTITLEMENT?

In the West, the right to live is commonly viewed as a negative right – that is, as the right to be spared a violent death. A statement on human rights issued by the Information Office of the State Council of the People's Republic of China puts a different spin on the matter. It asserts, "It is a simple truth that, for any country or nation, the right to subsistence is the most important of all human rights, without which the other rights are out of the question.... To solve their human rights problems, the first thing for the Chinese people to do is ... to secure the right to subsistence."[48]

This statement can be construed as suggesting that the right to subsistence – that is, the right to have access to those things such as food that are essential for survival – is a right of entitlement (positive right). The statement does not go on to specify whose job it is to make

[48] Information Office of the State Council of the People's Republic of China, *Human Rights in China* (1991), 10–11, at http://news.xinhuanet.com/employment/200211/18/content_633179.htm (last accessed September 8, 2006).

certain that the Chinese people have access to food and the other things that are essential for survival, though it can be surmised that in a socialist country, which China is in theory if not in practice, it is the government that has the ultimate responsibility for these matters. As will be noted in greater detail in Chapter 4, the belief that the right to subsistence is the most basic right puts in a different light China's one-child policy, which has been widely criticized in the West for what many Westerners believe to be human rights violations. More on that later.

LIBERTY: ARE THERE LIMITS?

What about liberty? Is liberty an absolute natural right? If liberty is an absolute natural right, there is not a case to be made for incarcerating criminals because incarceration by its very nature interferes with liberty.

That, however, was surely not the intent of Jefferson and the other signers of the U.S. Declaration of Independence. Jefferson himself observed, "Of liberty I would say that, in the whole plenitude of its extent, it is unobstructed action according to our will. But rightful liberty is unobstructed action according to our will within the limits drawn around us by the equal rights of other."[49] A century-and-a-half later, U.S. Supreme Court Justice Oliver Wendell Holmes, Jr. (1841–1935) is reported to have said, "My right to swing my fist ends where the other man's nose begins."[50] Article 29 of the Universal Declaration of Human Rights states that in the exercise of rights and freedoms, "everyone should be subject only to such limitations as are determined by law solely for the purpose of securing due recognition and respect for the rights and freedoms of others...." In a frequently quoted passage in *A Theory of Justice*, Harvard philosopher John Rawls (1921–2002) proposes that "each person is to have an equal right to

---

[49] Thomas Jefferson, *Letter to Isaac H. Tiffany (1819)*. Quoted in *Thomas Jefferson on Politics & Government* at http://etext.virginia.edu/jefferson/quotations/jeff0100. htm (last accessed October 26, 2007).

[50] Though the quotation is frequently attributed to Holmes, the source is never identified, making it difficult to ascertain whether or not the statement was actually made by him.

the most extensive basic liberty compatible with a similar liberty for others."[51]

And so it is quite common to suggest that we do not have absolute liberty but rather liberty within limits, with the limits defined by respect for the rights and liberty of others. This view is not entirely compatible with the ringing words of the U.S. Declaration of Independence, which, if our liberty is not unlimited liberty (and our right to live is not an unlimited right), would have to be redrafted to read, "We hold these truths to be self-evident, that all men are created equal, that they are endowed by their Creator with certain unalienable Rights, that among these are Life (within certain limits), Liberty (within certain limits) and the pursuit of Happiness (within certain limits)." That is not a statement likely to resonate through the halls of history. Nevertheless, the view that our liberty is not absolute liberty but rather liberty within limits defined by respect for the rights and liberty of others has at least some degree of plausibility.

There is, however, another way of looking at this, a way that draws upon the distinction between *prima facie* and actual obligations noted previously. This approach begins with the assertion that everyone has a basic right to complete liberty and we all have a *prima facie* obligation to respect the liberty of others. However, we also have other *prima facie* obligations such as the obligation to stand with those who are threatened and help defend them. Sometimes these competing *prima facie* obligations take priority over our *prima facie* obligation to respect the right of others to complete liberty, particularly in cases in which some might be using this liberty to harm their fellow human beings. This second approach has the advantage of facilitating a more nuanced approach to the question of when limiting liberty is appropriate, one that allows different types of judgments in different situations.

The desirability of a nuanced approach is underscored by Justice Holmes, who delivered the opinion of the Supreme Court of the United States in *Schenk v. United States* and *Baer v. United States*. (It is from this opinion that the oft-quoted statement that "[t]he most stringent protection of free speech would not protect a man in falsely

---

[51] John Rawls, *A Theory of Justice* (Cambridge, MA: The Belknap Press of Harvard University Press, 1971), 60.

shouting fire in a theatre and causing a panic" comes.) In these two decisions, issued jointly, the Court upheld the conviction of the defendants, who were charged with violating the Espionage Act of June 15, 1917, by distributing leaflets opposing the military draft. Justice Holmes stated in the opinion:

> The question in every case is whether the words used ... are of such a nature as to create a clear and present danger.... It is a question of proximity and degree. When a nation is at war many things that might be said in time of peace are such a hindrance to its effort that their utterance will not be endured so long as men fight and that no Court could regard them as protected by any constitutional right.[52]

SOME CONCLUSIONS

While philosophical discussions can – and often do – continue forever, all chapters in all books must in time come to an end. And so we of necessity must come to some summary conclusions. Based on the foregoing and in an effort to bring as much clarity as possible to what is often a very confused discussion, we propose the following:

1. *The right to live is the most basic human right.*

We deliberately use the phrase "the right to live" rather that the phrase "the right to life" for two reasons. One is that the phrase "the right to life" has been coopted by one side in the often bitter abortion debate. While the question of when the life of an individual human being begins is an important one, we do not wish to digress from our discussion of human rights and the ethics of globalization to address a question that has no completely satisfactory answer.[53]

The second and more significant reason that we have chosen to use the phrase "the right to live" is that any meaningful notion of basic human rights, at least within Western philosophical and political traditions, must encompass more than simply biological existence. It is more than just being alive. It also has to do with the way that one is

---

[52] Supreme Court of the United States, *Schenck v. United States; Baer v. United States*, 249 U.S. 47 at 52.

[53] One of the authors of this volume has addressed the question of when the life of an individual human being begins in Daniel E. Lee, *Freedom v. Intervention: Six Tough Cases* (Lanham, MD: Rowman & Littlefield Publishers, Inc., 2005), 37–62.

able to live one's life. And indeed, that is precisely what Locke and Jefferson had in mind when they spoke, not just of a right of life, but also of liberty and the pursuit of happiness (or property, in Locke's case, though his notion of property encompasses far more than just material possessions[54]). Thus liberty, including freedom of speech, freedom of religion, and the other basic liberties enshrined in the Bill of Rights, are intrinsic to the notion of being able to live one's life as one sees fit.

2. *The right to live is best understood as a natural right, rather than as a conferred right.*

As noted previously, the epistemological claim made by natural law theorists – namely, the claim that "an intelligence common to all of us" enables determining that certain things are right and other things are wrong – is deeply flawed. However, rejecting the epistemological claim that natural law theorists make does not by implication suggest that there is really not anything that is right or wrong. Being value noncognitivists, which we are, does not automatically make us subjectivists on the ontological level. When one looks at the horrors of the Holocaust, it is difficult, if not impossible, to conclude that morality is "simply in the eye of the beholder" and that Nazi morality is just as good as any other system of morality. Sartre's assertion that "no signs are vouchsafed in this world" and "[y]ou are free, therefore choose – that is to say, invent" leaves us with little moral traction. Some things are so appalling, so horrific, that it is inconceivable that they could even remotely be morally acceptable. The Holocaust is a case in point.

And so rejecting the epistemological claim that natural law theorists make does not automatically lead to rejection of the claim that there really are some things that are right and some things that are wrong. Being value noncognitivists, however, does mean that when making value claims, in the final analysis we can do more than say of the ultimate values that give rise to the ethical claims we make that we firmly believe that these values are the appropriate ones. That might be what Jefferson had in mind when drafting the U.S. Declaration of Independence. It is interesting to note that in Jefferson's rough draft,

[54] See footnote 11.

"self-evident" does not appear. Rather, Jefferson states, "We hold these truths to be sacred & undeniable; that all men are created equal & independent, that from that equal creation they derive rights inherent & inalienable, among which are the preservation of life, & liberty, & the pursuit of happiness...."[55] The phrase "hold these truths to be sacred & undeniable" can be construed simply as a strong statement of belief.

In any event, it makes eminent sense to view the right to live as a natural right, rather than as a conferred right – that is, as a right that is "inherent & inalienable," rather than as a right that is contingent on institutional guarantees or on the actions of others. Indeed, to view the right to live as something that is contingent on the actions of others would cheapen the notion beyond recognition.[56]

 3. *Natural rights are best understood as negative rights (rights of forbearance), rather than as positive rights (rights of entitlement).*

Jefferson and the other drafters of the U.S. Declaration of Independence were wise to view natural rights as negative rights (rights of forbearance) – that is, as rights that are respected simply by staying out of the way of others and refraining from interfering in their lives. The drafters of the U.S. Declaration of Independence were not trying to get rid of King George III of England. They certainly were not suggesting that he ought to be beheaded. They simply wanted him to leave them alone so that they could live their lives as they saw fit and came to the reluctant conclusion that independence was necessary if that was to be realized.

The problem with expansive lists of natural or basic rights that include positive rights (rights of entitlement) is that the result is often a laundry list that is so lacking in precision that it is at best confusing and, in many cases, well nigh meaningless. The Universal Declaration of Human Rights is a case in point. The laundry list of human rights

[55] "Jefferson's 'original Rough draught' of the U.S. Declaration of Independence," 423. Some believe that the change of "sacred & undeniable" to "self-evident" was made at the suggestion of Benjamin Franklin, though that is far from being a settled matter (*ibid.*, n.2., 427).
[56] In suggesting that the right to live is a natural right, we are not by implication suggesting that this right, or any other right, can be derived from a study of nature; we are merely suggesting that it exists independent of anything that someone else might or might not do.

delineated in this document includes "the right to rest and leisure" (Article 24), "the right to a standard of living adequate for the health and well-being of himself and of his family, including food, clothing, housing and medical care and necessary social services" (Article 25), "the right to security in the event of unemployment, sickness, disability, widowhood, old age or other lack of livelihood in circumstances beyond his control" (Article 25), and "the right to education" which "shall be free, at least in the elementary and fundamental stages" (Article 26).

All of these are morally praiseworthy sentiments. All are goals worth striving to achieve. The problem, however, is that the document does not go on to address the all-important question of whose job it is to make good on these rights of entitlement. There is a fundamental difference between statements of ideals portraying the world as we would like to see it and statements of basic rights. Statements of ideals can be, and often are, directed toward inspiring and motivating others. As such, they perform a very useful function.[57] Statements of basic rights that include rights of entitlement, however, must go beyond rhetoric and address the practical question of whose responsibility it is to ensure that these rights are realized. In *Flores v. Southern Peru Copper Corporation*, the 2nd Circuit Court of Appeals was correct when, after examining the Universal Declaration of Human Rights and other international declarations, it concluded that the aspirations given expression in these documents are too amorphous to be considered binding rules of international law.[58]

At the same time, the importance of aspirations should not be underestimated. Lyndon Baines Johnson, the thirty-sixth president of the United States (1963–1969), was fond of quoting the King James version translation of Proverbs 29.18: "Where *there is* no vision, the people perish...."[59] The human condition is such that we wither away

---

[57] In *A World Made New*, Glendon observes, "The Universal Declaration charted a bold new course for human rights by presenting a vision of freedom as linked to social security, balanced by responsibilities, grounded in respect for equal human dignity, and guarded by the rule of law"(235).

[58] *Flores v. Southern Peru Copper Corporation*, 414 F.3d 233, 254 (2nd Cir. 2003).

[59] The King James version is a rather loose translation of the text. A more accurate translation of Proverbs 29.18 can be found in the New Revised Standard Version of the Bible: "Where there is no prophecy, the people cast off restraint...."

and perish when we have no aspirations, when there is no vision of what might be. The Universal Declaration of Human Rights is an inspiring vision of what might be. It is, above all else, an affirmation of hope.

> 4. *In some cases, conferred rights, many of which are positive rights (rights of entitlement), are just as important as natural rights.*

None of the foregoing is intended to suggest that conferred rights are always less significant than natural rights.[60] Indeed, in some situations it might even be the case that conferred rights are necessary if natural rights are to be realized. Take, for example, the right to vote. Jefferson and the other visionaries who were present at the creation of the United States realized that democracy is the best defense against incursions on individual rights by abusive authoritarian forms of government. Thus, the right to vote ends up being important not just because the opportunity to participate in governance enhances freedom but because it can be, and often is, a way of securing and protecting other rights.

Martin Luther King, Jr. (1929–1968) was keenly aware of the importance of full participation in the processes of governance. On August 28, 1963, standing on the steps of the Lincoln Memorial in Washington, D.C., he eloquently stated:

In a sense we have come to our nation's capital to cash a check. When the architects of our republic wrote the magnificent words of the Constitution and the U.S. Declaration of Independence, they were signing a promissory note to which every American was to fall heir. This note was a promise that all men, yes, black men as well as white men, would be guaranteed the unalienable rights of life, liberty, and the pursuit of happiness. It is obvious today that America has defaulted on this promissory note insofar as her citizens of color are concerned.... Now is the time to make real the promises of democracy. Now is the time to rise from the dark and desolate valley of segregation to the sunlit path of racial justice. Now is the time to lift our nation from the quick sands of racial injustice to the solid rock of brotherhood. Now is the time to make justice a reality for all of God's children.

---

[60] This is not to imply that all conferred rights are of equal significance. For example, the right to park in a parking lot reserved for faculty and staff is hardly of the same magnitude as voting rights (though to those desperately looking for a place to park that might seem to be so at the time).

Then, setting aside his prepared text and speaking from the heart, he went on to say that "even though we face the difficulties of today and tomorrow, I still have a dream. It is a dream deeply rooted in the American dream. I have a dream that one day this nation will rise up and live out the true meaning of its creed: 'We hold these truths to be self-evident: that all men are created equal....'"[61] King's inspiring words captured the conscience of the nation.

5. *Rights claims do not exhaust all there is to say about ethics; in some cases, it makes more sense simply to talk about moral obligations, rather than attempt to subsume everything under the rubric of rights.*

In a thought-provoking book entitled *Rights Talk: The Impoverishment of Political Discourse*, Glendon cautions, "As various new rights are proclaimed or proposed, the catalog of individual liberties expands without much consideration of the ends to which they are oriented, their relationship to one another, to corresponding responsibilities, or to the general welfare." She adds, "Our rights talk, in its absoluteness, promotes unrealistic expectations, heightens social conflict, and inhibits dialogue that might lead toward consensus, accommodation, or at least the discovery of common ground."[62]

Glendon is right. The language of rights has been greatly overextended. Like Glendon, we prefer narrower, more precise definitions of rights – narrower, more precise definitions that will salvage the language of rights from the tangled wilderness of utter confusion.

---

[61] Martin Luther King, Jr., "I Have a Dream" at http://www.usconstitution.net/ dream.html (last accessed October 27, 2007). This website has the exact text of the speech as it was delivered, transcribed from recordings. By using language such as "promissory note" to refer to the statements of rights in the U.S. Declaration of Independence and the Constitution of the United States, King might be departing from the traditional understanding of freedom as a negative right (right of forbearance) and instead suggesting that "the unalienable rights of life, liberty and the pursuit of happiness" are positive rights (rights of entitlement). While it might be possible to argue that life, liberty and the pursuit of happiness are at the same time both negative rights and positive rights, it makes more sense to interpret King's speech as suggesting that government has a duty to stand with those who are threatened to protect them from those interfering with their basic rights – that is, that government functions as a guarantor of rights and that this is the promissory note to which King makes reference.

[62] Mary Ann Glendon, *Rights Talk: The Impoverishment of Political Discourse* (New York: The Free Press, 1991), x, 14.

It is for this reason that we insist that one should refrain from making claims about rights of entitlement unless one is also prepared to address the question of whose job it is to make good on those rights of entitlement.

There are other reasons as well for preferring a more modest approach to the use of the language of rights. As Glendon correctly points out, rights claims are by their very nature confrontational, leading in many cases to litigation. To be sure, neither she nor we are suggesting that confrontation is never appropriate. The Civil Rights Movement would never have happened had King and others not been willing to confront the entrenched power that was perpetrating the injustices of racial discrimination and unequal treatment. And in the last chapter of this volume we suggest that litigation under the provisions of the Alien Tort Claims Act can be a useful tool for encouraging U.S. multinational corporations to refrain from acts harmful to those living in the countries in which they operate.

As Glendon and others realize, however, we will all be better off if we can foster the values of community, rather than only the values of confrontation – if we can rediscover what it is to be a neighbor, rather than just a naysayer. None of this is easy to accomplish. Indeed, it is far easier to make rights claims of a confrontational nature than it is to weave the fabric of community, fabric that includes the bonds of obligations and responsibilities as well as affirmations of individual rights. The task of weaving the fabric of community is even more daunting in an era of globalization in which we have, to use the language of the theologian Karl Barth, both near neighbors and distant neighbors.[63] Taking on this daunting challenge forms the agenda for the next chapter.

[63] Karl Barth, *Church Dogmatics*, Vol. 3, Part 4, *The Doctrine of Creation*, trans. A.T. MacKay et al. (Edinburgh: T. & T. Clark, 1961), 285–302. One should not assume, however, that Barth would have agreed with the conclusions reached in Chapter 2. He was using the terms in a somewhat different context.

2

Near Neighbors, Distant Neighbors, and the Ethics of Globalization

In the prologue we asked whether Paulette Johnson's job is more important than Yun Liu's job or vice versa. (Paulette Johnson was one of 4,500 workers making Fieldcrest, Cannon, and Royal Velvet sheets and towels at Pillowtex Corporation's plant in Kannapolis, North Carolina, but lost her job when the company shut down the plant because it could not compete with imports from countries such as China; Yun Liu left the poverty-stricken rural area in China where she grew up and went to work for the Huafang Cotton Weaving Company, one of China's largest textile mills, a mill that supplies the export market.) If one accepts an ethic of universal human rights that affirms the dignity and worth of each person and asserts that all people living in all countries in all parts of the world should be viewed as possessing equal rights, the answer to this question can succinctly be stated: Paulette Johnson's job and Yun Liu's job are of equal importance. Yun Liu has just as much right to be employed as Paulette Johnson and vice versa. In short, when it comes to the importance of having a job, there are no distinctions to be made between our near neighbors and our distant neighbors, between ourselves, our families, and those who live down the street from us, on the one hand, and, on the other hand, those who live some distance from us.

There is, however, a related question that is far more complex: Are there any distinctions to be made about the obligations and responsibilities we might have with respect to our family members and those who live near to us, compared to our obligations and responsibilities with respect to those who live in distant countries? Take, for example, the matter of providing funding for a college education. If one assumes that each person is of equal significance, does this mean that whatever obligations we might have to pay for the college educations of our own sons and daughters are of equal magnitude to whatever obligations we might have to pay for college educations for young men and women in Ethiopia and Liberia?

Some, of course, might simply approach these matters on the basis of self-interest, arguing that we ought to give priority to funding the college educations of our own sons and daughters because if we do not, they might never leave the nest and could continue to be financial burdens to us for years to come. Similarly, they might argue that helping find new jobs for the unemployed who live down the street from us is far more important than trying to find jobs for the more than 75 percent of the workforce in Liberia that is unemployed, because if the unemployed in the towns and cities in which we live do not find jobs, we will end up having to pay more in taxes for unemployment benefits and other social programs, while what happens to the unemployed in Liberia has little, if any, impact on us.

An ethic of universal human rights that affirms the worth and dignity of each person, however, does not allow this type of crass ethical egoism. Nor does it allow a type of utilitarianism that might rationalize writing off those in other countries if so doing could be shown to contribute to the greater good. It might be added that trying to apply the utilitarian principle of the greatest good for the greatest number to issues related to globalization is risky in other ways as well. If one interprets the principle of the greatest good for the greatest number as suggesting that one ought to support economic policies that maximize the number of people who are employed, while minimizing the number who are unemployed, a case can be made for moving all factories to less-developed countries, where labor-intensive forms of production made possible by low wages typically involve employing more people than capital-intensive forms of production in the United States and Western Europe, where robots have, in many cases, been replacing assembly-line workers. That, however, is not an argument that we wish to make.

In short, an ethic of universal human rights that affirms the worth and dignity of each person does not allow approaching issues related to globalization either on the basis of simple self-interest or on the basis of calculating forms of utilitarianism that are quite willing to sacrifice individuals, including, in some cases, large numbers of individuals. Instead, a human rights–based ethic of globalization insists that everyone counts. Such an ethic demands a more nuanced and discerning approach.

NEGATIVE RIGHTS AND THE ETHICS OF GLOBALIZATION

We begin with the simpler part of the equation. In Chapter 1, we noted that negative rights (rights of forbearance) are essentially rights of noninterference that are respected by refraining from interfering with the liberty of others or otherwise harming them. We also suggested that natural rights – that is, rights that people possess simply because they are human beings, quite apart from contractual arrangements or anything else that someone else might do – are best understood as negative rights. This notion of rights quite readily lends itself to articulating at least the beginnings of an ethic of globalization. Quite simply stated, it asserts that anything that we or anyone else might do that hurts other people is wrong, regardless of who they are or where they live.

This very basic ethical guideline calls into question, for example, practices by multinational corporations that result in the contamination of streams and rivers – pollution that can adversely affect the health and well-being of the local population, thereby violating their most basic rights.[1] (A case in which it is alleged that indigenous

---

[1] For purposes of our discussion, we need not here develop a full-blown environmental ethic. Suffice it to say that when environmental pollution harms other people, it is a human rights issue. More detailed discussions of environmental ethics can be found in the following books: Dale Jamieson, *Ethics and the Environment: An Introduction* (New York: Cambridge University Press, 2008); Robert Elliott, ed., *Environmental Ethics: Oxford Readings in Philosophy* (New York: Oxford University Press, 1995); Christine E. Gudorf and James Edward Huchingson, *Boundaries: A Casebook in Environmental Ethics* (Washington, DC: Georgetown University Press, 2003); Louis Pojman, *Global Environmental Ethics* (Mountain View, CA: Mayfield Publishers, 2000); Ben A. Minteer, ed., *Nature in Common? Environmental Ethics and the Contested Foundations of Environmental Policy* (Philadelphia: Temple University Press, 2009); Walter Kennedy Dodds, *Humanity's Footprint: Momentum, Impact, and Our Global Environment* (New York: Columbia University Press, 2008); Marti Kheel, *Nature Ethics: An Ecofeminist Perspective* (Lanham, MD: Rowman & Littlefield, 2008);

groups in Ecuador were harmed by industrial pollution is discussed in Chapter 9.) These, however, are the easy cases (though holding multinational corporations accountable for such activity is far easier said than done, matters that are also discussed in Chapter 9). Far more complex and difficult are market relationships that are detrimental to various individuals – market relationships in which, to varying degrees, we all participate. An example is provided by the world coffee market. As will be noted in Chapter 6, a glut of coffee on the world market resulted in plummeting coffee prices, which was disastrous for coffee farmers in Ethiopia and elsewhere, particularly for the small farmers who account for a significant portion of world coffee production.

Some might respond by saying, "But we had nothing to do with that. We aren't the ones responsible for the glut of coffee on the world coffee market." And in a certain literal sense, that, of course, is true. However, matters that at first glance appear to be simple rarely are when examined in greater detail. If we purchase coffee or any other commodity exclusively on the base of price without giving any consideration to what is received by the farmer who produced the commodity or the miners who extracted it from the earth, we are part of the problem, even though we were not intentionally trying to harm small farmers struggling to survive and miners who are paid very little for long hours of backbreaking labor.[2] The same is true with respect

---

John O'Neil, *Markets, Deliberation, and the Environment* (London: Routledge, 2007); Charles S. Brown and Ted Toadvine, eds., *Nature's Edge: Boundary Explorations in Ecological Theory and Practice* (Albany: State University of New York Press, 2007), Robert D. Bullard, ed., *The Quest for Environmental Justice: Human Rights and the Politics of Pollution* (San Francisco: Sierra Club Books, 2005), Richard P. Hiskes, *The Human Right to a Green Future: Environmental Rights and Intergenerational Justice* (New York: Cambridge University Press, 2009), Paul W. Taylor, *Respect for Environmental Ethics* (Princeton, NJ: Princeton University Press, 1986), Thomas L. Friedman, *Hot, Flat, and Crowded: Why We Need a Green Revolution – and How It Can Renew America* (New York: Farrar, Straus, and Giroux, 2008); Kristin Schrader-Frechette, *Environmental Justice: Creating Equality, Reclaiming Democracy* (New York: Oxford University Press, 2002); and Holmes Rolston III, *Environmental Ethics: Duties to and Values in the Natural World* (Philadelphia: Temple University Press, 1988).

[2] The question of whether – and to what extent – intent affects the morality of an act is a complicated matter. In both law and ethics, intent often plays a role. For example, premeditated murder is typically considered to be a more serious offense than involuntary manslaughter even though the end result is the same, namely, the death of a human being. However, even if one allows that intent (or lack thereof) can have

to purchasing jeans, shirts, or anything else that is manufactured by poorly paid workers in sweatshops located in China and elsewhere. It is for this reason that organizations such as Oxfam International,[3] the Fair Trade Federation,[4] and United Students Against Sweatshops[5] are working hard to increase consumer awareness and encourage consumers to purchase fair trade products that provide a decent return to the farmers and workers who produce them. And it is for this reason that advocacy groups have promoted films such as *Black Gold: A Film about Coffee and Trade*[6] and *China Blue*, a film about the blue jeans business in China that aired on PBS as part of the Independent Lens series.[7]

Much of what happens, of course, is market driven. The owner of the blue jeans factory profiled in *China Blue* is not portrayed as an evil person who is indifferent to the plight of his employees. Rather, he finds himself in a difficult situation. To get a new order from a British buyer, he must agree to very low prices and a very tight delivery schedule, which forces him to reduce his workers' pay and require them to work around the clock to meet the delivery deadline.

Sometimes it is possible to change market realities in ways that will be beneficial to small farmers and those working for low wages. Some ways of doing this are noted in Chapters 5 and 6, respectively – forming unions to negotiate more favorable wages and working conditions, as has been done in the case of Firestone workers in Liberia (discussed in Chapter 5), joining together in cooperatives to improve market position (discussed in Chapter 6), and trademarking high-quality

---

an impact on the seriousness of the offense, this does not by implication suggest that it is acceptable to unintentionally harm others. As the notion of involuntary manslaughter serves to remind us, certain things, such as killing innocent people, are wrong, even if done unintentionally.

[3] Information about Oxfam International can be accessed at http://www.oxfam.org/en/about.

[4] Information about the Fair Trade Federation can be accessed at http://www.fairtradefederation.org/ht/d/sp/i/197/pid/197.

[5] Information about United Students Against Sweatshops can be accessed at http://www.studentsagainstsweatshops.org//index.php?option=com_content&task=view&id=20&Itemid=27.

[6] Additional information about "Black Gold: A Film about Coffee and Trade" can be accessed at http://www.blackgoldmovie.com.

[7] Additional information about "China Blue" can be accessed at http://www.pbs.org/independentlens/chinablue.

products, as producers of specialty coffees in Ethiopia are attempting to do (also discussed in Chapter 6). In other cases, however, it is
not possible to restructure market realities in ways that are favorable
to less-advantaged workers and producers. In these cases, appealing
to the moral sentiments of consumers, as the fair trade movement
is attempting to do, is often the most practical course of action.
Sometimes it is the only course of action. (In Chapter 6, we discuss
the fair trade movement and appealing to moral sentiments in relation to Adam Smith's *The Theory of Moral Sentiments*.)

HOW MIGHT FAIR TRADE BE DEFINED?

Free market economists are quick to point out that in a competitive market economy, the market price of a good is determined by
the interplay of the forces of supply and demand. If there is greater
demand for a particular good, and supply does not keep pace with
this greater demand, the price of the good is bid up. On the other
hand, if there is an increase in the supply of a good without a corresponding increase in the demand for that good (as happened a few
years ago on the world coffee market), the market price drops.

There are, however, no market mechanisms for determining what
might constitute a fair trade price for a commodity or product. Rather,
it essentially ends up being whatever those giving fair trade certification to a commodity or product think it is.

This is not to suggest that that fair trade prices are arbitrarily chosen. Rather, fair trade certifiers typically have carefully defined criteria that they use to determine what they identify as fair trade prices for
various goods and commodities. Fairtrade Labelling Organizations
International (FLO), a consortium of fair trade labeling organizations in Europe, Canada, the United States, Japan, Australia, and New
Zealand, defines fair trade as follows: "Fair Trade is a trading partnership, based on dialogue, transparency and respect, that seeks greater
equity in international trade. It contributes to sustainable development by offering better trading conditions to, and securing their rights
of, disadvantaged producers and workers – especially in the South."[8]

---

[8] Fairtrade Labelling Organizations International, "What is Fair Trade" at http://
www.fairtrade.net/about_fairtrade.html (last accessed September 3, 2008).

More specific criteria are delineated in a forty-three-page document entitled *Generic Fairtrade Standards for Small Farmers' Organizations* and a document of similar length entitled *Generic Fairtrade Standards for Hired Labour*,[9] which set both minimum requirements and progress requirements for participation in their certification programs. The minimum requirements are intended to ensure that:

1. Fair trade benefits reach the small farmers and/or workers.
2. The small farmers' organization and/or the workers has/have potential for development.
3. Fair trade instruments can take effect and lead to development that cannot be achieved otherwise.

FLO further specifies progress requirements "on which producer organizations must show permanent improvement," with reporting to be done on an annual basis.[10] In addition to the generic standards, FLO issues fair trade standards for coffee and other products specifying both the Fairtrade minimum price and the Fairtrade premium that participating traders are expected to pay for different varieties of coffee and other commodities.[11] For example, the Fairtrade minimum price, which went into effect June 1, 2008, for washed Arabica coffee beans is $1.25 a pound with a Fairtrade premium of ten cents a pound.[12] (The premium goes to a fund used to finance projects beneficial to participating organizations, with allocation decisions made democratically by these organizations.[13])

---

[9] Both *Generic Fairtrade Standards for Small Farmers' Organizations* and *Generic Fairtrade Standards for Hired Labour* can be accessed on Fairtrade Labelling Organizations International's website at http://www.fairtrade.net/producer_standards.html.

[10] Fairtrade Labelling Organizations International, "Generic Fairtrade Standards for Small Farmers' Organizations," 3.

[11] FLO's fair trade pricing standards for coffee and other commodities can be accessed at http://www.fairtrade.net/producers.html.

[12] Fairtrade Labelling Organizations International, "Fairtrade Standards for Coffee for Small Farmers' Organizations," 6. The pricing guidelines note that if the market price, as established by the New York commodities market, should exceed the fair trade price, the market price should take priority.

[13] Fairtrade Labelling Organizations International, "Generic Fairtrade Standards for Small Farmers' Organizations," 6. To participate in the fair trade certification program, FLO requires that small farmers and workers be organized, be it in the form of a farm cooperative, a labor union, or in some other way.

The somewhat imprecise nature of fair trade standards does not mean they are not of significance. Though there might be room for debate as to what constitutes a fair price for a commodity or product, there is little room for debate about the core of the fair trade argument, namely, the claim that if we are to treat all people with respect and dignity and are to refrain from actions harmful to others, we ought to refrain from buying products from producers who marginalize their workers by not paying them enough to provide a decent living for their families. If consumers looked beyond the price tag when purchasing blue jeans, the market for blue jeans produced in sweatshops, such as the one profiled in *China Blue*, would dry up and the British purchasing agents could no longer demand extremely low prices and very tight delivery schedules. Fair trade certification allows consumers to look beyond the price tag and purchase only products with pricing structures that ensure that the small farmers and workers who produce them are not harmed by being underpaid or otherwise exploited. Granted, this results in higher costs for consumers in affluent countries such as the United States and those in Western Europe (albeit costs that are voluntarily assumed). But is this not preferable to being unwitting accomplices to economic practices that harm our fellow human beings in less-developed countries? An ethic of universal human rights that mandates treating all people with respect and dignity suggests that it is.

An additional observation is in order. It is far easier for most of us to refrain from harming our near neighbors than to refrain from harming our distant neighbors. When we learn to know our near neighbors, we quickly come to realize that they, like we, are human beings who know times of hope and times of despair, times of joy and times of sorrow, times of success and times of failure. In contrast, there is a pronounced tendency to ignore the humanity of our distant neighbors, most of whom we never see. It is very easy to overlook the fact that they, like we, are also human beings who know times of hope and times of despair, times of joy and times of sorrow, times of success and times of failure (though, it should be added, for many in Liberia, Ethiopia, and elsewhere, the measure of despair and sorrow far exceeds the measure of hope and joy). And when we ignore their humanity – when their needs and concerns do not even show up on our radar screens – it is very easy to act with indifference toward them and, because of this indifference, do things that are harmful to them.

In short, if an ethic of universal human rights that calls upon us to treat all of our fellow human beings with respect and dignity is to have any traction with respect to our distant neighbors, we must increase awareness that they, like we, are human beings who know times of hope and times of despair, times of joy and times of sorrow, times of success and times of failure. How might this be accomplished? Films like *Black Gold* and *China Blue* can help increase awareness of the plight of others. Indeed, just attaching a name to a face helps. Watching *China Blue*, which tells the story of Jasmine, a seventeen-year-old factory worker who left the rural village where she was born to go to a large urban area to work in the blue jeans factory, puts a human face on the plight of workers in garment factories in China. In a certain sense, Jasmine comes to symbolize all exploited workers in similar situations and, by so doing, makes us aware of their humanity.

Awareness of the humanity of our distant neighbors can be gained in other ways as well. International study programs that take us to less-developed countries and introduce us to people who live there (experiences in which both of the authors of this volume have participated) and other international programs help, as does international travel and experiences such as visiting a center for war refugees. Because most of us do not routinely have the needs and concerns of our distant neighbors on our radar screens, awareness of their needs and concerns and of their humanity is something that must constantly be fostered and nurtured.

RELATIONAL RIGHTS AND OUR NEAR AND DISTANT NEIGHBORS

In Chapter 1, we noted the difference between natural rights, which people have quite independent of anything that anyone else might do, and conferred rights, which are conferred by action of some sort such as signing a contract. We further noted that conferred rights are a type of relational rights because they are the result of a relationship of some sort that has been established such as a contractually defined employment relationship. We also noted that there are other types of relational rights, such as those involved in the parent-child relationship, that are inherent in the relationship itself, quite independent of any contracts that might or might not have been signed. Finally, we noted that in many cases, both conferred and inherent relational rights are positive rights (rights of entitlement) that specify certain things that identifiable individuals or groups of individuals have the obligation to provide to the possessor of the right. For example, as noted in Chapter 1, in an employer-employee relationship in which the employee is entitled to compensation, someone – the payroll clerk or some other identifiable individual – has the obligation to cut the check for the amount that the employee is entitled to receive and, by so doing, make good on that right of entitlement.

Both conferred and inherent relational rights are of significance for constructing an ethic of globalization. Both offer guidelines for understanding our obligations with respect to our near neighbors and our distant neighbors, respectively. For example, rubber plantation workers in Liberia have certain clearly defined rights of entitlement under the 2008 labor agreement the company signed with the Firestone Agricultural Workers Union of Liberia (FAWUL), the union that represents Firestone's workers. As specified by the contract, rubber tappers (workers who collect the latex from rubber trees) are entitled to wage increases of 24 percent over three years retroactive to January of 2007. Under the terms of the contract, the company is obligated to make good on that commitment. (The Firestone agreement is discussed in greater detail in Chapter 5.) If contractual language conferring specified rights is clear, as it should be, there is nothing more to consider in this more generic portion of our discussion other than to note that once rights of entitlement are clearly specified, all that remains are the question of compliance (i.e., the question of whether all parties to the agreement make good on the commitments they have made) and the question of enforcement if there are compliance problems.

The nature of conferred rights is such that they must be granted knowingly and intentionally, whether in the form of a mutually agreed-upon contract or in the form of official action taken by the individual or institution granting the rights of entitlement – for example, a personnel policy approved by top management that grants employees a specified number of personal leave days. The situation with respect to inherent relational rights is somewhat more complex because they sometimes stem from a relationship that the obligated party did not intentionally – perhaps not even knowingly – enter. While becoming a parent is something that ideally ought to be the result of a deliberate decision, and often is, there are numerous instances of couples, including married couples, unexpectedly becoming parents. This does not in any way diminish the rights of entitlement the child has or the obligations of the parents to make good on these rights of entitlement. Regardless of whether the child is the result of a planned pregnancy or an unplanned pregnancy, the child is entitled to a protective, nurturing, and supportive environment, and the parents are the ones with the primary responsibility to make good on these entitlements. Indeed, these obligations and responsibilities are inherent in the nature of the parent-child relationship. The same can be said with respect to the obligation of adult children to do what they can to ensure the well-being of aged parents; from the perspective of the child, the parent-child relationship is never intentionally chosen but rather is something in which the child simply finds herself or himself.

Though often overlooked, there are inherent rights of entitlement in a wide range of the relationships in which business entities engage, among them the employer-employee relationship, the supplier-customer relationship, and relationships with investors and many others. Indeed, there is a certain sense in which the very nature of business is such that it is about relationships. (More on that in the next chapter.) If there are rights of entitlement inherent in various types of business relationships, it is incumbent on business entities and other participants in these relationships to make good on these rights of entitlement when the responsibility for doing so falls on their shoulders, even if these rights of entitlement are not specified in a written contract. This is true regardless of whether the company is operating in Michigan or Mauritania, California or China.

To be sure, there are sometimes differences of opinion as to what these inherent rights of entitlement might entail. Nevertheless, there is broad consensus that the employer is entitled to receive an honest day's work from each employee and that the employee is entitled to have a safe work environment that is free from sexual harassment or other types of harassment – in short, an environment where he or she is treated with respect and dignity. Similarly, it is plausible to argue that customers ought to be treated with respect and dignity and that integrity in business transactions ought to be maintained, both by the buyer and by the seller. (There is no place for the old notion of *caveat emptor* – let the buyer beware – in a rights-oriented ethic of mutual respect.) The same is true with respect to relations with investors and the whole range of other relationships in which business entities engage, matters that will be discussed in greater detail in the next chapter.

Because contractual rights and inherent relational rights stem from relationships of various sorts, our obligations related to them typically involve near neighbors, rather than distant neighbors. It might be added, however, that the very nature of globalization is such that distant neighbors in many cases become near neighbors. When Firestone established rubber plantations in Liberia under the terms of the 1926 concession agreement, Liberians – at least those hired by Firestone and those living in the areas in which the rubber planta- tions are located – became for them near neighbors. The same is true for the companies that have built factories or opened retail outlets in China, Mexico, or any of a number of other countries in which vari- ous multinational corporations have established operations.

This is not to suggest that with globalization everyone becomes a near neighbor. Even in an age of Internet and other forms of telecom- munication, there are some who remain distant. Moreover, because "near" and "distant" are nothing more than opposite ends of a far- ranging spectrum, nearness admits of degrees. Both geographically and otherwise, the person who lives next door is nearer to us than someone who lives on the other side of town while the person on the other side of town is nearer to us than someone who lives on the other side of the earth. That having been said, however, it bears underscor- ing that globalization, in many different ways, brings distant neigh- bors nearer to us.

CONCENTRIC CIRCLES OF RESPONSIBILITY

To summarize: We have argued that (a) natural rights are best under- stood as negative rights (rights of forbearance), (b) because natural rights have been historically viewed as applying to all people living in all parts of the world, our obligations related to them, such as refraining from harming others, pertain to our distant neighbors as well as to our near neighbors, and (c) positive rights (rights of entitlement), are best understood either as rights that are contractually conferred or as rights that derive from certain types of relationships such as the parent-child relationship and the employer-employee relationship. We now return to the question posed earlier in this chapter: Are whatever obligations we might have to pay for college educations for young men and women in Ethiopia and Liberia of equal magnitude to whatever obligations we might have to pay for the college educations of our own sons and daughters?

If positive rights (rights of entitlement) are understood as deriving from relationships of various types, be they contractual relationships or other types of relationships, there is a strong case to be made for suggesting that the duties and obligations pertaining to rights of entitlement are concentric in nature. In short, as parents and as fellow citizens we have a greater obligation to provide for the educations of our sons and daughters and the sons and daughters of our near neighbors, be it directly or indirectly via taxation, than for the sons and daughters of distant neighbors, though helping cover the costs of the education of the sons and daughters of our distant neighbors might well be morally praiseworthy.[14] When mapping out the differences between negative rights (rights of forbearance) and positive rights (rights of entitlement) in Chapter 1, we noted that claims with respect to positive rights make no sense whatsoever unless one also addresses the question of whose job it is to make good on them. While negative rights and the obligations of noninterference related to them are universal in nature, positive rights and the obligations related to them are particular in nature. We do not have the same level of obligation with respect to the children of our distant neighbors as to our own children (though, of course, it is plausible to argue that distant neighbors who are parents have obligations to their children

---

[14] We stop short of suggesting that parents have an absolute obligation to pay for post-secondary education for their children. As Immanuel Kant reminds us, the ought implies the can. Some parents are not in a position financially to pay college costs for their children. There are also some who believe that working to pay for one's college education can build strength of character, even in situations (some might say particularly in situations) where parents have ample financial resources to pay college costs for their daughters and sons.

commensurate with our obligations to our children). Similarly, asserting that an employer has a contractually defined obligation to provide health benefits to its employees, does not by implication suggest that employers have an obligation to provide similar benefits for those who are not employees or members of employees' families, even though it might be morally praiseworthy if business entities helped fund universal health coverage. Hence, the notion of concentric circles of responsibility. It might be added that using the tax system to finance universal health care coverage for all Americans – a goal of many political liberals – does not by implication suggest that we should use our tax system to finance universal health care coverage for everyone living anywhere in the world, even though health care coverage that is really universal – that is, is world wide – is certainly an ideal worth pursuing. Once again the notion of concentric circles of responsibility comes into play.

MORE THAN RIGHTS

We place strong emphasis on human rights because we firmly believe that all human beings are of significance and because we are persuaded that a strong ethic of human rights can provide useful guidelines in an age of globalization, helping protect the lives, dignity, and well-being of our fellow human beings regardless of who they are or where they live. That having been said, however, we also need to note that an ethic of human rights is, at best, an incomplete ethic, be it within the context of globalization or in any other context. Toward the end of Chapter 1, we suggested that we would do well to avoid overextending the language of human rights by trying to address all ethical questions under the rubric of human rights. The time has come to be more explicit about what we meant by that.

While we again strongly emphasize that we believe that notions of human rights are exceedingly important – and indeed have become even more important in an age of globalization that has seen widespread exploitation and abuse of human beings – notions of human rights, at least as they are rooted in the Age of Enlightenment, have some limitations. One is that they are essentially confrontational in nature. While confronting those who are harming others is often both necessary and appropriate, the ethical ideal must be to move beyond confrontation and establish a real sense of community.

This brings us to a second limitation of notions of human rights as they have been developed in our political traditions. As originally conceived in the Age of the Enlightenment, rights claims are basically directed toward protecting the individual from intrusion or mistreatment by government or by other individuals (notions which, as noted in Chapter 1, have in the post-World War II years been extended to protecting individuals from mistreatment by multinational corporations and other social institutions). John Locke, who played a key role in the development of the natural rights tradition and strongly influenced the thought of Thomas Jefferson and the other drafters of the U.S. Declaration of Independence, saw government as little more than a contrivance to protect the life, liberty, and property of the individual. In a state of nature, he suggested, there would be no government. Everyone would be completely free, subject to no one "for all being kings as much as he, every man his equal...." However, because "the greater part [of humankind are not] strict observers of equity and justice, the enjoyment of the property he has in this state is very unsafe, very unsecure." He continues:

This makes him willing to quit a condition which, however free, is full of fears and continual dangers; and it is not without reason that he seeks out and is willing to join in society with others who are already united, or have a mind to unite, for the mutual preservation of their lives, liberties, and estates, which I call by the general name 'property.'[15]

There is a contrasting philosophical tradition, one that dates back to antiquity, where it is rooted in the thought of Aristotle. This contrasting tradition views human beings not as isolated individuals who band together for no reason other than to protect their property, but rather as social creatures who experience self-realization by living and participating in society. In a passage in *The Politics* that contrasts sharply with the position Locke was to take two millennia later, Aristotle observes that "it is evident that the state is a creation of nature, and that man is by nature a political animal."[16] This is not

---

[15] John Locke, *The Second Treatise of Government*, ed. Thomas P. Peardon, Library of Liberal Arts Edition (Indianapolis: Bobbs-Merrill Company, Inc., 1952), 70–71 (IX, 123).

[16] Aristotle, *The Politics*, rev. trans. Jonathan Barnes, ed. Stephen Everson (Cambridge: Cambridge University Press, 1988), 3 (I, 1253^{a}1–2). Barnes's translation is a revision of the translation by Benjamin Jowett.

to suggest that the state is some preexisting entity. Rather, Aristotle believes there is something built into human beings that cannot fully be realized apart from living and participating in society. He adds, "And he who by nature and not by mere accident is without a state, is either a bad man or above humanity; he is like the '[t]ribeless, lawless, heartless one,' whom Homer denounces – the natural outcast is forthwith a lover of war...."[17] (When referring to the state, Aristotle has in mind the city–state such as he knew at Athens, which he viewed as the most highly developed social structure.[18])

The notion of experiencing growth and development leading to self-realization and the related notion of achieving excellence as a member of society are reflected in Aristotle's concept of the virtues, which he views as skills that are developed through practice, much as a violinist achieves excellence through endless hours of practice and a tennis player achieves excellence by practicing and practicing until switching from the forehand to the backhand, when the situation calls for so doing, becomes second nature and can be done without having to stop and think about how to do it. (The four traditional cardinal virtues – prudence, justice, temperance, and fortitude – are rooted in the thought of Aristotle, though prudence, temperance, and fortitude involve far more in Aristotle's understanding of them than the English terms we use to identify them might suggest.[19]) Justice, Aristotle suggests, is complete excellence because it benefits others and not just the person who is just:

[17] *Ibid.* The quotation from Homer comes from his *Iliad* (IX, 63). We need not be concerned with the question of what the true state of nature might have been. In the writings of both Locke and Aristotle (and those of many other authors as well), the state of nature is not a historical state of affairs that actually existed but rather a rhetorical device used to make a point.

[18] Though Aristotle spent much of his life in Athens, the fact that he was a Macedonian precluded his being a citizen of Athens. As a resident alien, his rights were limited, even to the extent that he had to get a special dispensation to lease land for his school. It is interesting to note that though Aristotle served as a tutor to Philip of Macedon's son, Alexander, who became known as Alexander the Great when he succeeded his father as king and conquered much of the known world, Aristotle finds the participatory city–state vastly preferable to an empire ruled by one person (Steven Everson, "Introduction," *The Politics*, x-xi).

[19] See, for example, the comments of J.A.K. Thomson interspersed in his translation of *The Nicomachean Ethics* (*The Ethics of Aristotle* [Baltimore: Penguin Books, 1953], 93, 102, 109, 116).

It is complete because he who possesses it can exercise his excellence toward others too and not merely by himself.... [J]ustice, alone of the excellences, is thought to be another's good, because it is related to others; for it does what is advantageous to another.... Now the worst man is he who exercises his wickedness both toward himself and toward his friends, and the best man is not he who exercises his excellence toward himself but he who exercises it towards another; for this is a difficult task. Justice in this sense, then, is not part of excellence but excellence entire, nor is the contrary injustice a part of vice but vice entire.[20]

Another way of putting this is to suggest that developing our moral skills is an important part of self-realization and experiencing the good life,[21] just as a violinist or a tennis player who achieves excellence experiences a greater measure of the fullness of life.[22] To put this in slightly different words, to experience self-realization and fullness of life is to flourish.

LIVING IN COMMUNITY AND BEING A NEIGHBOR

We deliberately chose to use the term "neighbor" to refer to other people because neighbor carries with it the connotation of community. Granted, the word "community" is used in all sorts of different ways – the community in which we live, the business community, the academic community, and even the world community. The strand that runs through all of these varied usages, however, is the notion of having something in common. Indeed, *communis*, the Latin word from which the English word community is derived, means "fellowship, community of relations or feelings."[23] What we have in common with

---

[20] Aristotle, *The Nicomachean Ethics* in *The Complete Works of Aristotle: The Revised Oxford Translation*, Vol. II, ed. Jonathan Barnes (Princeton, NJ: Princeton University Press, 1984), 1783 (V, 1129^{b}30–1130^{a}11). Thomson's translation, which is an older translation, uses "virtue" rather than "excellence." For example, Thomson's translation reads, "Thus righteousness or justice, so understood, is not a part but the whole of virtue, while injustice, its opposite, is not a part but the whole of vice" (V, 1, 142).

[21] For Aristotle, the ultimate goal is experiencing *eudaimonia*, which has often been translated as "happiness," though a fuller, more accurate translation might be "the good life" or "the fullness of life."

[22] A caveat is in order here. If the violinist or the tennis player who achieves excellence does so as the result of obsessive ambition that is destructive of family and friends, achieving excellence does not equate with experiencing the fullness of life.

[23] *Oxford English Dictionary Online* at http://dictonary.oed.com/cgi/entry/50045241?q ueryword=community& ... (last accessed September 8, 2008).

our near neighbors and our distant neighbors alike is our common humanity, even as, in many cases, we speak different languages, have different religious and political views, and live in different parts of the world. It is as we become aware of and respect and affirm the humanity of our near neighbors and our distant neighbors alike that we gain a sense of community.

Perhaps the reason that the language of rights – in particular the language of rights of entitlement – has been so widely used in recent years is that it might seem to some that it is less humiliating and more dignified to claim that something is owed them, as opposed to asking for help as an act of charity. There is something to that.

At the same time, to try to make everything one might need or otherwise desire a right of entitlement is to overlook the fact that part of our common humanity is that we all need to experience charity. That takes some explaining. When we hear the word "charity," we often think about giving money to those who are less fortunate – for example, donating money to the local food pantry or to an international relief organization. Helping those who are less fortunate is an important part of charity. But it is only a small part of what charity entails. Charity, in its fullest sense, involves living in and experiencing community. It involves understanding others and being understood. It involves treating others with respect and dignity, and being treated with respect and dignity ourselves.[24]

---

[24] The English word "charity" comes from the Old French word *charité*, which carried with it the notions of fondness, affection, and valuing greatly – connotations that are today often associated with the English word "cherish." Also of etymological significance is the Latin word *caritas*, which was often used to translate the Greek word *agápe*, found both in the love commandment ("You shall love your neighbor as yourself," which first appears in Deuteronomy 6.5 and Leviticus 19.18 in the Hebrew Bible and is quoted in Matthew 22.39 and Luke 10.27 in the New Testament) and the apostle Paul's reference to faith, hope and love in I Corinthians 13. *Caritas* is often defined as "dearness, love founded on esteem" (*Oxford English Dictionary*, 3:42.25). The Greek verb from which *agápe* is derived is customarily defined as "to treat with affection" and "to regard with brotherly love" as when treating a stranger as if he or she were a member of the family. Ancient Greeks, it might be added, did not use the term *agápe* to refer to giving money to those less fortunate; rather, they used the term *eleemosyne*, from which the English word "alms" is derived. *Eleemosyne* involved pity, which *agapé* did not (*An Intermediate Greek-English Lexicon*, based on the seventh edition of Liddell and Scott's *Greek-English Lexicon* [Oxford: The Clarendon Press, 1961], 4, 248).

To suggest that we all need to experience charity – that is, be treated in a charitable manner – is not to suggest that we should all receive food stamps to buy groceries. The vast majority of those of us living in more affluent countries are perfectly capable of putting food on the table without any financial assistance from the government. However, we all do need charity – charity in the traditional sense of the term. Charity understood as being treated with respect and dignity. Charity understood as being taken seriously. Charity understood as having others put the most charitable construction on all that we do. In short, charity involves discovering and affirming the humanity of others – that of our distant neighbors as well as that of our near neighbors – and discovering and affirming our own humanity in the process. Respecting and defending the rights of others is part of that. But only part, for far more is necessary if people are to flourish.

SUMMING IT ALL UP

Before going on to a discussion of ethical guidelines for business organizations in an age of globalization, which forms the agenda for the next chapter, summarizing the conclusions that have been reached in this chapter is useful. We have suggested that:

- jobs are just as important for workers in other countries, as for those in the country in which we live – that is, for our distant neighbors as well as for our near neighbors;
- negative rights (rights of forbearance) apply equally to our distant neighbors and to our near neighbors; our obligation to refrain from harming others is universal – that is, it pertains equally to harm that might be done to our distant neighbors, as well as to harm that might be done to our near neighbors;
- rather than contribute to harm done to our neighbors, be they distant neighbors or near neighbors, we would do well to refrain from purchasing products, the production of which has involved exploitation of small farmers, factory workers and/or others; purchasing fair trade certified products provides an alternative;
- positive rights (rights of entitlement) are best understood as relational rights stemming from various types of relationships, be they

contractual relationships or relationships such as the parent-child relationship;

- such being the case, the obligations that we have to make good on, that to which others are entitled, are directly linked to various types of relationships in which we are involved;
- because we are more likely to be involved in rights-defining relationships with our near neighbors than with our distant neighbors, the affirmative duties we have to make good on the rights of entitlement others have are often greater with respect to our near neighbors than with respect to our distant neighbors – hence the notion of concentric circles of responsibility;
- the nature of globalization is such that in many cases, as when a company builds a production facility in another country, distant neighbors become near neighbors;
- while concepts of human rights provide useful guidelines when constructing an ethic of globalization, simply affirming and calling for the recognition of human rights is not all that is needed if people are to flourish; living in community and being treated in a charitable manner are also part of what is necessary if people are to flourish.

The stage is set for identifying ethical guidelines for business organizations in an age of globalization, a task to which we now turn.

3

Constructing an Ethic for Business
in an Age of Globalization

As in the case of so many other ethical issues, the categorical imperative of Immanuel Kant (1724–1804), the renowned German philosopher of the Enlightenment, provides a useful starting point for constructing a business ethic that can serve as a framework for discussions of the ethics of globalization. In the *Groundwork of the Metaphysic of Morals*, published in 1785, Kant admonishes, "For, all rational beings stand under the *law* that each of them is to treat himself and all others *never merely as means* but always *at the same time as ends in themselves.*"[1]

This formulation of the categorical imperative has been misconstrued sometimes as suggesting that we should never use other people as means to help accomplish whatever we might be attempting to accomplish. That, however, is not what it says. Rather, Kant states that each person should "treat himself and all others *never merely as means* but always *at the same time as ends in themselves.*" For example, if we hire someone to rake the leaves from our lawn, we are using that person as the means of getting that particular job done. Kant would have no

---

[1] Immanuel Kant, *Groundwork of the Metaphysic of Morals*, trans. Mary Gregor (Cambridge: Cambridge University Press, 1998), 41 (4:433). In *Groundwork*, Kant gives two other formulations of the categorical imperative and insists that the "three ways of representing the principle of morality are at bottom only so many formulae of the very same law ..." (43; 4:436). We leave to Kant scholars the question of whether Kant's various formulations of the categorical imperative are indeed interchangeable.

problem with this but would insist that we should not view the person we hire simply as a means of getting the job done.

Sketched in practical terms, this suggests that we should bear in mind at all times a very basic fact of life, namely that those we employ or do business with are human beings just as we are. People with hopes and fears, times of joy and times of sorrow. People with a need for food, clothing, shelter, and everything else that is involved in being a human being. People for whom being treated with respect and dignity is of great importance. And, as Kant's categorical imperative also serves to remind us, we ought not lose sight of our own personhood for if we simply "sell ourselves to the company" we have undercut the very nature of our own humanity.

WHAT IS THE BUSINESS OF BUSINESS?

As Kant's categorical imperative also suggests, ethics involves both questions about ends and questions about means. When applied to the business world, this means both questions about what ends or objectives are appropriate and questions about what means are appropriate when trying to accomplish these ends or objectives. To put the first part of this in slightly different words, what is the business of business? Or, if you prefer, what are the marks of a successful business?

A very traditional answer to the question of "what is the business of business" is to say that the business of business is making money. And indeed, many in business, if they are honest when responding to this question, would acknowledge that the hope of making money is precisely why they went into business. Among the most stalwart defenders of this particular view is Nobel laureate Milton Friedman, who in *Capitalism and Freedom*, which was first published in 1962, asserts, "Few trends could so thoroughly undermine the very foundations of our free society as the acceptance by corporate officials of a social responsibility other than to make as much money for their stockholders as possible."[2] In a widely reprinted article entitled "The Social Responsibility of Business Is to Increase Its Profits" that originally appeared in *The New York Times Magazine*, Friedman argues:

---

[2] Milton Friedman, *Capitalism and Freedom* (Chicago: University of Chicago Press, 1962), 133.

Insofar as [a corporation executive's] actions in accord with his "social responsibility" reduce returns to stockholders, he is spending their money. Insofar as his actions raise the price to customers, he is spending the customers' money. Insofar as his actions lower the wages of some employees, he is spending their money.[3]

Was Nobel laureate Milton Friedman right about what the business of business is? Not if one affirms an ethic of business responsibility that encompasses more than pursuit of profits. Not if one has a broader vision of what business enterprises should be doing.

Ryuzaburo Kaku, the former president and chairman of Canon, Inc., has argued that *kyosei*, a concept with roots in traditional Japanese culture, provides useful ethical guidelines for business. He made *kyosei* the central feature of Canon's corporate philosophy.[4] The company defines *kyosei* and its corporate philosophy as follows:

The corporate philosophy of Canon is *kyosei*. A concise definition of this word would be 'Living and working together for the common good,' but our definition is broader: 'All people, regardless of race, religion or culture, harmoniously living and working together into the future.' Unfortunately, the presence of imbalances in our world in such areas as trade, income levels and the environment hinders the achievement of *kyosei*.

Addressing these imbalances is an ongoing mission, and Canon is doing its part by actively pursuing *kyosei*. True global companies must foster good relations, not only with their customers and the communities in which they operate, but also with nations and the environment. They must also bear the responsibility for the impact of their activities on society. For this reason, Canon's goal is to contribute to global prosperity and the well-being of humankind, which will lead to continuing growth and bring the world closer to achieving *kyosei*.[5]

Others share this broader vision of what the business of business might entail. A few years ago, the Caux Round Table, a group comprised of business executives from the United States, Europe, and

---

[3] Milton Friedman, "The Social Responsibility of Business Is To Increase Its Profits" in Lisa H. Newton and Maureen M. Ford, eds., *Taking Sides: Clashing Views on Controversial Issues in Business Ethics and Society*, 9th ed. (Guilford, CT: McGraw-Hill/ Dushkin, 2006), 88.

[4] Ryuzaburo Kaku, "The Path of *Kyosei*," *Harvard Business Review* Vol. 75, No. 4 (July–August 1991), 55–63.

[5] *Canon Corporate Philosophy: Kyosei*, at http://www.canon.com/about/philosophy/ index.html (last accessed October 27, 2006).

Japan, mapped out a set of principles for business – principles rooted in two basic ethical ideals: *kyosei* and human dignity. In contrast to Friedman, who focuses almost exclusively on obligations to shareholders, the business executives who drafted the Caux Round Table Principles for Business prefer to speak of responsibilities to several groups of individuals who have a stake in what a company does. In addition to owners and investors, these stakeholders include customers, employees, suppliers, competitors, and the communities in which companies operate.[6]

Robert W. Lane, chairman and chief executive officer of Deere & Company, put this in slightly different words in a talk entitled "The Great Corporation: Vigorous Competition, Cardinal Virtues, and Value Creation" in which he suggested that "the ultimate objective of economic organizations in society should be the overarching good of human flourishing...."[7]

Implicit in all of these views is the notion that serving others is what business is ultimately all about. This is true even in the case of Friedman's rather narrowly defined approach in which he, in effect, suggests that the business of business is serving shareholders by maximizing profits for them.

We concur with the view that business enterprises should not exist just for the sake of existing but rather that they exist to serve. But whom should they serve? Just the shareholders, as Friedman suggests? Or other groups and constituencies as well, as the Caux Round Table principles suggest? We prefer a broader vision of the business of business – one that suggests that the groups and constituencies that business enterprises are called to serve include, but are not limited to, the following: shareholders, customers, employees, suppliers, and the communities in which facilities owned by the company are located.[8]

---

[6] *Caux Round Table Principles for Business*, included in *American Business Values: A Global Perspective* (5th ed.) by Gerald F. Cavanagh (Upper Saddle River, NJ: Pearson/ Prentice Hall, 2006), 356–361. The Caux Round Table Principles can also be accessed at http://www.cauxroundtable.org/principles.html.

[7] Robert W. Lane, "The Great Corporation: Vigorous Competition, Cardinal Virtues, and Value Creation," The Ellwood F. Curtis Family Lectureship in Public Affairs, Augustana College, Rock Island, Illinois, October 28, 2003 (http://www.deere. com/en_US/compinfo/speeches/2003/031028augustana.html [last accessed September 23, 2005]).

[8] We do not include, as did the Caux Business Roundtable, competitors on this list. While it is plausible to argue that competitors should be treated fairly and with

We like very much Lane's suggestion that "the ultimate objective of economic organizations in society should be the overarching good of human flourishing...."

In the paragraphs and pages that follow, we map out what business organizations might do to serve each of the five groups noted previously – shareholders, customers, employees, suppliers, and the communities in which company facilities are located. In all cases, this involves respecting the rights that they have simply by virtue of the fact that they are human beings (i.e., their natural rights) by refraining from harming them. In a book entitled *The Ethical Investor* that was published several years ago but is still a good read, John G. Simon, Charles W. Powers, and Jon P. Gunnemann observe, "We know of no societies ... whose moral codes do not contain some injunction against harming others." Moreover, they suggest, there is an obligation to correct any injury that one does to others. They conclude, "In sum, we would affirm the prima facie obligation of all citizens, both individual and institutional, to avoid and correct self-caused social injury."[9]

Similarly, there is a strong case to be made for arguing that business entities have a clear obligation to respect contractually conferred and other relational rights. Helping people flourish, however, involves more than just respecting and affirming their rights. It also involves helping create those conditions that enable people to grow and develop and experience self-realization. More on that later in this chapter.

BOTH MEANS AND ENDS

Before going on to map out some more specific ethical guidelines, it is useful to note that each of the five constituent groups listed previously can be viewed – and, we believe, ought to be viewed – both as means and ends, just as, if we are to take the second formulation of Kant's categorical imperative seriously, we ought to view the person

---

respect and dignity, that is not the same as to say that it is the responsibility of other business enterprises to serve them.

[9] John G. Simon, Charles W. Powers, and Jon P. Gunnemann, *The Ethical Investor: Universities and Corporate Responsibility* (New Haven, CT: Yale University Press, 1972), 20–21.

we hire to rake the leaves from our lawn not only as a means of getting the job done but also as an end – i.e., as a human being whom we
ought to treat with respect and dignity. Shareholders and other investors are one of the means of securing the capital needed to purchase
new equipment, build new factories, and improve existing facilities.
At the same time, they are also one of the constituencies business
organizations ought to be serving. Customers purchasing products
and services provide the flow of income needed to maintain profitability while at the same time being an important constituency for
business enterprises to serve. Employees are key components of the
means of production; they are the ones who fabricate the goods and
provide the services marketed to customers while at the same time
being another important constituency. Suppliers provide raw materials, components, and other items needed to produce the goods and
services the company markets while at the same time being real, live
people who ought to be treated fairly and with respect and dignity.
Residents of the communities in which business organizations have
facilities help provide the supportive milieu for the company's operations while being yet another important constituency to serve.

There is nothing inherently contradictory about simultaneously
being both a means and an end. It does, however, necessitate some
careful thinking and deliberate attention to responsibilities and obligations, for the more complex the model of the function of business
organizations, the more difficult it is to keep things sorted out in a
coherent manner. We now turn to some more specific observations
and guidelines with respect to each of the five constituent groups
noted previously.

SHAREHOLDERS AND OTHER OWNERS AND INVESTORS

It is not unheard of for those critical of the business world to view
"profit" as a dirty word evoking images of greedy corporate Scrooges
thinking about nothing other than piling up as much money as they
can get their hands on. As the revelations with respect to Bernie Madoff
and others enmeshed in scandal suggest, there is some truth to that
caricature. It is, however, at best an incomplete picture. Moreover, it
is very misleading, for there are many in business – probably the vast
majority – who think about far more than making money.

No business executive worth her or his salt, however, can ignore profitability. The reality is that without maintaining profitability, business enterprises cannot in any meaningful way serve any of the constituencies noted previously. It is no overstatement to say that profits are the lifeblood of business enterprises. Richard C. Chewning, John W. Eby, and Shirley J. Roels, who believe that business success should be defined in terms of service, put it this way: "Profit is necessary. Without profit a business cannot survive. It will not provide a return for owners and investors who take risks to keep it going. Nor will it have resources to invest in further growth. Profit is not a dirty word!"[10]

Paying dividends to shareholders is what irritates some social critics the most. Is that not just channeling money into the pockets of the wealthy? Not necessarily. Pension funds and other institutional investors such as colleges and universities with endowments are major players on Wall Street, owning nearly two-thirds of the outstanding shares of Standard and Poors 500 Index (S&P 500) companies.[11] Is paying dividends on stocks owned by pension funds simply padding the pockets of the wealthy? Not when viewed from the perspective of retirees and future retirees who are the beneficiaries of those pension funds.

The question of what constitutes a fair return on investment is somewhat more complicated. This is not just a matter of what levels of dividends should be paid, though that is certainly part of the equation. The question of a fair return on investment also encompasses what the company might do to maintain and increase the value of the stock owned by shareholders, which, among other things, is a function of the profitability of the company, perceptions about how well the company is managed, and prospects with respect to the future of the company.

---

[10] Richard C. Chewning, John W. Eby, and Shirley J. Roels, *Business through the Eyes of Faith* (San Francisco: Harper & Row, Publishers, 1990), 15, 199–200.

[11] Norbert Michel, "Most Stocks Are Held by Private Investors," *The Heritage Foundation WebMemo No. 265*, April 18, 2003 (http://www.heritage.org/Research/Taxes/loader.cfm?url=/commonspot/security/getfile.cfm&PageID=40188 [last accessed March 24, 2006]). Michel adds, however, that when all publicly traded companies are considered, the percentage of stocks owned by institutional investors is somewhat lower.

Moreover, deciding what the return on investment should be involves far more than ethical considerations. In a competitive market economy, the parameters within which managers can operate are, in substantial measure, defined by market factors. If pension fund managers and others who make investment decisions conclude that a particular company's stock does not provide a sufficient return, be it in the form of dividends or prospects for appreciation, they will sell it and buy stock in a company they view as more promising. The result will be a decline in the value of the stock of the underperforming company, which will make it more difficult for that company to raise the capital it needs to modernize production facilities or do whatever else needs to be done. In short, to decide that paying shareholders, say, a 5 percent return on their investment might not be realistic within the parameters defined by prevailing market factors.

Inherent in the shareholder-business organization relationship are certain rights of entitlement that go beyond simple return on their investment. Chief among these is the right to receive the information needed to make carefully considered investment decisions. This can, in many cases, go beyond the mandatory information included in the company's annual report. And, to state the obvious, it is incumbent on managers when disclosing information to shareholders and other investors, as well as to the public, to maintain absolute integrity in their disclosure statements, something managers at AIG and other troubled companies failed to do. Maintaining absolute integrity includes releasing all relevant information, rather than painting a misleading picture by withholding information that is essential if investors are to make carefully considered, informed decisions.

Finally, managers would do well to keep in mind that even though they might view the company as their company, it is the shareholders who own the company (though, to be sure, managers who own stock in the company are part owners of the company, though only, in most cases, minority owners). Thus, managers of the publicly owned modern corporation are stewards of property that is mostly owned by others. This means that it is incumbent on managers to take good care of the property of others with which they have been entrusted, managing it wisely in ways that will conserve and increase the value of these assets, while avoiding reckless decisions that will risk loss of assets with which they have been entrusted.

To summarize, moral responsibilities of managers of modern business corporations with respect to shareholders and other investors include, but are not limited to, the following:

1. managing corporate assets wisely to provide an appropriate return to investors;
2. practicing good stewardship with respect to assets and property owned by shareholders; and
3. maintaining integrity in relationships with shareholders and other investors by disclosing to them the information they are entitled to receive in order to make informed investment decisions.

CUSTOMERS

To suggest that part of the business of business is serving customers by providing the goods and services they desire at competitive prices is not breaking new ground. Just about every business organization has a statement of some sort about that in its list of goals and objectives. There is, however, more to the equation. If business organizations are to make good on their responsibilities to their customers, it is essential that they maintain integrity in their relations with customers by refraining from misrepresenting the product or withholding information potential customers need to make informed decisions about the product. It might be added that affirming an ethic that mandates integrity in relations with customers calls into question image advertising that associates such things as career success and sex appeal with use of the product, even though in practice there is no evidence to suggest that such is the case. Space does not allow detailed discussion of this matter in the present volume.

There is, however, another issue that needs to be addressed – the question of whether companies should sell products that harm other people, even if there is market demand for these products. Examples include gas-guzzling SUVs that contribute to global warming (which in time will have tremendous human costs) and blue jeans that are manufactured in sweatshops in China and elsewhere.[12] There is no

---

[12] *China Blue*, a film to which reference has already been made, and to which we will return in the next chapter, documents some of the human costs associated with factories of this type.

question that there is a market demand for gas-guzzling SUVs (or at least there was before the price of gasoline went up). And there is no question that consumers often do not look beyond the price tag when making purchasing decisions, which is why there is a market for blue jeans and other apparel produced in low-wage sweatshops in other countries. But is it ethical for companies to respond to this consumer demand by selling these products, even though there are social costs associated with them?

We believe that it is not ethical for companies to sell products that harm other people, be it in the production or the use of them. It is for this reason that we favor supplier codes of conduct that set standards that have to be met by suppliers when a company purchases components and/or finished products from outside suppliers. (The use of supplier codes of conduct is discussed in greater detail later in this chapter and in the next chapter, which addresses the ethics of doing business in China.)

Similarly, we believe that companies have a prima facie obligation to refrain from selling products that damage the environment, which gas-guzzling SUVs do by contributing to global warming (though we realize that industrywide standards requiring greater fuel efficiency are necessary to level the playing field and prevent competitive disadvantage – industrywide standards that companies that claim to be socially conscious ought to be supporting, rather than fighting). It might be added that gas-guzzling SUVs and other vehicles that are not fuel efficient impose social costs in other ways as well by increasing our dependence on imported oil, which has both economic and political consequences.[13]

To summarize, we believe that responsibilities and obligations relating to customers include the following:

1. serving customers by providing the goods and services that they desire (with the exception noted below) at competitive prices;
2. maintaining integrity in relationships with customers by not misrepresenting products, by providing customers and

---

[13] We realize that there are some who have legitimate needs for large SUVs, four-wheel-drive trucks, and other vehicles that are not fuel efficient. Industrywide standards requiring greater fuel efficiency, however, can encourage automakers to develop more fuel-efficient SUVs and trucks.

potential customers with the information they need to make informed purchasing decisions, and by refraining from manipulative advertising that attempts to persuade potential customers to purchase the product for reasons that have nothing at all to do with the product itself; and

3. refraining from selling products that harm other people in their production and/or use, even if there is consumer demand for these products (with industrywide regulation minimizing any resulting competitive disadvantage).

EMPLOYEES

It is with respect to employees that some of the most challenging and difficult ethical questions for business organizations arise – and where some of the greatest abuses occur when employers view their employees simply as means to other ends, rather than also as ends themselves. We begin by noting that it is essential that employers respect the basic rights of their employees by refraining from doing things harmful to them such as forcing them to work in an unsafe or threatening work environment that places at risk their lives, health, and/or well-being. This responsibility includes maintaining a work environment that is free from sexual harassment or any other type of harassment that threatens the well-being of employees. This also includes practicing nondiscrimination by ensuring that factors such as race, gender, religious affiliation, and nationality do not play a role in hiring and promotion decisions when they are not bona fide occupational qualifications (BFOQs).[14] We further note that it is

---

[14] In the United States, federal law allows consideration of these factors if it can be demonstrated that they are in some way related to the job. For example, a Baptist church hiring a new pastor can give preference to candidates who are Baptists and a ballet company auditioning dancers for the role of the Sugar Plum Fairy in Peter Tchaikovsky's *The Nutcracker* can limit auditions to female dancers. In cases such as these, factors such as religious affiliation and gender are BFOQs. On the other hand, if the manager of an auto repair facility is hiring someone to repair fuel injection systems, it is irrelevant whether that person is Buddhist or Baptist, male or female. Somewhat more difficult are cases that are somewhere along the middle of the spectrum – for example, hiring teachers for the lower elementary grades in a school district in which (a) a substantial majority of the teachers already on staff are female, and (b) a significant number of the students that school district serves come from single-parent families that lack positive male role models.

incumbent on employers to make good on the rights of entitlement specified in contractual agreements and official personnel policies, both with respect to current employees and with respect to retirees and other former employees.[15]

The importance of respecting the rights of employees is underscored by various international sets of guiding principles, among them Caux Round Table Principles for Business (to which reference has already been made), the United Nations Global Compact's *Ten Principles*,[16] the Global Sullivan Principles of Social Responsibility,[17] and the OECD Guidelines for Multinational Enterprises.[18] All of these statements of principle include strong affirmations of human rights. Signatories of the Global Sullivan Principles of Social Responsibility, for example, pledge the following:

Accordingly, we will:

- Express our support for universal human rights and, particularly, for those of our employees, the communities within which we operate, and parties with whom we do business.

A significant question for multinational corporations is the question of the extent to which nationality should be a consideration when making hiring and promotion decisions, particularly with respect to the upper levels of management. There has been a historic tendency for multinational corporations to reserve upper-level management positions for managers from the country in which the company is incorporated, rather than for managers from the countries in which production and/or retail facilities are located. As will be noted in our discussion of Firestone in Liberia in Chapter 5, this is one of the issues addressed in the negotiations that led to the 2008 contract with the labor union that represents Firestone employees.

[15] Our focus in this chapter is on the obligations that business organizations have with respect to their employees. It is, however, a two-way street with employees also having obligations to respect the rights of their employers – for example, property rights and other negative rights (rights of forbearance), which mandate that employees respect their employer's property rights by refraining from vandalizing company property and from stealing from their employers by slipping company-owned tools into their lunch boxes when going home at the end of the day, as well as refraining from other injurious or unwarranted acts that are costly to the company. Similarly, as noted in Chapter 2, employers have certain rights of entitlement inherent in the employer-employee relationship, among them a right of entitlement to receive a full day's work from the employee in return for a full day's pay.

[16] The United Nations Global Compact's *Ten Principles* can be accessed at http://www.unglobalcompact.org/AboutTheGC/TheTenPrinciples/index.html.

[17] The Global Sullivan Principles can be accessed at http://globalsullivanprinciples.org/principles.htm.

[18] The OECD Guidelines for Multinational Enterprises can be accessed at http://www.oecd.org/dataoecd/12/21/1903291.pdf.

- Promote equal opportunity for our employees at all levels of the company with respect to issues such as color, race, gender, age, ethnicity, or religious beliefs, and operate without unacceptable worker treatment such as the exploitation of children, physical punishment, female abuse, involuntary servitude, or other forms of abuse.
- Respect our employees' voluntary freedom of association.
- Compensate our employees to enable them to meet at least their basic needs and provide the opportunity to improve their skill and capability in order to raise their social and economic opportunities.
- Provide a safe and healthy workplace, protect human health and the environment, and promote sustainable development.[19]

Respecting the rights of employees, however, is only part of what companies must do if their employees are to flourish. They must be provided with work environments where they are respected and treated with dignity, where their ideas are taken seriously, and where they have opportunities to grow, develop, and experience self-realization. There have been some constructive developments in recent years as companies have moved away from the traditional model of management from the top-on-down and instead have adopted more participatory styles of management that open the door to greater employee involvement in management decisions. The result is often not only improved employee morale but increased productivity. Put in slightly different words, helping employees flourish is often an effective way of helping the company flourish.

Transplanting participatory models of management to overseas operations poses unique challenges, particularly in countries such as China, where authority is often viewed as coming from the top on down – countries where workers have been conditioned for years to be submissive to authority figures. Moreover, there is often discomfort, at times active resistance, from authoritarian governments that view empowering workers as a threat. We believe, however, that multinational corporations can be a constructive force for change, a matter

---

[19] *Ibid.* As will be noted in greater detail in the next chapter when we discuss the ethics of investment in China, the Global Sullivan Principles provide useful general guidelines but lack the specificity needed for particular cases.

we will examine in greater detail in the following chapter, which discusses the ethics of investment in China.

We have saved until last the most difficult question pertaining to employer-employee relations – that of compensation. Of necessity, compensation levels are, at least in part, market driven. No wise manager would ignore market realities when setting compensation levels or when negotiating a collective bargaining agreement. However, simply leaving the determination of compensation levels to the law of supply and demand in a competitive labor market is not acceptable if one is to take any recognizable notion of justice seriously, particularly in an age of globalization in which the labor market has increasingly become a world market, rather than one that is localized. Simply allowing market factors to determine compensation levels can result in a company being accomplices to – perhaps even practitioners of – exploitative labor practices such as sweatshops harmful to those who are the victims of these practices. Hence, it is essential that all employers in general, and companies with overseas operations in particular, give deliberate and conscientious attention to questions of justice pertaining to compensation levels.

In practice, this is far easier said than done. It is relatively easy to articulate principles such as equal pay for equal work. What this means in practice might be relatively clear with respect to workers in the same job category in the same factory who have worked there the same number of years. Most today would agree, in contrast to what was widely practiced prior to the equal rights movement, that factors such as gender should not come into play in these situations. That might be straightforward enough. Applying the principle of equal pay for equal work is far more difficult to accomplish, however, when attempting to determine compensation levels for employees working in the same plant but in different job categories. It is even more difficult to determine what this principle might mean when comparing employees working in factories in different parts of the country – or in different countries – where costs of living might vary greatly. Does "equal pay for equal work" mean giving each employee the same dollar amount, when determining compensation levels? Or does it mean giving each employee the same purchasing power, with the actual dollar amount varying relative to the cost of living in the part of the country – or the part of the world – where she or he lives and works?

This, however, does not mean that we should not attempt to address questions of justice related to levels of compensation. A place to begin is by noting that if one is to adhere to an ethic that calls for treating all people with respect and dignity, there is a moral minimum as to what employers can do in good conscience in the area of compensation. That moral minimum is providing each full-time employee with a level of compensation sufficient to support a family of average size in the community in which she or he lives and works – a level of compensation that will provide for a baseline standard of living, defined as having food, shelter, basic health care, and access to educational opportunities on at least the primary and secondary levels. This might not all be provided in the form of wages. Some companies, such as Firestone Natural Rubber Company in Liberia (discussed in Chapter 5), provide health care and educational opportunities directly to employees and members of their families, rather than indirectly via wages that must then be used to purchase these services. The dollar equivalent of this morally minimal level of compensation, of course, will vary relative to the cost of living in the communities in which companies have operations and where employees live. The importance of this morally minimal level of compensation, however, can be succinctly stated: If companies are not willing to provide at least a morally minimal level of compensation for their employees, they have no business being in business.

Providing a morally minimal level of compensation for employees at the bottom of the wage scale does not fully resolve questions of equity related to compensation. There are also questions of equity pertaining to relative levels of compensation for various members of the organization, including top management. Recent years have seen significant increases in compensation levels for CEOs and other senior company officials, both in absolute terms and relative to what other employees are paid. At a bare minimum, this is not politically wise at a time when jobs are being shifted overseas to plants in low-wage countries and workers in plants in this country are being asked to accept reduced levels of compensation and less generous health-care benefits. This huge disparity in compensation can also be questioned on ethical grounds. Even if one believes, as did Aristotle in Book V of *The Nicomachean Ethics*, that wealth and other things viewed as desirable should be allocated on the basis of merit, is there any way

that it is plausible to argue that chief executive officers of U.S. companies are, on the average, 120 times more meritorious than the average factory worker,[20] even in years in which the company is performing poorly? Is there any reasonable standard of justice that can support such a disparity? In an article that appeared in the *New York Times*, Joe Nocera observes that "executive compensation is a socially corrosive issue, especially when the middle class is struggling."[21]

Fairness in compensation is part of treating people with respect and dignity – most of us would say a very important part. However, there is far more to creating and sustaining environments that enable people to flourish. In the United States, there has been an unfortunate tendency to equate affluence with quality of life and prospering with flourishing. That is rather misleading. While no one would idealize abject poverty that leaves those experiencing it desperately struggling to survive (hence the argument that companies should provide at least a morally minimal level of compensation for their employees), it does not follow that quality of life is simply determined by the level of affluence that one experiences. There is much more to quality of life. When all things are considered, the quality of the interpersonal relationships that one experiences has far more to do with quality of life than how much money one has. We suggested earlier that business is really about relationships – relationships with investors, customers,

---

[20] In 1980, the average CEO's salary was forty-two times that of the ordinary factory worker. Today it is more than 120 times that of the ordinary factory worker. This compares with a ratio of 16:1 in Japan, 21:1 in Germany, and 33:1 in the United Kingdom (Gerald F. Cavanagh, *American Business Values: A Global Perspective*, 5th ed. [Upper Saddle River, NJ: Pearson/Prentice Hall, 2006], 257).

[21] Joe Nocera, "What if C.E.O. Pay Is Fair?" *New York Times*, October 13, 2007. Defenders of high levels of pay for top management frequently suggest that compensation levels are market driven. Among those who defend high levels of compensation is Marc Hodak, who states in an article entitled "CEOs Aren't Overpaid" that appeared on *Forbes.com*, "The possibility that executive pay is largely driven by supply and demand for scarce executive talent is rarely mentioned. But it happens to be true" (*Forbes.com*, May 8, 2008, at http://www.forbes.com/2008/05/08/ceos-not-overpaid-ent-competition08-cx-mh_0508hodak_print.html [last accessed September 16, 2008]). Nocera takes issue with that view, arguing that the market is rigged: "Chief executives sit on one another's boards, so they have an incentive to take care of one another. Directors are predisposed to want to make the chief executive happy since, after all, he or she is the one who picked them for the board. Far too often, a chief executive's pay isn't the result of an arms-length negotiation, but a result of a kind of corporate buddy system."

employees, suppliers, and the communities in which facilities are located. In substantial measure, it is the quality of the employment relationship that determines quality of life for employees. Compensation is important. However, simply buying off employees with high wages and salaries while ignoring the quality of the workplace experience, as was once common, does little to contribute to employees' quality of life. If employees are to flourish in the workplace, they need more than just a paycheck, which is why employee involvement and other participatory measures noted previously are so important.

To summarize, moral responsibilities of managers of modern business corporations with respect to employees include, but are not limited, to the following:

1. respecting workers' basic rights by maintaining a safe workplace that minimizes risks to their health and well-being;
2. protecting workers from sexual harassment and other forms of harassment injurious to them;
3. practicing nondiscrimination by ensuring that factors such as race, gender, religious affiliation, and nationality do not play a role in hiring and promotion decisions when they are not bona fide occupational qualifications (BFOQs);
4. maintaining integrity in employee relations by respecting contractual agreements and making good on rights of entitlement contractually specified and/or specified in personnel policies;
5. maintaining a work environment where workers are provided with information of significance to them and where their ideas are respected and welcomed; and
6. maintaining equitable levels of compensation.

SUPPLIERS

As are all other business relationships, relationships with suppliers are a two-way street. Suppliers serve companies involved in manufacturing by providing the raw materials and components they need to make the finished product and companies involved in the retail business with products to put on their shelves. In return, companies buying materials or products from other companies provide suppliers with a market for their products.

The basic obligations of companies to their suppliers can be summarized as follows:

1. giving potential suppliers a fair opportunity to bid on contracts;
2. providing potential suppliers with product specifications and the other information they need to make competitive bids;
3. specifying delivery deadlines that are realistic for suppliers to meet; and
4. paying suppliers in a timely manner.

Making good on these obligations, however, does not exhaust the moral responsibilities companies have that are inherent in their relationships with suppliers. If a company is to take its social responsibilities seriously, it must insist that suppliers treat their employees fairly and refrain from practices harmful to their employees and others. It is for this reason that a number of companies have adopted codes of conduct for suppliers. Among the companies that have adopted codes of conduct for suppliers is retailing giant Target. The company states:

Specifically, we seek to do business with Vendors, including suppliers and manufacturers, who share our commitment to high ethical standards. We require our vendors to:

- Provide employees with a safe and healthy workplace,
- Adopt nondiscrimination principles and limit work hours,
- Pay fair wages,
- Renounce forced or other compulsory labor and abstain from its use,
- Refrain completely from use of child labor. We define child labor as being below the minimum legal working age according to local law, or under the age of fourteen, whichever is greater. We do make an exception for legitimate apprentice programs.[22]

Target is one of more than 300 companies that signed the National Retail Federation's (NRF's) Statement of Principles on Supplier Legal Compliance. The NRF, which is the largest retail trade association in the world, organized the "Clothes Made in Sweatshops Aren't Our Style" campaign in 1996. The organization has not hesitated to speak

---

[22] Target Corporation, "Global Compliance: Business Ethics Practices for Vendors and Trading Partners" at http://sites.target.com/site/en/corporate/page.jsp?contentId=PRD03-004392 (last accessed September 12, 2008).

out against reported human rights abuses in other countries. For example, in August of 2008, the NRF issued a statement demanding that Uzbekistan end the use of child labor in the harvesting of cotton and warning that companies that are members of the federation could boycott products made from Uzbek cotton if the use of child labor is not ended.[23]

In 2004, NRF, in cooperation with several other organizations, was instrumental in establishing the Fair Factories Clearing House (FFC), which houses a global database of factory information and social compliance audit reports. FFC, which is based in New York, is funded by member contributions and by a grant from the U.S. Department of State Bureau of Democracy, Human Rights, and Labor.[24]

COMMUNITIES IN WHICH COMPANY FACILITIES ARE LOCATED

Business organizations serve the communities in which company-owned and operated facilities are located simply by virtue of the fact that they provide jobs and pay state and local taxes. Numerous studies indicate that every dollar in payroll is multiplied by a factor of at least three as it makes its way around the community – the employee spends it at the local supermarket, the local supermarket uses the money to pay their employees, their employees spend it at the mall, and so on. Just by doing business in a particular locale, business enterprises benefit that community.

The more difficult – and controversial – question is whether business organizations have philanthropic obligations that go beyond simply benefiting the broader community in the normal course of doing business. Friedman gives a very simple answer to that question. All corporate assets, he suggests, belong to shareholders. Money that is not needed to make payroll or invest in new equipment should go to shareholders in the form of dividends. Once they receive their

---

[23] National Retail Federation, "NRF Demands End to Use of Forced Child Labor to Harvest Cotton in Uzbekistan" at http://www.nrf.com/modules. php?name=News&sp_id=560&op=printfriendly&txt=National+Retail+Federatio n++- (last accessed September 12, 2008).

[24] Fair Factories Clearing House, "FFC Home" at http://www.fairfactories.org/ (last accessed September 12, 2008).

dividends, it is their decision whether to keep that money for themselves or give it to charitable organizations or other worthy causes. Friedman comments:

One topic in the area of social responsibility that I feel duty-bound to touch on, because it affects my own personal interests, has been the claim that business should contribute to the support of charitable activities and especially to universities. Such giving by corporations is an inappropriate use of corporate funds in a free-enterprise society.

The corporation is an instrument of the stockholders who own it. If the corporation makes a contribution, it prevents the individual stockholder from himself deciding how he should dispose of his funds.[25]

Others take a broader view, suggesting that business organizations should view themselves as citizens of the communities in which they operate, with the responsibilities of citizenship including supporting the arts, educational institutions, athletic programs, housing programs, and other programs. Target Corporation, for example, states, "At Target, we don't define the success of our business simply by the bottom line. We also measure our company's achievement based on our role in the communities we serve." Since 1946, the company has contributed 5 percent of annual income to support education, the arts, and social services in local communities, which today totals more than $3 million each week.[26]

Robert J. Ulrich, Target Corporation's chairman and chief executive officer, served as a member of the Committee Encouraging Corporate Philanthropy (CECP), a group of CEOs and chairpersons working together to raise the level and quality of corporate philanthropy. CECP's philosophy, as stated on the organization's website, is as follows:

Giving back, when conceived and executed thoughtfully, creates a win-win scenario for business and the public. From eradicating disease and improving childhood literacy rates to boosting employee job skills, opening new markets and heightening brand recognition – business and society both stand to benefit greatly if companies can demonstrate programmatic

---

[25] Friedman, *Capitalism and Freedom*, 135.
[26] Target Corporation, "Corporate Responsibility" at http://sites.target.com/site/en/corporate/page.jsp?contentId=PRD03–004325 (last accessed September 12, 2008).

effectiveness, fiscal accountability, and good stewardship in their philan-thropic contributions.[27]

The late Paul Newman – movie star, race car driver, chairman of Newman's Own, Inc., and one of the founders of CECP – stated, "I helped to start CECP with the belief that corporate America could be a force for good in society."[28]

The business leaders who are members of CECP believe that cor-porate philanthropy involves more than writing a check. A CECP publication observes:

In the last few years, companies have begun to adopt a more holistic approach to corporate philanthropy. Cash contributions remain significant, but companies are increasing other types of contributions that draw on more of the company's resources.... [N]early as many companies support employee volunteering as make cash contributions, for example. Some of the most innovative programs make use of an even broader array of resources, including corporate matches, product donations, capacity sharing, and asset leveraging.[29]

It might be added that while contributions to the community such as those Target makes can, on one level, be viewed as charitable contri-butions, they are not devoid of benefit to the company. By support-ing the arts, education, and athletic programs, companies help make the communities in which they have facilities the sort of communities where people want to live, thereby aiding recruiting efforts. Moreover, people who are happy with the communities in which they live are more likely to be happy in the workplace and hence more productive. Additionally, corporate charitable contributions frequently generate significant good will for companies – good will that would cost a lot of advertising dollars to buy, good will that can lead to a greater number of customers entering their doors.[30]

---

[27] Committee Encouraging Corporate Philanthropy, "About CECP: An Overview" at http://www.corporatephilanthropy.org/membership/ (last accessed September 15, 2008).

[28] Quoted in *ibid.*

[29] Committee Encouraging Corporate Philanthropy, *Business's Social Contract: Cap-turing the Corporate Philanthropy Opportunity*, 13, at http://www.corporatephilan-thropy.org/research/pubs/SocialContract.pdf (last accessed September 15, 2008).

[30] Because companies are keenly aware of the public relations dividends that can result from supporting community organizations, institutions, and activities, it is

A few years ago, Curtis C. Verschoor and Elizabeth A. Murphy, both members of the faculty of DePaul University, did a study of the top 100 U.S. corporations for *Business Ethics* magazine's 2001 list of Best Corporate Citizens, all of which were included in Standard and Poors 500 Index (S&P 500), to see how their financial performance compared with that of S&P 500 companies not on *Business Ethics* magazine's 2001 list. They discovered that the financial performance of companies on *Business Ethics* magazine's 2001 list of Best Corporate Citizens compared favorably to that of other S&P 500 companies. VerSchoor and Murphy conclude:

> Based on the findings in this study, there is unbiased and rather conclusive empirical evidence that demonstrates that firms that are simultaneously committed to social and environmental issues that are important to their stakeholders also have superior financial performance and superior reputations as well.... These findings (like prior studies) should continue to encourage more corporations to increase their emphasis on accountability to all stakeholders, not just shareholder profitability. They should also encourage the growth of investment in socially and ethically responsible corporations.[31]

ESTABLISHING PRIORITIES

If one maps out a far-ranging list of corporate goals and objectives, as we have done here, it is very easy to come up with a laundry list of obligations and responsibilities that far exceed what is possible for any business organization to do, even one with substantial resources at its disposal. As Immanuel Kant is frequently credited with reminding us,

---

not surprising that they like to see the company name in some way associated with the contribution, such as the name of a building if the contribution is a substantial one. If a contribution is listed as "anonymous," it is a pretty good guess that it came from an individual donor, rather than from a business organization.

[31] Curtis C. VerSchoor and Elizabeth A. Murphy, "The Financial Performance of Large U.S. Firms and Those with Global Prominence: How Do the Best Corporate Citizens Rate?" *Business & Society Review* Vol. 107, No. 3 (Fall 2002), 378. As statisticians are quick to remind us, correlation does not establish causality. It is likely that corporation executives who have breadth of vision with respect to social issues also have breadth of vision with respect to research and development, marketing, and other factors that contribute to profitability. However, it is certainly plausible to argue that the good will generated by social involvement and the greater productivity of employees who view the company positively also contribute to better financial performance.

the ought implies the can – that is, in order to claim in any meaning-ful way that someone is obligated to do something, it must be possible for that person to do what it is suggested that he or she ought to do.[32] For example, it does not make sense to assert that someone ought to give $5 million to help fund a new center for the performing arts if that person's net assets total less than a thousand dollars. In like manner, it makes no sense to identify any goal or objective that is impossible for a particular company to achieve. We believe that all of the obligations and responsibilities noted previously in relation to investors, customers, employees, suppliers, and communities in which facilities are located are potentially doable.

In many situations, however, it might not be possible for a com-pany to do everything that it ideally ought to do, even if each particu-lar obligation, when viewed in isolation, is doable. In such situations, priorities must be established. When competing obligations involve competition for scarce resources, be they monetary or any other type of resource, questions of distributive justice come into play – that is, questions about what constitutes an appropriate distribution of available resources. In *The Nicomachean Ethics*, Aristotle advocates a proportionate distribution of scarce resources based on merit "for all men agree that what is just in distribution must be according to merit in some sense, though they do not all specify the same sort of merit...."[33] Aristotle goes on to suggest that if what is being allo-cated is undesirable, those who are less meritorious should receive a

---

[32] Though Immanuel Kant is frequently credited with saying that "the ought implies the can," that exact statement cannot be found in his writings. The following pas-sage, however, is to be found in his *Critique of Pure Reason*: "Pure reason, then, con-tains, not indeed in its speculative employment, but in that practical employment which is also moral, principles of the *possibility of experience*, namely, of such actions as, in accordance with moral precepts, *might* be met with in the *history* of mankind. For since reason commands that such actions should take place, it must be possible for them to take place" (A807/B835). The quotation comes from the translation by Norman Kemp Smith, which is now in the public domain and can be accessed at http://arts.cuhk.edu.hk/Philosophy/Kant/cpr/. It does not follow, of course, that the can implies the ought. The fact that we could go to the nearest casino and gamble away every penny we have saved, along with the grocery money and the money needed to make next month's mortgage payment, in no way suggests that we ought to do so.

[33] Aristotle, *The Nicomachean Ethics* in *The Complete Works of Aristotle: The Revised Oxford Translation*, Vol. II, ed. Jonathan Barnes (Princeton, NJ: Princeton University Press, 1984), 1785 (V, 1131ª10–33).

greater share – that is, that costs should be allocated in inverse order of merit.

Using merit criteria for allocation decisions does make sense in a certain range of situations. For example, it is common for employers in the business world, as well as employers in other sectors of the economy, to use merit criteria, at least in part, when determining the magnitude of increases in compensation for salaried employees.[34] Merit criteria, however, do not work as well when making allocation decisions in other areas such as charitable contributions to community organizations. Here other criteria such as need, often coupled with assessments of the efficacy of the organization, are more appropriate. Nor do merit criteria provide useful reference points for establishing priorities or otherwise weighting obligations with respect to the other constituencies noted previously.

There is no precise mathematical formula that can be used to determine exactly how resources and/or costs should be allocated among these various constituencies. It is essential, however, that business organizations (and other organizations as well) have in place strategic plans that provide a framework for addressing these allocation and priority questions when they arise. It is almost always a serious mistake to ignore these questions until forced to address them in the immediacy of the situation. What often happens if no prior attention has been given to these matters is that decisions end up being made in a piecemeal manner without any serious attention being given to questions of priority and relative importance.

A FINAL MATTER TO BE NOTED

Before proceeding to Part II of this volume, where, drawing upon the guiding principles we have mapped out in these first three chapters, we will examine in detail the ethics of investment in China and other countries, one final matter remains to be addressed. Both in Chapter 1 and in Chapter 2 we suggest that if one approaches ethical issues related to globalization (or any other ethical issues, for that matter) from a rights-oriented perspective that emphasizes the dignity and

---

[34] This is routinely done notwithstanding the fact that, as Aristotle noted, not everyone agrees as to what constitutes merit.

worth of each person, harming other people is always wrong. In real life, however, things are not quite that simple. As those in the business world know, there are times when imposing costs on other people is unavoidable – for example, when business takes a turn for the worse and it is no longer economically feasible to keep everyone on payroll, as has been the case in the worldwide recession that began in 2008. While there is perhaps a distinction to be made between unavoidably imposing costs on other people and deliberately harming them, this is not a distinction that makes much sense to the person who loses her or his job or to those living in a once-quiet neighborhood, the tranquility of which is destroyed by truck traffic going to and from a new factory that has been built nearby.

While it is sometimes possible to ameliorate these costs – for example, by covering the cost of constructing a new road so that truck traffic can be diverted from the once-quiet neighborhood – in other cases, such as layoffs necessitated by a downturn in business, it is not possible to do so. In still other cases, the pressure of international competition in this age of globalization might force decisions detrimental to workers such as John Ester, who, as noted in the introduction to this volume, worked for twenty-six years making refrigerators at the Maytag plant in Galesburg, Illinois, but saw his job disappear when the company decided to move production of refrigerators to a plant in Mexico.[35] As also noted previously, in a book entitled *The Ethical Investor*, John G. Simon, Charles W. Powers, and Jon P. Gunnemann affirm a "prima facie obligation of all citizens, both individual and institutional, to avoid and correct self-caused social injury."[36] To this we would add that even if social injury cannot be avoided, there is still an obligation to correct it, be it in the form of outplacement programs for displaced employees or in some other way.

SUMMING IT ALL UP

We have argued that business decisions ought not be made solely on the basis of the bottom line, though maintaining profitability is

---

[35] Steven Greenhouse, "City Feels Early Effects of Plant Closing in 2004," *New York Times*, December 26, 2002, A26.
[36] Simon, Powers, and Gunnemann, *The Ethical Investor*, 20–21.

important if the company is to survive. Rather, consideration ought to be given to what is best for all of the constituencies the organization is called to serve – not just investors but also customers, employees, suppliers, and the communities in which company facilities are located – that is, all those who have a stake in what the company does. As the more specific cases we will consider in the chapters that follow illustrate, this is seldom easy, with many shades of gray in a world beset with ambiguity. It is far preferable, however, that business organizations (and all other organizations and institutions) struggle with what is the right thing to do, rather than just take the easy road – the road that might offer the least resistance but a road that sells short what the business of business ideally ought to be.

PART II

PRACTICAL APPLICATIONS

4

Human Rights and the Ethics of Investment in China

Beijing today looks much like Chicago, Toronto, Brussels, or any other modern city – high-rise office buildings clad in glass, streets packed with automobiles and trucks, and billboards, many of them in English,[1] advertising name-brand products, many of them U.S. name brands, though that, of course, does not necessarily mean they were manufactured in the United States. The same can be said of Shanghai, Nanjing, and a number of other Chinese cities.

The U.S presence in China, which is apparent even to the most casual observer, is growing rapidly. From 1993 to 2002, direct investment in China by U.S. companies increased by a factor of ten, making the United States the second largest foreign investor in China. (Hong Kong, though nominally a part of China but with a separate economic and political structure, is the largest foreign investor.) A substantial portion of the U.S. investment (approximately 60 percent) is in the manufacturing sector, which turns out vast quantities of merchandise, some of it sold in the rapidly expanding Chinese market, some of it exported for sale in the United States and elsewhere.[2]

---

[1] English is rapidly becoming the second language of China. Chinese school children are required to study English and delight in practicing their English by seeking out and talking with visiting Americans.

[2] United States General Accounting Office, *World Trade Organization: U.S. Companies' Views on China's Implementation of Its Commitments* (GAO-04-508, March 2004), 42.

But as was the case with U.S. direct investment in South Africa three decades ago, human rights activists and others concerned about social justice have raised questions about the role that U.S. companies play in China, for, as was the case with South Africa prior to the end of apartheid, China's record on human rights is far from unblemished. Should U.S. companies continue to invest in China? And if so, what ethical guidelines should govern their practices? Do the Global Sullivan Principles of Social Responsibility, drafted by the Rev. Leon Sullivan in 1997 at the request of world and industry leaders, provide useful guidelines? Or are more specific guidelines, comparable to those drafted by Sullivan in the mid-1970s with respect to South Africa, needed? In an era of widespread outsourcing, what responsibilities do U.S. and other multinational companies have to ensure that their suppliers comply with relevant human rights standards? To what extent – if at all – are codes of conduct for suppliers enforceable? Before responding to these and other questions pertaining to the ethics of investing in China, it is useful to look at China's human rights record.

HUMAN RIGHTS IN CHINA

The official position of the government of China is that they are strongly committed to human rights. Article 35 of the Constitution of the People's Republic of China, which was adopted on December 4, 1982, states, "Citizens of the People's Republic of China enjoy freedom of speech, of the press, of assembly, of association, of procession and of demonstration." A constitutional amendment approved by the Tenth National People's Congress on March 14, 2004, added the words "The State respects and preserves human rights" to Article 33.[3] A lengthy statement issued by the Information Office of the State Council of the People's Republic of China in 1991 asserts:

The Constitution [of the People's Republic of China] provides for a wide range of political rights to citizens. In addition to the right to vote and to be elected ... citizens also enjoy freedoms of speech, the press, assembly, association, procession and demonstration. There is no news censorship in

---

[3] *Constitution of the People's Republic of China*, at http://english.peopledaily.com.cn/constitution/constitution.html (last accessed October 13, 2006).

China.... The Constitution also rules that citizens have the right to criticize and make suggestions regarding any state organ or functionary and the right to make to relevant state organs complaints or charges against, or exposure of, any state organ or functionary for violation of the law or dereliction of duty. The Constitution provides that freedom of the person of citizens of the People's Republic of China is inviolable. Unlawful detention or deprivation of citizens' freedom of the person by other means and unlawful search of the person of citizens are prohibited; the personal dignity of citizens is inviolable, and insult, libel, false accusation or false incrimination directed against citizens by any means is prohibited; the residences of citizens are inviolable and unlawful search of, or intrusion into, a citizen's residence is prohibited; freedom and privacy of correspondence are protected by law, and those who hide, discard, damage or illegally open other people's letters, once discovered, shall be seriously dealt with, and grave cases shall be prosecuted.[4]

If this statement could be taken at face value, there would be no human rights issues to discuss with respect to China. But because it is not unusual for official Chinese government statements (or those of many other governments) to take liberties with the facts, one should not assume that everything in this statement is factually accurate. And indeed, organizations and agencies as diverse as the U.S. Department of State and Amnesty International question the veracity of China's claim that human rights are consistently and universally respected in China. An Amnesty International document notes, "The revision of China's constitution in March 2004 to include the clause 'the state respects and safeguards human rights' suggests an intent on the part of Chinese authorities to take seriously the task of improving human rights in China. Despite these promises, serious violations of human rights continue in China."[5] The 2009 U.S. Department of State report on human rights practices in China (issued March 11, 2010 by the Bureau of Democracy, Human Rights, and Labor) states:

The [Chinese] government's human rights record remained poor and worsened in some areas. During the year the government increased its severe cultural and religious repression of ethnic minorities in Tibetan

---

[4] Information Office of the State Council of the People's Republic of China, *Human Rights in China* (1991), 10–11, at http://news.xinhuanet.com/employment/200211/18/content_633179.htm (last accessed September 8, 2006).
[5] Amnesty International, "People's Republic of China: The Olympics Countdown – Three Years of Human Rights Reform?" (August 5, 2005), at http://web.amnesty.org/library/Index/ENGASA17021205 (last accessed September 8, 2006).

areas and the Xinjiang Uighur Autonomous Region (XUAR). Tibetan areas remained under tight government controls. The detention and harassment of human rights activists increased, and public interest lawyers and law firms that took on cases deemed sensitive by the government faced harassment, disbarment and closure. The government limited freedom of speech and controlled the Internet and Internet access. Abuses peaked around high-profile events, such as the twentieth anniversary of the Tianamen Square uprising, the fiftieth anniversary of the Tibetan uprising, and the sixtieth anniversary of the founding of the People's Republic of China.... Individuals and groups, especially those deemed politically sensitive by the government, continued to face tight restrictions on their freedom to assemble, practice religion, travel.... The government failed to address serious social conditions that affected human rights, including endemic corruption, trafficking in persons, and discrimination against women, minorities, and persons with disabilities. The government continued its coercive birth limitation policy, in some cases resulting in forced abortion and sterilization. Workers cannot choose an independent union to represent them in the workplace, and the law does not protect workers' right to strike.[6]

The dissonance between official Chinese government statements on human rights and what happens in practice is underscored by the 2008 arrest and subsequent conviction of human rights activist Huang Qi. On May 12, 2008, a violent earthquake in Sichuan Province killed more than 80,000 people, among them several thousand school children who were crushed when school buildings collapsed. A month later, police detained Huang, a longtime civil rights activist who ran a website that had been critical of the Chinese Communist Party's restrictions on human rights, and charged him with illegally possessing state secrets. Huang had supported parents who claimed that shoddy and corrupt building practices had contributed to the collapse of the school buildings that claimed the lives of their children. In November of 2009, Huang was sentenced to three years in prison (the verdict coming days after U.S. President Barack Obama's visit to China).[7]

---

[6] U.S. Department of State Bureau of Democracy, Human Rights, and Labor, *2009 Human Rights Report: China* (issued March 11, 2010) at http://www.state.gov/g/drl/rls/hrrpt/2009/eap/135989.htm (last accessed April 30, 2010).
[7] Reuters, "Man Charged After Quake in China Gets 3 Years," *New York Times*, November 23, 2009, A10.

Because space does not allow detailed discussion of all areas of concern, more specific comments will be limited to three areas – reproductive rights, religious freedom, and workers' rights. Concerns about reproductive rights and religious freedom, while not directly related to U.S. and other multinational corporations operating in China, are pertinent to the cultural context in which multinational corporations must operate while concerns about workers' rights interface directly with international business activity in China.

REPRODUCTIVE RIGHTS

When Chinese leader Deng Xiaoping, in an effort to control China's rapid population growth, introduced the controversial one-child policy in 1979, it was characterized as a temporary measure. Today, more than a quarter of century later, it remains in effect. Zhang Weiqing, minister of the National Population and Family Planning Commission, stated in March of 2008 that China will not make major changes in family planning policy for the next decade, at which time an anticipated surge in births is expected to end.[8]

For urban residents and government employees, the policy is strictly enforced, with exceptions to the one-child restriction seldom given. (An exception is sometimes granted in cases in which both parents are only children.) In rural areas, where more than half of the Chinese population lives, a second child is more frequently allowed, particularly if the first child is a girl.[9] For example, Anhui Province allows some who had a child in a previous marriage, coal miners, and some farm couples to have a second child.[10]

Those who violate the policy are assessed a "social compensation fee," which can be as much as ten times a person's annual income. These fees are set and assessed on the local level. Other penalties may

---

[8] Jim Yardley, "China Sticking with One-Child Policy," *New York Times*, March 11, 2008.

[9] Therese Hesketh, Li Lu, and Zhe Wei Xing, "The Effect of China's One-Child Family Policy after 25 Years," *New England Journal of Medicine* 353:1171–1176 (September 15, 2005), at http://content.nejm.org/cgi/content/full/353/11/1171 (last accessed October 15, 2006).

[10] U.S. Department of State Bureau of Democracy, Human Rights, and Labor, *2006 Human Rights Report: China*.

include job loss or demotion, loss of opportunities for promotion, and expulsion from the Communist Party (membership in which is required for certain jobs). The central government formally prohibits the use of physical coercion to force pregnant women to undergo abortions or sterilization, though, as the U.S. Department of State Bureau of Democracy, Human Rights, and Labor notes in its most recent report on China, there continue to be reports of coerced abortion and sterilization.[11] Officials at all levels are subject to rewards or penalties for meeting or failing to meet the population goals set by their administrative region.[12]

While reports of forced abortion and involuntary sterilization are difficult to verify, they have been made with sufficient frequency to suggest that there is at least some basis in fact for such allegations. Even if it is the case that physical coercion does not occur as frequently as some of the critics of China's one-child policy suggest, the huge "social compensation" fees assessed on those who choose to have a second child can plausibly be construed as economic duress and hence contrary to Western notions of the rights of individuals. Thus, it is not surprising to encounter comments such as that made by Thomas R. Jackson, a physician affiliated with Ireland Army Community Hospital in Fort Knox, Kentucky, who stated in a letter to the editor published in the *New England Journal of Medicine*, "The policy of one child per family has been a terrible violation of the personal rights of millions of Chinese women. All that is necessary for the draconian policy to be removed ... is for the Chinese government to make the decision to stop such repressive measures and start dealing with the problems posed by an expanding population through moral means."[13]

When all things are considered, however, the situation is not quite that simple. In certain crucial respects, the Chinese notion of human rights is quite different from Western notions of human rights. For example, the statement on human rights issued by the Information Office of. the State Council of the People's Republic of China (to

---

[11] U.S. Department of State Bureau of Democracy, Human Rights, and Labor, *2009 Human Rights Report: China*.

[12] *Ibid.*

[13] Thomas R. Jackson, "China's One-Child Family Policy (Letter to the Editor)," *New England Journal of Medicine* 354:877 (February 23, 2006), at http://content.nejm. org/cgi/content/full/354/8/877 (last accessed October 15, 2006).

which we have already made reference) asserts, "It is a simple truth that, for any country or nation, the right to subsistence is the most important of all human rights, without which the other rights are out of the question.... To solve their human rights problems, the first thing for the Chinese people to do is ... to secure the right to subsistence."[14]

In short, the Chinese government sees the one-child policy, not as a violation of human rights, but as something that is necessary if what they view as the most basic of human rights – the right of subsistence – is to be realized. Therese Hesketh, who is affiliated with the Institute of Child Health in London, and Zhu Wei Xin, who is affiliated with Zhejiang University in Hangzhou, China, (two of the authors of the article with which Dr. Jackson took exception), respond to his comments as follows:

We agree that the one-child policy is a violation of the human right to reproductive choice, as we acknowledge in our article. It is precisely for this reason that it is so controversial. But we should not judge the Chinese by Western standards. Few Chinese see the policy as a human rights violation. Most (though not all) accept it with equanimity, even in the cities where the one-child rule is enforced.... The Chinese authorities would argue that the policy has contributed to improvements in human rights by lifting more than 200 million people out of poverty and by raising living standards for the majority of the population. In an increasingly interdependent world, where available natural resources per capita are decreasing, the Chinese government should perhaps be applauded for having the courage to take unpopular measures to control population growth.[15]

This exchange underscores a very important question: To what extent is it appropriate for us to use our notion of human rights to judge what other people in other countries and cultures do? This question, of course, is not uniquely related to reproductive rights in China. It also comes up with respect to a number of other controversial matters, among them the practice of female genital mutilation in Africa and the plight of women in countries ruled by Islamic fundamentalists.

[14] Information Office of the State Council, *Human Rights in China*.
[15] Therese Hesketh and Zhu Wei Xing, "China's One-Child Family Policy (Letter to the Editor: The Authors Reply)," *New England Journal of Medicine* 354:877 (February 23, 2006), at http://content.nejm.org/cgi/content/full/354/8/877 (last accessed October 15, 2006).

Space does not allow detailed discussion of these cases. Suffice it to say that (a) if people are being harmed by practices and policies in other countries, and (b) we are able to do something about it (recalling the Kantian dictum that ought implies can), there is a strong moral argument to be made for standing with those who are threatened and doing what we can to prevent or diminish the harm being done to them.

The human rights equation with respect to China, however, is somewhat more complicated, for here whatever harm might be done to those wishing to have more than one child can be construed as contributing to the greater good. In short, there are utilitarian arguments that can be made in support of China's one-child policy. Those of us with strong commitments to Western notions of human rights find such arguments unpersuasive. But it at least behooves us to understand as best we can the reasons for China's one-child policy.

RELIGIOUS FREEDOM

The official position of the Chinese government is that freedom of religion is a constitutionally guaranteed right. What happens in practice, however, is quite a different story.

The Chinese government officially recognizes five main religions: Buddhism, Taoism, Islam, Protestantism, and Catholicism. New regulations, which went into effect March 1, 2005, require religious groups to register places of worship and reaffirm the authority of the government to determine what is "normal" and hence lawful.[16]

There are about thirty officially sanctioned Protestant and Roman Catholic churches in Beijing,[17] among them the Beijing Kuanjie Protestant Christian Church, which President George W. Bush attended during his 2008 visit to China, Gangwashi Church,

---

[16] U.S. Department of State Bureau of Democracy, Human Rights, and Labor, *China Human Rights Report – 2006*. See also Philip P. Pan, "Protestant Pastor in China Convicted for Printing, Distributing Bibles," *Washington Post*, November 9, 2005, A22, and China Aid Association, Inc., "House Churches in Beijing and Jilin, China, Raided," at http://www.thegreatseparation.com/newsfront/2006/01/house_churches_.html (last accessed October 8, 2006).

[17] Maureen Fan, "Beijing Curbs Rights It Says Citizens Have to Worship; Christian Activists Detail Harassment, Even Arrests," *Washington Post*, August 10, 2008, A12.

which President Bush visited when he was in China in 2005,[18] and Chongwenmen Church, which Presidents Bill Clinton and George H.W. Bush attended while visiting Beijing during their presidencies.[19] Attendance at the officially sanctioned churches in Beijing and elsewhere in China is growing, with crowded sanctuaries forcing many worshipers to go to the basement and watch the service on closed circuit television. An editorial that originally ran in the *Economist* entitled "Holier than Mao – Chinese Christians Might Outnumber Communists," speculates that the number of Christians in China might be greater than the number of communists.[20] Though reliable statistics on church attendance are not available, it is possible that the writer of the editorial is right. The official website of the Communist Party of China states by the end of 2007, the party had 74,153,000 members.[21] The government officially estimates that there are 21 million Christians in China (16 million Protestants, 5 million Catholics), though outside observers believe that the number of practicing Christians in China is much higher – perhaps as many as 130 million – when attendance at the unofficial house churches is taken into account.[22]

The officially sanctioned churches are carefully controlled by the Chinese government. In a piece entitled "China's Catholics Caught between Church, State" that ran on National Public Radio, Anthony Kuhn noted that when the time came to select a new bishop for the Hengshui diocese in Hebei province (where many of China's Roman Catholics live), local church members submitted three names both to the Vatican and to the Chinese Patriotic Catholic Association in

[18] Peter Baker and Philip P. Pan, "Bush Attends Beijing Church, Promoting Religious Freedom," *Washington Post*, November 20, 2005, A18.

[19] Embassy of the People's Republic of China in the United States of America, "President Clinton Attends Sunday Church Service in Beijing," at http://www.china-embassy.org/eng/zmgx/zysj/kldfh/t36226.htm (last accessed October 8, 2006).

[20] "Holier than Mao – Chinese Christians Might Outnumber Communists," *Gazette* (Montreal), October 6, 2008, A17. The article originally ran in the *Economist* October 4, 2008, with the title "Sons of Heaven: Christianity in China."

[21] "Communist Party of China" at http://www.chinatoday.com/org/cpc/ (last accessed October 23, 2009).

[22] "Holier than Mao – Chinese Christians Might Outnumber Communists." Even if the 130 million figure is accurate, however, that represents no more than 10 percent of China's population of more than 1.3 billion.

Beijing. In time, both the Vatican and the Chinese Patriotic Catholic Association (which is the government-sanctioned Roman Catholic organization) approved the selection of Peter Feng as bishop. While the Vatican recognizes most of the bishops sanctioned by the Chinese Patriotic Catholic Association, the two prongs of the approval process are entirely independent of each other.[23] The Chinese Patriotic Catholic Association does not recognize the authority of the Holy See to appoint bishops but does allow discreet input from the Vatican. A substantial majority of the bishops appointed by the government via the Chinese Patriotic Catholic Association has received official approval from the Vatican.[24]

In an article entitled "China Opens Door to Christianity – of a Patriotic Sort" that ran in the *Christian Science Monitor,* Robert Marquand, commenting on the growth of Christianity in China, notes, "The change is part of a new official formula that is fitfully taking shape [in China]: a basic and perhaps grudging acceptance of faith, including low-level experiments with religious exchange abroad – so long as Chinese believers profess loyalty and patriotism to the state."[25]

While officially sanctioned churches are experiencing growth, Protestant and Catholic "house churches" and other unregistered groups are believed to be growing even faster.[26] With the government wishing to control religious activity, unregistered groups can be, and often are, subjected to harassment by government officials.[27] While the way that local authorities respond to unregistered groups varies, leaders of unregistered groups have been subjected to physical abuse and detention. For example, in late 2005, the Beijing People's Intermediate Court sentenced Cai Zhuohua, a prominent pastor in the underground Protestant Church, to three years in prison for

[23] Anthony Kuhn, "China's Catholics Caught between Church, State," National Public Radio, March 16, 2006, at http://www.npr.org/templates/story/story.php?storyId=5284707 (last accessed October 8, 2006).
[24] U.S. Department of State Bureau of Democracy, Human Rights, and Labor, *2008 Human Rights Report: China.*
[25] Marquand, "China Opens Door to Christianity – of a Patriotic Sort."
[26] *Ibid.*
[27] See, e.g., China Aid Association, Inc., "House Churches in Beijing and Jilin Raided; Public Security Denied Jailed Beijing Pastor to Meet with his Mother; Five Detained Church Leaders in Xinjiang Released," January 16, 2006 Press Release, at http://www.chinaaid.org/english_site/press_release_detail.php?id=118 (last accessed October 8, 2006).

"illegal business practices" after he was charged with and convicted of illegally printing and distributing Bibles and other religious literature (a sentence that was imposed shortly before President Bush's visit to China).[28] In May of 2008, government officials showed up at the Shou Wang house church in the western part of Beijing, announced that the service was an illegal assembly, and wrote down the names, employers, and cell phone numbers of those in attendance. Shortly thereafter, those attending the worship service received phone calls from religious officials and employers ordering them to stop attending the house church, which most refused to do.[29]

The Chinese government's treatment of groups such as Falun Gong is even harsher. Viewed by the Chinese government as a cult, the Falun Gong movement, founded in 1992 by Li Hongzhi, emphasizes meditation techniques and physical exercise to achieve good health and peace of mind. Though drawing upon concepts and techniques rooted in Buddhism and Taoism, Falun Gong members insist that their movement is not a religion. Li Hongzhi contends that Falun Gong members can be of many different faiths because, he argues, Falun Gong does not contradict any faith.[30]

The movement spread rapidly, gaining several million practitioners in China and elsewhere. Estimates of practitioners range from a few million to several hundred million. In early 1999, when the Chinese government renewed efforts to suppress nonsanctioned spiritual movements, Falun Gong responded with a silent, nonviolent protest in front of Communist Party headquarters in Beijing. Reportedly, over 10,000 people participated in this illegal protest. Startled by the size of the protest and the failure of the secret police to provide intelligence about the event, the Chinese government outlawed the movement on July 22, 1999.[31]

Disregarding the International Covenant on Civil and Political Rights, which China signed,[32] the Chinese government has resorted

---

[28] Pan, "Protestant Pastor in China Convicted for Printing, Distributing Bibles."

[29] Fan, "Beijing Curbs Rights It Says Citizens Have to Worship."

[30] *Falun Gong* at http://religiousmovements.lib.virginia.edu/nrms/falungong.html (last accessed October 20, 2006). See also Falun Gong's website: http://www.falun-dafa.org.

[31] *Ibid.*

[32] The International Covenant on Civil and Political Rights states, "Everyone shall have the right to freedom of thought, conscience and religion. This right shall include

to harsh measures in an effort to suppress the Falun Gong. The government established a website intended to discredit Falun Gong beliefs and practices while Falun Gong countered with their own website (http://www.faluninfo.net/index.asp) with reports of brutality, including allegations that thousands of Falun Gong practitioners have been secretly put to death so that their organs could be used for transplant. A very active Falun Gong Human Rights Working Group (http://www.faluninfo.net/index.asp) posts on its website reports of atrocities and advocates corrective action.

While the harsh treatment of Falun Gong practitioners has received significant press coverage in the United States and other Western countries, Falun Gong is by no means the only spiritual group with which the Chinese government has dealt harshly. The government has also cracked down on Tibetan Buddhists, Muslim Uyghurs (Altaic-speaking Sunni Muslims of Turkish descent, most of whom live in Xinjiang province, which they refer to as "Eastern Turkestan"), and a number of smaller groups they view as cults.[33] While there are constitutional guarantees of freedom of religious belief, the level of repression of Tibetan Buddhists increased significantly after the March 2008 unrest. The Chinese government tends to equate reverence for the Dalai Lama with political opposition to the central government and the Chinese Communist Party. Similarly, the government fears that the support of Muslim Uyghurs for regional autonomy threatens the authority of the central government.[34]

WORKERS' RIGHTS

China's constitution provides for freedom "of association, of procession and of demonstration." In practice, however, workers have

freedom to have or to adopt a religion or belief of his choice, and freedom, either individually or in community with others and in public or private, to manifest his religion or belief in worship, observance, practice and teaching." (http://www1.umn.edu/humanrts/instree/b3ccpr.htm, last accessed December 15, 2006). China signed the covenant October 5, 1998 but has not yet ratified it (http://www1.umn.edu/humanrts/research/ratification-china.html, [last accessed December 15, 2006]).
[33] U.S. Department of State Bureau of Democracy, Human Rights, and Labor, *2006 Human Rights Report: China.*
[34] U.S. Department of State Bureau of Democracy, Human Rights, and Labor, *2008 Human Rights Report: China.*

enjoyed very little freedom to organize or to join unions of their own choosing. The All-China Federation of Trade Unions (ACFTU), which is controlled by the Communist Party of China (a high-level party official is the head of ACFTU), keeps a tight rein on union activities. While labor law permits collective bargaining, the rigid ACFTU control of all union activities has meant that in practice there has been very little collective bargaining. A number of labor activists have been arrested. Among them are Kong Jun and Li Xintao, who were employees of the state-owned Huamei Garment Company, which experienced bankruptcy. In May 2005, they were convicted of disturbing social order and government institutions because they asked the Shandong provincial government to take action against the Huamei Garment Company for failure to pay workers' wages.[35]

The enfeebled status of labor unions in China might be changing. Intent on presenting the best possible face during the build-up to the 2008 Olympics, the Chinese government, as part of a crackdown on sweatshops and other labor abuses, proposed for consideration a new law that would give labor unions real power for the first time. This initiative became possible when the Chinese Communist Party endorsed new approaches for dealing with the human costs of the country's economic expansion. In a move unusual for China, the government invited comment on the proposal.[36]

Rather ironically in view of the fact that the United States for years has put pressure on China to improve its human rights practices, including those related to workers' rights, the American Chamber of Commerce (AmCham), which represents U.S. companies with overseas operations, spoke out against the proposed law. AmCham warned that increases in levels of compensation for Chinese workers might cause some U.S. companies to pull out of China. AmCham also feared that the new law, if enacted, would make it difficult to fire underperforming employees.[37]

Joined by the United States-China Business Council (USCBC), a membership-supported private organization of U.S. companies doing

---

[35] *Ibid.*
[36] David Barboza, "China Drafts Law to Empower Unions and End Labor Abuse," *New York Times*, October 13, 2006, A1.
[37] *Ibid.*

business in China, and various U.S. companies with operations in China, AmCham succeeded in persuading the Chinese government to modify some provisions of the proposed legislation. In a prepared statement issued in January 2007, USCBC, while recommending additional changes, stated that the revised draft "makes significant improvements to the previous draft and strengthens protections for both employees and employers."[38]

Others were less sanguine in their assessment. In an article entitled "Chinese Heat is on US Sweatshop Lobby" that ran in the online version of Asia Times, Brendan Smith, Tim Costello, and Jeremy Brecher charged, "Despite successfully removing important pro-worker provisions from the first draft, the business community has launched a major new lobby effort to further gut the legislation...."[39]

Even without the proposed law in place, the All-China Federation of Trade Unions became more aggressive in attempting to organize facilities operated by foreign companies. For example, union activists organized unions in all Wal-Mart outlets in China, a monumental accomplishment at a retailing giant that has fought hard to keep unions out of its retail operations. (Wal-Mart, which currently operates nearly 150 stores in China with more than 70,000 employees,[40] is poised to become the largest foreign-owned retailer in China as the result of its purchase of a 35 percent stake in Bounteous Company, a

[38] U.S. China Business Council, "Comments on the Draft People's Republic of China Law on Employment Contracts (Draft of December 24, 2006" at http://www.uschina.org/public/documents/2007/01/comments-employment-contracts-english.pdf (last accessed April 6, 2007).

[39] Brendan Smith, Tim Costello, and Jeremy Brecher, "Chinese Heat Is on US Sweatshop Lobby," *Asia Times* (April 5, 2008) at http://www.atimes.com/atimes/China_Business/ID05Cb01.html (last accessed April 6, 2007). The article is adapted from a report entitled "Undue Influence: Corporations Gain Ground in Battle over China's New Labor Law" issued by Global Labor Strategies in March 2007 (at http://laborstrategies.blogs.com/global_labor_strategies/files/undue_influence_global_labor_strategies.pdf). In what has become a heated exchange, the United States-China Business Council (USCBC), in a statement issued April 5, 2007, has taken sharp exception to the Global Labor Strategies article, asserting that Global Labor Strategies has "repeatedly mischaracterized" the USCBC position on the proposed Chinese Law (United States-China Business Council,"The US-China Business Council's Position on China's Proposed Labor Contract Law" at http://www.uschina.org/public/documents/2007/04/proposed-labor-contract-law-position.html [last accesesed April 6, 2007]).

[40] "Latest Counts of Wal-Mart" at http://wal-martchina.com/english/news/stat.htm (last accessed October 24, 2009).

Taiwan-based company with more than 100 retail outlets in mainland China.[41]) Guo Wencai, an ACFTU organizer, called the success in organizing Wal-Mart a "breakthrough" and predicted that the success at Wal-Mart would lead to success at Eastman Kodak, Dell, and other companies.[42] A number of other U.S. companies with outlets in China, including McDonald's and Yum! Brands (which owns KFC, Pizza Hut, Long John Silver's, and Taco Bell), have followed Wal-Mart's lead in agreeing to unionization.[43]

The contract labor law, with some revision, was adopted and went into effect January 1, 2008. The law requires that employers give all employees a written contract that complies with applicable minimum wage and safety requirements. It also makes it more difficult for companies to use temporary workers and to dismiss employees, and it gives the ACFTU greater power to negotiate employment agreements on behalf of the employees it represents.[44] With the new law in place, the ACFTU, with the encouragement and support of the Chinese government, has demanded that all foreign-owned multinational companies operating in China allow their workers to organize and join the ACFTU (which continues to be the only labor organization the Communist Party of China allows). Even though far more Chinese workers are employed by Chinese-owned companies than by foreign-owned multinational companies, the ACFTU is focusing on the latter.[45] In an interview with a *New York Times* reporter, Wang Ying, an ACFTU official, stated, "Some foreign companies in China haven't behaved well in dealing with their workers' interests and rights. As the economy and society develops, China needs to improve workers' legal rights and interests, which is a demand of a civilized society."[46]

Whether unions that are affiliated with ACFTU will effectively protect workers' rights remains to be seen. Anita Chan, a visiting

---

[41] David Barboza, "Wal-Mart Buys Stake in Retail Chain to Gain Stronger Presence in China," *New York Times*, February 27, 2007.
[42] David Lague, "Official Union in China Says All Wal-Marts Are Organized," *New York Times*, October 13, 2006, C6.
[43] David Barboza, "China Tells Businesses to Unionize," *New York Times*, September 12, 2008.
[44] U.S. Department of State Bureau of Democracy, Human Rights, and Labor, *2008 Human Rights Report: China*.
[45] Barboza, "China Tells Businesses to Unionize."
[46] Quoted in *ibid.*

research fellow at Australian National University in Canberra who is an authority on labor issues in China, observes, "It all depends on how they are set up. After you set up a union, these groups have to know how to become representatives of the workers, and really collectively bargain."[17]

Even though the contract labor law in theory gives workers greater protection, there are reports that the law is widely ignored and that conditions have actually deteriorated in many of the export-oriented factories located in southern China.[48] Zhang Zhiru, director of the Shenzhen Chungfen Labor Dispute Service, a worker advocacy group, observes, "The economic downturn has given regulators the perfect excuse to ignore the law."[49] Some local governments have issued competing rules or interpretations of the contract labor law in an effort to aid factory owners. Liu Cheng, a law professor at Shanghai Normal University who helped draft the law, observes, "Many local governments want to develop their own versions of the law"[50] – a development that has had the practical effect of weakening the law. As noted previously, the contract labor law requires all employers to give their employees a written contract that complies with minimum wage and safety requirements. However, Liu Kaiming, who is the director of a labor rights group based in Shenzhen, reports, "The employment contract in many factories here is a mere scrap of paper [that is ignored]."[51]

During the recession that began with the collapse of credit markets in 2008, China, while taking a hit because of declining consumer demand worldwide, succeeded in securing a larger piece of the shrinking pie. Reducing prices by slashing wages of factory workers, many of them migrant workers, has enabled China to undersell factories in Mexico and elsewhere and, by so doing, gain market share.[52]

---

[17] Quoted in *ibid*.
[48] David Barboza, "Growth, but at a Price," *New York Times*, June 23, 2009, B1.
[49] Quoted in *ibid*.
[50] Quoted in *ibid*.
[51] Quoted in *ibid*.
[52] David Barboza, "In Recession, China Solidifies Its Lead in Global Trade," *New York Times*, October 14, 2009. Barboza reports that China's exports during the first half of 2009 totaled $521 billion, which was 22 percent less than exports during the first half of 2008. That, however, compares favorably to other exporters. In the same period, German exports fell by 34 percent while Japanese exports were down by 37 percent and U.S. exports by 24 percent.

There is no national minimum wage law. Labor law, however, does require local governments to specify minimum wage requirements, which must be consistent with standards promulgated by the Ministry of Human Resources and Social Security. These standards include the minimum cost of living for workers and their families in that locality and other factors. Local minimum wage laws are unevenly enforced. Factory owners frequently undercut these laws by imposing arbitrary fines and wage deductions on their workers for alleged breaches of company rules. Many employers set unrealistic production targets that force workers to work overtime without additional compensation in order to meet the production target[53] – a practice documented in *China Blue*, which, as noted in Chapter 2, aired on PBS as part of the Independent Lens series.[54]

Chinese labor law prohibits forced labor. Though the Chinese government denies that forced labor occurs, it has worked to resolve cases in which it is alleged that products made with prison labor have been exported for sale in other countries. Chinese labor law also prohibits child labor, defined as employment of children under the age of sixteen, though reports of child labor are not infrequent.[55] For example, family members allege that child labor was widely employed at the Lihua Textile Factory in Hebei Province, where five teenage girls living in factory dormitories died of asphyxiation.[56] In March 2008, police in Heilongjiang Province rescued thirty-three migrant workers, several of whom reportedly had mental disabilities, from confinement in a ninety-eight-square-foot room. The following month, police in Guangdong Province rescued more than 100 youths following reports that labor brokers were supplying under-age workers to factories and workshops in violation of labor, child welfare, and antitrafficking laws.[57] Also in 2008, police in Anhui

---

[53] U.S. Department of State Bureau of Democracy, Human Rights, and Labor, *2008 Human Rights Report: China.*

[54] Independent Lens, "China Blue" at http://www.pbs.org/independentlens/china-blue/film.html (last accessed September 18, 2008).

[55] U.S. Department of State Bureau of Democracy, Human Rights, and Labor, *2005 Human Rights Report: China* (March 8, 2006), at http://www.state.gov/g/drl/rls/hrrpt/2005/61605.htm (last accessed October 7, 2006).

[56] U.S. Department of State Bureau of Democracy, Human Rights, and Labor, *2007 Human Rights Report: China.*

[57] U.S. Department of State Bureau of Democracy, Human Rights, and Labor, *2008 Human Rights Report: China.*

province freed thirty mentally handicapped workers from what was described as "slave conditions" in a brick kiln.[58] After an international nongovernment organization (NGO) reported that some factories licensed to make goods bearing the 2008 Olympics logo were practicing child labor, police in Guangdong Province determined that the Lekit Stationery Company had hired students under the age of sixteen, which resulted in the company's loss of the license to produce goods bearing the Olympic logo. In October 2008, authorities in Hubei Province announced a crackdown on workshops that reportedly employed underage workers.[59]

Though the number of industrial accidents has declined in recent years, the State Administration for Work Safety (SAWS) acknowledges that occupational health and safety problems continue to be serious.[60] According to official statistics, in 2006 industrial accidents killed 14,382 workers, though that was 9.4 percent fewer deaths than in the previous year.[61] Between January and October 2007, official statistics indicate that industrial accidents killed 11,109 workers, a decrease of 6.1 percent from the previous year. The coal industry accounted for 3,770 of the reported fatalities (which is perhaps the reason that the Anhui provincial government allows coal miners to have more than one child). On December 5, 2007, 105 miners were killed in a coal mine in Shanxi Province. About two-thirds of the coal mine accidents occurred in small mines, which account for only one third of China's coal production.[62] SAWS reports that deaths from coal mine accidents declined from a peak of 6,995 in 2002 to 2,630 in 2009, a decline of 62.4 percent. Independent labor groups, however, claim that the actual casualty figures are much higher than what SAWS reports.[63]

Pneumonoconiosis, a chronic respiratory disease caused by inhaling mineral or metallic particles, continues to be the most prevalent

[58] Barboza, "Growth, but at a Price."
[59] U.S. Department of State Bureau of Democracy, Human Rights, and Labor, *2008 Human Rights Report: China.*
[60] *Ibid.*
[61] U.S. Department of State Bureau of Democracy, Human Rights, and Labor, *2007 Human Rights Report: China.*
[62] *Ibid.*
[63] U.S. Department of State Bureau of Democracy, Human Rights, and Labor, *2009 Human Rights Report: China.*

occupational disease in China. The government has reported that 440,000 workers have the disease, though some observers believe that far more Chinese workers have this particular disease.[64] In February 2008, 130 workers at a lead refinery in Shaanxi Province, which the government had ordered closed in November 2007, reportedly suffered lead poisoning and sought compensation after being dismissed from their jobs. In July 2008, workers at a battery factory in Jiangsu Province sought compensation, reporting that they suffered from cadmium poisoning.[65]

The situation is particularly difficult for rural-to-urban migrants who have moved to China's cities in search of work. Many are denied access to health care and decent housing and do not receive the state benefits available to permanent urban residents. An Amnesty International report states, "They experience discrimination in the workplace, and are routinely exposed to some of the most exploitative conditions of work. [Their] insecure legal status, social isolation, sense of cultural inferiority and relative lack of knowledge of their rights leaves them particularly vulnerable, enabling employers to deny their rights with impunity."[66] Wang Yuancheng, a rural-to-urban migrant who experienced a greater degree of success than most migrants, observes, "[T]he lives of migrant workers are miserable. They have to live in makeshift shelters, eat the cheapest bean curd and cabbage. They have no insurance and their wages are often delayed. And most of all, they are discriminated against by urban people."[67] The Chinese government estimates that as a result of the recession that began in 2008, 20 million migrant workers have lost their jobs.[68] Because pension benefits are not portable, many had to forfeit the bulk of social insurance contributions made on their behalf.[69]

---

[64] U.S. Department of State Bureau of Democracy, Human Rights, and Labor, *2006 Human Rights Report: China.*

[65] U.S. Department of State Bureau of Democracy, Human Rights, and Labor, *2008 Human Rights Report: China.*

[66] Amnesty International USA, "Internal Migrants: Discrimination and Abuse" at http://www.amnestyusa.org/document.php?lang=e&id=ENGASA170082007 (last accessed September 23, 2008). See also U.S. Department of State Bureau of Democracy, Human Rights, and Labor, *2008 Human Rights Report: China.*

[67] Quoted in *ibid.*

[68] Barbaroza, "Growth, but at a Price."

[69] U.S. Department of State Bureau of Democracy, Human Rights, and Labor, *2008 Human Rights Report: China.*

An estimated 130 million workers are on the move in China, many of them young women, many of them teenagers. The plight of these rural-to-urban migrants is documented in *China Blue*. The young women who work for a factory that makes blue jeans live together in crowded dormitories where water has to be carried upstairs to their living spaces in buckets. Seventeen-year-old Jasmine, the central character in the documentary, shares a room with twelve other girls. Meals and rent are deducted from their wages, which amount to less than a dollar a day. They work every day from 8:00 A.M. until 2:00 A.M. the next morning removing lint and snipping loose threads from the seams of the blue denim jeans the factory produces.[70]

In short, China's human rights record is far from exemplary, a reality that was underscored during the summer of 2008 when the Chinese government harshly suppressed demonstrations in Llasa and elsewhere in Tibet, demonstrations that were intended to call attention to the Tibetan desire for greater autonomy. Yet there are indications that some progress is being made. Susan Greenhalgh, an anthropologist and women's rights activist who has visited China on numerous occasions, has observed that "despite the heavy costs China's restrictive population policy has imposed and continues to impose on women and girls, important pro-woman changes are occurring...." Greenhalgh concludes that there are "promising developments that open up opportunities for new forms of constructive engagement by Americans that support the reform tendencies already in place."[71] At the same time, as the October 2006 arrest of human rights lawyer Gao Zisheng[72] and the suppression of peaceful demonstrations in Tibet serve to remind us, the path is not one of unrelenting progress. President Bush struck the right balance of concern and constructive engagement when he stated during a joint appearance with Chinese President Hu Jintao at the Great Hall in Beijing, "It's

[70] Independent Lens, "China Blue."

[71] Susan Greenhalgh, "Women's Rights and Birth Planning in China: New Spaces of Political Action, New Opportunities for American Engagement" (testimony prepared for the Congressional Executive Commission on China), at http://www.cecc.gov/pages/roundtables/092302/greenhalgh.php (last accessed October 20, 2006).

[72] Joseph Kahn, "China Charges a Lawyer with Inciting Subversion," *New York Times*, October 15, 2006, A10.

important that social, political and religious freedoms grow in China and we encourage China to continue making their historic transition to greater freedom."[73]

IDENTIFYING AN ETHICAL FRAMEWORK
FOR INTERNATIONAL INVESTMENT

And so, when all things are considered, China's human rights record is far from unblemished, though there is constitutional affirmation of human rights. What does this mean with respect to the ethics of international investment in and trade with China?

Prior to the dismantling of the apartheid system in South Africa, there were strong voices for social justice calling for U.S. and other multinational companies to refrain from investing in South Africa and, if there, to divest. Those who asserted that multinational companies had no business being involved in the land of apartheid typically argued that by being there and paying taxes to the apartheid government, they were implicitly supporting apartheid.

We do not hear similar voices calling for divestment from China. Why not? There are significant differences between South Africa during the days of apartheid and China today. In South Africa, apartheid was the law of the land, supported by various structures of government. In China today, as noted previously, statements affirming human rights are included in the country's constitution, as well as in other official government documents. While these statements might be window dressing primarily intended to deflect external criticism, they do provide a framework for addressing issues of human rights.

Does this then mean that it is fine for U.S. and other multinational companies to invest in China, guided only by what is good for the bottom line? Was Nobel laureate Milton Friedman right when he asserted, "Few trends could so thoroughly undermine the very

---

[73] Quoted by Baker and Pan in "Bush Attends Beijing Church, Promoting Religious Freedom." In contrast to his predecessors, President Obama said very little about human rights issues when he visited China in November 2009. He signaled his more conciliatory approach several weeks before his visit to China when he chose not to meet with the Dalai Lama in order to avoid offending China's leaders (Helene Cooper, "China Holds Firm on Major Issues in Obama's Visit," *New York Times*, November 18, 2009, A1).

foundations of our free society as the acceptance by corporate officials of a social responsibility other than to make as much money for their stockholders as possible" (a view that is perhaps reflected in the American Chamber of Commerce's opposition to the contract labor law).[74] Not if one affirms, as we did in Chapter 3, an ethic of corporate responsibility that entails more than blind pursuit of profits. Not if one agrees with Ryuzaburo Kaku, the former president and chairman of Canon, Inc., who has argued that business enterprises should be guided by *kyosei*, a concept with roots in traditional Japanese culture that can be defined as "living and working together for the common good."[75]

In short, there is a middle path between, on the one hand, refusing to invest in countries with questionable human rights records, and, on the other hand, letting the bottom line determine everything. The middle path is that of constructive engagement.

THE SULLIVAN PRINCIPLES

In 1971, the Reverend Leon H. Sullivan, a prominent civil rights leader, was invited to join the board of directors of General Motors, which at that time was the largest employer of blacks in South Africa. Sullivan decided to use his position on the board to move General Motors in the direction of placing economic pressure on the government of South Africa in an effort to end apartheid.[76] Six years after joining the General Motors' board of directors, he drafted a set of principles that became an international standard for companies operating in South Africa. In their original form, the Sullivan Principles called upon U.S. companies and other foreign companies operating in South Africa to commit to:

---

[74] Milton Friedman, *Capitalism and Freedom* (Chicago: University of Chicago Press, 1962), 133.

[75] *Canon Corporate Philosophy: Kyosei*, at http://www.canon.com/about/philosophy/index.html (last accessed October 27, 2006). The notion of *kyosei* is one of the basic ethical ideals (along with the notion of human dignity) in which the Caux Round Table Principles of Business are rooted (accessible at http://www.cauxroundtable.org/principles.html).

[76] "The Sullivan Principles" at http://www.revleonsullivan.org/principled/principles.htm (last accessed October 27, 2006).

1. nonsegregation of the races in all eating, comfort, and work facilities
2. equal and fair employment practices for all employees
3. equal pay for all employees doing equal or comparable work for the same period of time
4. initiation and development of training programs that will prepare, in substantial numbers, blacks and other nonwhites for supervisory, administrative, clerical, and technical jobs
5. increasing the number of blacks and other nonwhites in management and supervisory positions
6. improving the quality of life for blacks and other nonwhites outside the work environment in areas such as housing, transportation, school, recreation, and health facilities[77]

In 1984, Sullivan added a seventh principle that called upon businesses to commit to working "to eliminate laws and customs that impede social, economic, and political justice."[78] In all cases, Sullivan insisted, progress must be measurable.

In 1987, discouraged with the rate of progress, Sullivan called upon U.S. companies to divest their businesses in South Africa. In 1990, Nelson Mandela, a leader of the African National Congress dedicated to ending apartheid, was released after being imprisoned for twenty-seven years. In 1994, he was elected president of South Africa, and the apartheid structure was dismantled.[79]

Though originally drafted to combat apartheid in South Africa, the Sullivan Principles live on in the form of the Global Sullivan Principles of Social Responsibility, drafted by Sullivan in 1997 at the request of world and industry leaders. Intended to provide guidance for multinational corporations in a global economy, the Principles challenge companies to make a strong commitment to human rights. They state:

As a company which endorses the Global Sullivan Principles we will respect law, and as a responsible member of society we will apply these Principles

---

[77] *Ibid.*
[78] *Ibid.*
[79] "Global Sullivan Principles: History and Evolution," at http://www.thesullivan-foundation.org/gsp/endorsement/history/default.asp (last accessed October 27, 2006).

with integrity consistent with the legitimate role of business. We will develop
and implement company policies, procedures, training and internal reporting structures to ensure commitment to these Principles through our organization. We believe the application of these Principles will achieve greater
tolerance and better understanding among peoples, and advance the culture of peace.

Accordingly, we will:

- express our support for universal human rights and, particularly,
  those of our employees, the communities within which we operate,
  and parties with whom we do business
- promote equal opportunity for our employees at all levels of the
  company with respect to issues such as color, race, gender, age, ethnicity, or religious beliefs, and operate without unacceptable worker
  treatment such as the exploitation of children, physical punishment, female abuse, involuntary servitude, or other forms of abuse
- respect our employees' voluntary freedom of association
- compensate our employees to enable them to meet at least
  their basic needs and provide the opportunity to improve their
  skill and capability in order to raise their social and economic
  opportunities
- provide a safe and healthy workplace, protect human health and
  the environment, and promote sustainable development
- promote fair competition including respect for intellectual and
  other property rights, and not offer, pay or accept bribes
- work with governments and communities in which we do business
  to improve the quality of life in those communities – their educational, cultural, economic, and social well being – and seek to provide training and opportunities for workers from disadvantaged
  backgrounds
- promote the application of these Principles by those with whom
  we do business
- be transparent in our implementation of these Principles and
  provide information which demonstrates publicly our commitment to them[80]

---

[80] *The Global Sullivan Principles of Social Responsibility* at http://globalsullivanprin-
ciples.org/principles.htm (last accessed October 27, 2006). Other statements
of principles for multinational corporations include the Caux Round Table

More than 150 companies have endorsed the Global Sullivan Principles. Endorsers with direct investment in China include American Airlines, T. Baird, Chevron, Coca-Cola, Ford, General Motors, Owens Corning, Pepsi Cola, Pfizer, and Procter & Gamble.[81]

ADAPTING THE SULLIVAN PRINCIPLES TO CHINA

In a piece that ran in the *Washington Post* with the headline "Business Can Change China," Jim Hoagland, characterizing the Sullivan Principles as "a turning point in the struggle against apartheid [in South Africa]," suggests that the South African experience provides a precedent for what U.S. companies might do in China. He notes, "The Sullivan Principles shifted the discussion from self-justifying theories about business advancing social change to the practical steps of what happened every day in the workplace." He adds, however, with respect to China, "Neither the original code of conduct nor the more general Global Sullivan Principles announced at the United Nations in 1999 fit the situation exactly. That is why U.S. firms need to develop a similar code of business conduct with Chinese characteristics."[82]

Principles of Business (accessible at http://www.cauxroundtable.org/principles. html) and the United Nations Global Compact's *Ten Principles*, which specify core values with respect to human rights, labor standards, the environment and anti-corruption (accessible at http://www.unglobalcompact.org/AboutTheGC/TheTenPrinciples/index.html). Like the Global Sullivan Principles of Social Responsibility, the Caux Round Table Principles of Business and the United Nations Global Compact's Ten Principles are somewhat general in nature and lack the specificity that characterized the original Sullivan Principles pertaining to investment in South Africa. Because situations vary from country to country, it is probably inevitable that global principles will have more the character of platitudes than concrete guidelines for practical action.

[81] *Ibid.*, and *American Representative Offices and Joint Ventures in Beijing, China,* at http://www.cbw.com/business/usco-beijing/index.html (last accessed October 27, 2006). See also a report issued by the Business Roundtable entitled *Corporate Social Responsibility in China: Practices by U.S. Companies* (February 16, 2000), at http://www.businessroundtable.org//publications/publication.aspx?qs=24A6BF807822B0F18D2. The report, issued at a time when Business Roundtable was lobbying to gain Congressional approval for permanent normal trade relations (PNTR) with China, is quite laudatory of the role that U.S. businesses play in China – perhaps excessively laudatory.

[82] Jim Hoagland, "Business Can Change China, *Washington Post* (March 12, 2006), B07. The view that the Sullivan Principles were a catalyst for change in South

Unfortunately, like newspaper columnists everywhere, Hoagland ran out of space before he got to the specifics. He is right, however, in suggesting that U.S. firms need to be involved in drafting such a set of guidelines. The Global Sullivan Principles can provide a framework. To be fully useful, however, they need to be augmented by guidelines more specifically tailored for China, just as the original Sullivan Principles were specifically tailored for South Africa. And they need to specify concrete courses of action that it is realistic for U.S. and other multinational companies to accomplish.

There would be considerable incongruity, of course, in (a) suggesting that U.S. and other multinational companies need to be involved in drafting these guidelines and (b) then proceeding to specify what these guidelines should be. It might be helpful, however, to bring up particular areas of concern to put on the table for discussion. These include the following:

1. compensation guidelines, including specification of minimum wage guidelines for areas of China that do not have such guidelines;
2. prohibition of practices such as levying fines on employees that reduce their take-home pay below levels specified by compensation guidelines;
3. specification of what "respect [for] employees' voluntary freedom of association" means with respect to the possibility of unionization and collective bargaining;
4. minimum workplace health and safety standards;
5. specification of responsibilities for improving the quality of life for employees outside the workplace;
6. appropriate ethical guidelines for suppliers; and
7. effective ways of monitoring compliance.

SUPPLIER CODES OF CONDUCT

The last two necessitate more detailed comment. In an era in which outsourcing is widespread, it is not simply a question of what U.S.

Africa is not universally held. Detractors charge that they were "more a public relations ploy than a force for peaceful change" (*Multinational Monitor* Vol. 6, No. 8, June 30, 1985, at http://multinationalmonitor.org/hyper/issues/1985/0630/sullivanprinciples.html, last accessed October 28, 2006).

companies' labor practices in China are. Concern about compliance with human rights standards must also extend to the suppliers that produce components or whatever else might be outsourced. Hence, the need for supplier codes of conduct – something that Deere & Company and several other companies have done.[83] For example, Deere & Company's supplier code of conduct states (in part):

Child Labor
John Deere will not engage in or support the use of child labor. Suppliers are expected to comply with applicable local child labor laws and employ only workers who meet the applicable minimum legal age requirement for their location. In the absence of local law, suppliers shall not employ children under the age of 14.

Forced Labor
John Deere will not engage in or support the use of forced or involuntary labor. John Deere will not purchase material or services from a supplier utilizing forced or involuntary labor.

Compensation and Working Hours
John Deere pays employees a competitive wage. Suppliers are expected to comply with all applicable wage and hour labor laws and regulations governing employee compensation and working hours.

Discrimination
John Deere supports diversity and equal opportunity in employment. Unlawful discrimination in the workplace is not tolerated. Suppliers are expected to comply with all applicable local laws concerning discrimination in hiring and employment practices....

Health and Safety
John Deere is committed to the safety and health of its employees and conducts its operations in compliance with applicable laws and regulations.

---

[83] See, e.g., Ford Motor Company, "Suppliers" at http://www.ford.com/en/company/about/sustainability/2005-06/relSuppliers.htm (last accessed November 1, 2006), PepsiCo, "Worldwide Code of Conduct" at http://www.pepsico.com/PEP_Citizenship/CodeofConduct/index.cfm# (last accessed November 1, 2006), and Proctor & Gamble, "Social Responsibility" at http://www.pg.com/company/our_commitment/sus_faqs.jhtml (last accessed November 1, 2006). As noted in Chapter 3, a number of retailers, among them Target Corporation, also have supplier codes of conduct in place, with many of them signatories of the National Retail Federation's (NRF's) Statement of Principles on Supplier Legal Compliance. NRF was instrumental in establishing the Fair Factories Clearing House (FFC),

Suppliers are expected to provide a safe working environment that supports accident prevention and minimizes exposure to health risks. Suppliers are expected to comply with all applicable safety and health laws and regulations in the countries in which they operate.[84]

MONITORING COMPLIANCE

When articulating the original Sullivan Principles pertaining to South Africa, Sullivan insisted on measurable progress, thus placing strong emphasis on monitoring compliance. Sullivan recognized that ethical guidelines for business mean nothing if they are ignored. Some companies do a conscientious job of internally monitoring compliance. In other cases, monitoring is far less rigorous.

A case can be made for external monitoring of compliance. Signatories of the original Sullivan Principles contracted with Arthur D. Little, Inc., to monitor compliance. Based on information included in annual reports and periodic on-site visits to signatories' facilities in South Africa, Arthur D. Little, Inc., rated signatories as "making good progress," "making progress," "needs to become more active," or as "failing to make progress."[85] Constructing a similar monitoring system for companies doing business in China merits serious consideration.

Groundwork done by the Global Reporting Initiative (GRI), a worldwide network of experts committed to sustainable development, might serve as a foundation for the construction of such a monitoring system. GRI has made available online a reporting framework that enables multinational corporations to assess and report their performance with respect to sustainable development. Their website notes, "GRI's vision is that reporting on economic, environmental,

---

which houses a global database of factory information and social compliance audit reports. Information about FFC can be accessed at http://www.fairfactories.org/
[84] "John Deere Supplier Code of Conduct" at http://www.deere.com/en_US/investinfo/media/pdf/corpgov/suppliercodeofconduct_english.pdf (last accessed October 30, 2006].
[85] International Labour Organization Bureau for Worker's Activities, "Corporate Codes of Conduct and Labour Standards" at http://www.itcilo.it/actrav/actrav-english/telearn/global/ilo/guide/jill.htm (last accessed October 28, 2006).

and social performance by all organizations [will be] as routine and comparable as financial reporting."[86]

Monitoring supplier compliance is not without its challenges. Liu Kaiming, who is with the Institute of Contemporary Observation in Shenzhen, China, observes, "The inspectors sent by multinational retailers rarely find problems. The factories get advance notice and coach their workers to lie to inspectors. They only want to reassure consumers, not to actually improve conditions."[87]

A few years ago, the Asia Monitor Resource Centre (AMRC), a Hong Kong–based independent nongovernment organization (NGO) that focuses on Asian labor concerns,[88] conducted a study to determine the impact of codes of conduct on foreign-owned shoe manufacturing companies in China. They discovered that notwithstanding the codes of conduct, working conditions had actually deteriorated. They reported, "All categories of the companies' codes of conduct – health and safety, freedom of association, wages and benefits, hours of work, overtime compensation, nondiscrimination, harassment and child labor – are being violated."[89] They added, "Moreover, most workers do not even know that there is a code of conduct that the factory is supposed to abide by. They are

[86] Global Reporting Initiative, "Reporting Framework" at http://www.globalreporting.org/ReportingFramework/AboutG3/G3GlossaryOfTerms.htm (last accessed December 1, 2006). Some companies find the GRI reporting requirements cumbersome. For example, Nokia, a socially concerned company that has been a signer and active supporter of the United Nations Global Compact since its inception, chose not to attempt full GRI compliance, though they have taken GRI indicators into consideration when structuring their reporting materials (http://www.nokia.com/A4149131, last accessed December 1, 2006). It might be noted the original Sullivan Principles pertaining to South Africa focused on only one set of social justice concerns – those pertaining to racial discrimination. When the social justice agenda is expanded to include a wider range of concerns, mechanisms for measuring corporate performance inevitably become more complex.
[87] Quoted in Independent Lens, "China Blue" at http://www.pbs.org/independentlens/chinablue/jeans.html (last accessed September 18, 2008).
[88] Asia Monitor Resource Centre, "About Us" at http://www.amrc.org.hk/text/about (last accessed November 24, 2008).
[89] Quoted by Alan Boyd in "Global Economy: Multinationals and Accountability," *Asia Times Online*, August 19, 2003 at http://www.atimes.com/atimes/Global_Economy/EH19Djo1.html (last accessed November 24, 2008).

unaware of their rights as workers and have no ways to channel their complaints and opinions."[90] Clearly there is need for improvement in the area of monitoring.

A final note: While monitoring of suppliers can be done, at least to some extent, monitoring of suppliers' suppliers is very difficult. Even with the best of intentions, monitoring systems tend to break down at this point.

Yet, doing what can be done to monitor compliance is better than ignoring compliance issues altogether. A glass half full is surely preferable to a glass that is entirely empty.

SOME CONCLUDING CONSIDERATIONS

In a country as large and complex as China, what needs to be done far exceeds what can be done. Moreover, while U.S. and other multinational corporations can and should help provide solutions to the problems facing China, there are limits to what it is reasonable to expect business enterprises to attempt to accomplish. While concepts of human rights and other ethical ideals provide important sign posts, constructive engagement must be defined in terms that are practical.

Some problems are clearly beyond the purview of U.S. and other multinational corporations. For example, U.S. and other multinational corporations are not really in a position to do anything about the Chinese government's repression of Uyghurs, who live on the western frontier of China far removed from the eastern parts of the country where the bulk of foreign investment is found. Moreover, even in Beijing, Shanghai, and other cities where there is a strong international presence, it is by no means a foregone conclusion that it is the job of U.S. and other multinational companies to serve as advocates for house churches or to call for reform of China's family planning laws.

Rather, the moral responsibilities of U.S. and other multinational companies are more narrowly focused. In particular, these

---

[90] Quoted in *ibid.* See also Asia Monitor Resource Center, *A Critical Guide to Corporate Codes of Conduct: Voices from the South* (2004) at http://www.amrc.org.hk/text/files/critical-guide-to-codeof-conduct.pdf (last accessed November 24, 2008).

responsibilities pertain to the ways that they conduct their own operations – matters such as treating their employees with respect and dignity, providing a safe work environment and appropriate levels of compensation, and, as noted earlier, doing what they can to ensure that their suppliers comply with appropriate ethical standards, threatening them, if need be, with termination of contracts if they fail to comply with the ethical standards specified in the company's supplier code of conduct. It also means that when they use their ability to influence government policy, which, as the case of the contract labor law illustrates, is far greater than many imagine, they ought to do so in ways that are supportive of their employees' rights and well-being. In short, what is needed is *con*structive engagement, not *de*structive engagement.

There is a related point to be made here as well. The more that the Chinese economy and our economy are intertwined, the more difficult it will be for the Chinese government to ignore our concerns with respect to human rights and other matters. Moreover, as participation in the global economy fosters the emergence of a rapidly growing Chinese middle class, the socioeconomic conditions will be in place for the Chinese people to demand a greater measure of freedom and more participatory forms of governance. Put in slightly different terms, while it might not be the job of U.S. and other multinational corporations operating in China to serve as advocates for house churches, contributing to the prosperity of the growing Chinese middle class might well help create a situation in which the Chinese government, with whatever degree of reluctance it might be inclined, gives in to growing social pressures and allows a greater measure of freedom of religion. The same is true with respect to freedom of speech, freedom of the press, freedom of assembly and other basic freedoms, as well as more democratic forms of governance. Hoagland is right. Business can change China.

China today: vibrant, rapidly growing, changing. A land of opportunity, but also a country with a flawed human rights record. Progress has been made in the struggle to ensure universal human rights for all those living in this, the most populous country in the world. Much, however, remains to be done. Guided by a revised set of Sullivan Principles specifically tailored for China and/or by internally generated codes of conduct that are specific and focused, U.S. and other multinational companies can be a positive force for change. Such is the vision of what is possible. And such is their obligation if they are to take seriously the most basic notions of social responsibility.[91]

[91] This chapter is a slightly revised version of an article entitled "Human Rights and the Ethics of Investment in China" that appeared in the Spring/Summer 2008 issue of the *Journal of the Society of Christian Ethics*.

5

Liberia and Firestone

A Case Study

Liberia was an American invention. Founded by American religious and philanthropic groups with the support and unofficial cooperation of the U.S. government, Liberia was envisioned as a place to which freed slaves could emigrate. The American Colonization Society (ACS) spearheaded the effort. Formed in Washington, D.C., in 1816, the organization's first president was George Washington's nephew, Bushrod Washington, who was an associate justice of the U.S. Supreme Court. Founding members included Speaker of the House of Representatives Henry Clay; Daniel Webster, who was to become a prominent U.S. senator known as a champion of American nationalism; Francis Scott Key, who penned the words to "The Star-Spangled Banner" a few years earlier during the War of 1812; and a number of other people of distinction. Thomas Jefferson, the drafter of the U.S. Declaration of Independence who had served two terms as president of the United States, and James Madison, Jefferson's successor, who was the president of the United States at the time that ACS was organized, lent their support.[1]

The founders and supporters of the American Colonization Society were motivated by a variety of concerns. Some saw colonization as a

[1] Robert Rinehart, "Historical Setting" in *Liberia: A Country Study*, ed. Harold D. Nelson (Washington, DC: United States Government, 1985), 8. The original name of the organization was the "American Society for Colonizing Free People of Color in the United States." This unwieldy name was shortened to the "American Colonization Society."

way to correct the injustices suffered by African Americans as a result of the practice of slavery. Others found the presence of free African Americans in the United States threatening (notwithstanding the fact that they numbered no more than 200,000[2] at a time when the population of the United States was more than 8 million.)[3] Still others believed that an African American colony in Africa would contribute to missionary work in Africa and help "civilize" indigenous tribes. Though colonization was limited to African Americans who were free, some ACS supporters hoped that in time their efforts would lead to the emancipation of large numbers of slaves.[4]

The founding of the ACS was set against the backdrop of the prohibition of the slave trade, first by Great Britain in 1807 and then by the United States the following year. Both the Royal Navy and the United States Navy assigned warships to intercept slave ships. The Royal Navy transported the freed slaves, who became known as "recaptives" because they had been recaptured, to Sierra Leone on the west coast of Africa, where a self-governing colony of freed slaves had been established in 1787. United States Navy ships transported the recaptives they freed either to Sierra Leone or to the United States for internment, where they became wards of the government. Along with providing a place to which free African Americans could emigrate, ACS founders and supporters saw colonization as a way of dealing with recaptives who had become wards of the U.S. government.[5]

FROM TENUOUS BEGINNINGS TO INDEPENDENCE

More than three years passed before the first group of colonists left New York aboard the brig *Elizabeth*, bound for the west coast of Africa. Reaching the coast of Africa, the *Elizabeth* entered the port of Freetown in Sierra Leone. The British governor, however, refused to allow the passengers to come ashore, compelling them to continue

---

[2] J. Gus Liebenow, *Liberia: the Quest for Democracy* (Bloomington, IN: Indiana University Press, 1987), 13.
[3] United States Bureau of the Census, *Historical Statistics of the United States, Colonial Times to 1957: A Statistical Abstract Supplement* (Washington, DC: Bureau of the Census, 1960), 8 (A6–8).
[4] Rinehart, "Historical Setting," 8.
[5] *Ibid.*, 7–8.

their journey by setting sail and following the coastline until they came to Sherbo Island, the site of an old British fort. Within a few weeks, tropical diseases felled twenty-two of the eighty-eight passengers who had crossed the Atlantic aboard the *Elizabeth*. A similar fate befell many of the passengers of the *Nautilus*, a second emigrant ship that followed the *Elizabeth* later in the year. In time, the survivors were allowed to return to Sierra Leone.[6]

A year passed before another ship, the *Augusta*, arrived in Sierra Leone with another group of colonists and retrieved the survivors from the *Elizabeth* and the *Nautilus*. Accompanied by a United States naval vessel, the *U.S.S. Alligator*, the *Augusta* sailed down the coast to Cape Mesurado, where ACS agents, who had reconnoitered the area several years earlier, had recommended a settlement site. Negotiations with local tribal leaders led to the purchase of a sixty-mile-long strip of land along the coast between the Mesurado and Junk Rivers in exchange for trade goods valued at approximately $300.[7] These included six firearms, a keg of gunpowder, a barrel of rum, a box of beads, and three pairs of shoes.[8]

By 1828, Liberia was a thriving colony of more than 1,200 African American settlers, their number augmented by a growing number of recaptives who chose to remain in the colony rather than return to the tribal areas from which they had been forcibly taken.[9] By 1846, there was talk of independence – not independence from a colonial power, as was the case with other countries in Africa and elsewhere, but rather independence from a private organization, namely the American Colonial Society (ACS). A year later, delegates to a constituting convention meeting in Monrovia, the capital of the colony (which was named after James Monroe, the fifth president of the United States), approved a declaration of independence, which was issued July 16, 1847. Patterned in substantial measure after the U.S. Declaration of Independence, the Liberian Declaration of Independence, stated, "We recognize in all men certain inalienable rights; among these are life, liberty, and the right to acquire, possess, enjoy, and defend

---

[6] Rinehart, "Historical Setting," 9–10.
[7] *Ibid.*, 10.
[8] Harold D. Nelson, "Introduction" in *Liberia: A Country Study*, xxiii.
[9] *Ibid.*, 11–14.

property." But then, in a stark reminder that the human rights record of the United States is far from unflawed, it stated in words both blunt and poignant:

We, the people of the Republic of Liberia, were originally inhabitants of the United States of North America.

In some parts of that country we were debarred by law from all rights and privileges of man – in other parts, public sentiment, more powerful than law, frowned us down.

We were excluded from all participation in the government.

We were taxed without our consent.

We were compelled to contribute to the resources of a country which gave us no protection.

We were made a separate and distinct class, and against us every avenue of improvement was effectively closed. Strangers from other lands, of a color different from ours, were preferred before us.

We uttered our complaints, but they were unattended to, or only met by alleging the peculiar institutions of the country.

All hope of a favorable change in our country was thus wholly extinguished in our bosoms, and we looked with anxiety for some asylum from the deep degradation.[10]

Great Britain was the first country to recognize the newly independent country, followed by most other European countries. The United States withheld recognition until 1862, according to some to avoid accrediting a black diplomat.[11]

AMERICO-LIBERIANS AND THE INDIGENOUS POPULATION

The seal of the new republic depicted a sailing ship approaching shore with the motto "The love of liberty brought us here." That might have been meaningful for the immigrants from the United States who came to Liberia in search of liberty and perhaps to their descendents as well, who became known as Americo-Liberians.[12]

---

[10] *The Liberian Constitutions: The U.S. Declaration of Independence* at http://onliberia. org/con_declaration.htm (last accessed April 26, 2008).

[11] Rinehart, "Historical Setting," 18.

[12] As part of a national unification policy, official use of the term was discontinued in the mid-1950s (Irving Kaplan et al., "The Society and Its Environment" in *Liberia: A Country Study*, ed. Harold D. Nelson [Washington, DC: United States Government, 1985], 88).

However, the seal and motto held no particular meaning for the indigenous population, most of whom had lived there for generations and comprised the vast majority of the population of Liberia. At no time did Americo-Liberians, who maintained American cultural traditions, comprise more than 5 percent of the population of Liberia. Most Americo-Liberians lived in urban areas along the coast, while the indigenous population mostly lived in inland areas that Americo-Liberians somewhat vaguely referred to as the "hinterlands." Some Americo-Liberians established large plantations reminiscent of those owned by whites in southern states in the United States prior to the Civil War. The owners of these plantations often used forced recruitment and compulsory labor practices to secure the services of the indigenous population from the hinterlands to work these plantations – labor practices eerily similar to slavery notwithstanding the fact that slavery was explicitly prohibited by the Constitution of 1847, as well as by all preceding documents of governance. It is an irony of history that at a time when the indigenous populations of other areas of Africa were being exploited by white minorities at the behest of Western European colonial powers, the indigenous population of Liberia was exploited by African Americans who had emigrated to Liberia and by their descendents.[13]

The export of native laborers, which was lucrative to the Americo-Liberians who engaged in it, was particularly pernicious. Cacao plantations on the island of Fernando Po, where a small Spanish colony was located, needed laborers to work in the fields. Because a reliable supply of workers was not legally available from nearby British and French colonies, Liberia agreed to provide the workers on contract, a practice that began in 1905 and was formalized in a treaty between Liberia and Spain nine years later. Liberian contractors were paid a fee for each worker they sent to Fernando Po, transported by German ships chartered to carry them. Most of the workers came from the Kru tribal groups, supplied to contractors by tribal leaders who were paid a per capita fee for providing the workers.[14]

---

[13] Nelson, "Introduction," xxiv.
[14] Rinehart, "Historical Setting," 43.

In the early 1920s, demand for plantation workers increased substantially. Liberia, which was teetering on the edge of bankruptcy,
welcomed the opportunity to expand revenue by increasing the sale
of contract labor. A syndicate that included several high-ranking government officials was formed to supply the increased number of workers needed by the plantations in Fernando Po.[15]

The matter came to the attention of the League of Nations, which
appointed a commission headed by Cuthbert Christy, a British jurist,
to look into the situation. The commission spent several months in
Liberia observing labor conditions and conducting interviews. The
Christy commission report, issued in 1930, accused high-ranking
Liberian government officials of complicity in procuring involuntary
labor by impressments and other illegal and questionable practices.
U.S. Secretary of State Henry L. Stimson wrote a sharply worded
note reiterating the charges and calling for punishment of guilty par-
ties. Liberian President Charles Dunbar Burgess King appointed a
Liberian commission to look into the matter. When evidence linked
Liberian Vice President Allen B. Yancey to the syndicate, both he
and President King resigned, with Liberian Secretary of State Edwin
James Barclay succeeding King as president.[16]

FIRESTONE COMES TO LIBERIA

Even though Liberia was an American invention, there was no
significant American investment in Liberia prior to 1926, when
Firestone Tire and Rubber Company signed a concessionary agreement with Liberia. Harvey S. Firestone, the president of Firestone
Tire and Rubber Company until his son, Harvey S. Firestone, Jr.,
succeeded him as head of the firm, was dismayed by the high
prices charged for raw rubber by British and Dutch producers in
Southeast Asia, who had a virtual monopoly on the world supply
of the commodity. Because of the tropical climate and abundant
supply of indigenous labor, Liberia, the Firestones believed, might
provide an alternative. Harvey Firestone, Jr., traveled to Liberia to
assess its suitability for producing raw rubber. He concluded that

[15] *Ibid.*
[16] *Ibid.*, 43–44.

the country would provide an appropriate environment for establishing rubber plantations.[17]

The younger Firestone handled the negotiations with the Liberian government and, once they were successfully concluded, headed up Firestone's operations in Liberia. Because the Liberian constitution limited land ownership to individuals of African descent, purchasing the land was not an option. Instead, Firestone Tire and Rubber secured a ninety-nine-year lease on one million acres of land at an annual rent of $.06 per acre (which was subsequently increased). In addition, the company agreed to pay a 1-percent tax on gross income from its Liberian operation (a tax that was also subsequently increased).[18] It was believed that if the rubber plantations were successful, the Liberian government would receive each year approximately two dollars per acre in revenues.[19]

At Firestone's insistence, a second agreement was also negotiated to protect the company's investment against the possibility of the government experiencing bankruptcy. Firestone raised $5 million from private sources, half of it provided by the Finance Corporation of America (FCA), a Firestone subsidiary created for the express purpose of purchasing the bonds that raised the funds. Half of the loan was to be used to redeem old bonds and pay off foreign obligations with the remainder earmarked for construction projects that would benefit both the country and Firestone. The loan left Liberia with an annual commitment of $300,000 to service the debt with the funds to come from customs and tax receipts that would be held in receivership by the FCA. In addition, Liberia was forced to accept the services of an American financial advisor and supervisor of customs.[20]

With French and British interests nipping at the borders, the Liberian government saw the agreements as a way of protecting the country from European colonial domination. Clarence L. Simpson, who served as secretary of state and later as vice president, characterized the agreements as "the lesser evil – that of veiled economic

[17] *Ibid.*, 42.
[18] *Ibid.*
[19] Charles Morrow Wilson, *Liberia: Black Africa in Microcosm* (New York: Harper & Row Publishers, 1971), 131.
[20] Rinehart, "Historical Setting," 42.

domination by a company belonging to a traditionally friendly country."[21]

It was economic domination that was to leave a bitter legacy. The plaque on the statue of President William V.S. Tubman erected in 1956 to commemorate repayment of the loan states, "This Monument erected by the people of Liberia is dedicated to the great relief brought to the Country by the Tubman administration in the retirement of the [1927] Loan with its humiliating and strangulating effects on the economy of the Nation."[22]

FIRESTONE'S LABOR PRACTICES

Firestone's labor practices were more enlightened than those of the Americo-Liberians engaged in the contract labor business. Rather than deal with contract labor agents, Firestone agents traveled to the interior themselves, often on foot, to meet and negotiate directly with tribal chiefs, taking care to spread out their recruiting efforts among all of the tribes, rather than deal primarily with one tribal group, as did the contract labor agents. All workers recruited to work on the Firestone plantations were free to leave and return to their tribal areas whenever they wished to do so. Workers could choose to receive part of their wages in food, which was provided at wholesale cost as a supplement to monetary compensation. All workers were provided with housing and medical care without cost to them. Many of the Firestone workers brought their families along with them.[23] Along with providing housing, medical care, basic foodstuffs, and educational opportunities for workers and members of their families, Firestone built roads, a rail line, port facilities, telephone and telegraph lines, and other important components of the country's infrastructure. The company also made a valuable contribution by sponsoring research in tropical medicine.[24]

Yet Firestone's record of labor relations was not beyond reproach. Former Firestone employee Arthur Hayman observed, "When the

---

[21] Quoted by Frank Chalk in "The Anatomy of an Investment: Firestone's 1927 Loan to Liberia," *Canadian Journal of African Studies* 1 (March 1967): 13.

[22] Quoted in *ibid.*, 32.

[23] Morrow, *Liberia*, 132–133.

[24] Rinehart, "Historical Setting," 42–43.

Firestone Company first came to Liberia it wanted to pay its native laborers the high wages, for Africa, of $1 a day. But the rulers insisted upon maintaining a coolie wage ... for men with money in their pockets would eventually have demanded the ballot and schools for their children...."[25] Firestone did build schools but complied with the ruling elite's desire to see wages kept at a low level.

THE LOAN CRISIS OF 1933

The planting of rubber trees of inferior stock got rubber production off to a slow start, though production increased when better trees were planted and, once they reached a waist-high diameter of five inches, could be tapped for the milklike latex that oozes from the layers of cells between the tree's outer bark and the cambium layer.[26] Far more serious were growing exports of raw rubber from the Dutch East Indies and the collapse of the export restrictions the British had imposed on their colonies, which substantially increased the supply of raw rubber on the world market just as the Great Depression in the United States (where automobile production had been booming) and economic collapse in other countries reduced the demand for rubber. Rubber prices plummeted. With rubber prices in the doldrums, Firestone, for a period of several years, did little more in Liberia than conduct small-scale scientific experiments and post watchmen on their plantations.[27]

Because of the economic slowdown, the Liberian government did not receive the revenues it expected to receive from the excise tax on rubber produced by Firestone, making it difficult to cover the cost of the debt service on the loan arranged by Firestone. As a result of declining revenues, the debt service, which had equaled 20 percent of total revenues in 1926, increased to 60 percent of total revenues in 1932, which led the Liberian government to place a moratorium on loan repayments to the FCA until revenues improved.[28]

---

[25] Quoted in the section on Harvey S. Firestone, Jr., in *Current Biography: Who's News and Why – 1944* (New York: The H.W. Wilson Company, 1945), 207.

[26] Morrow, *Liberia*, 134–135.

[27] Chalk, "Anatomy of an Investment," 31.

[28] Rinehart, "Historical Setting," 46.

Firestone and his lawyers were furious, demanding that the U.S. government send a warship to Monrovia to threaten the Liberian government with military action if loan payments were not resumed. Fortunately the loan crisis was resolved without the use of military force, though getting Liberia to resume payments did require a tremendous amount of diplomatic strong arming by U.S. Secretary of State Stimson.[29]

TROUBLED TIMES

The loan crisis of 1933 was but a small blip on the radar screen compared to the troubled times that were to follow. Troubled times that were the bitter fruit of the exploitation of the indigenous population by the Americo-Liberian minority. Troubled times that would eventually lead to a military coup d'état and civil war.

That did not happen immediately. There was an interim period during the lengthy presidency of William V.S. Tubman (1944–1971) and that of his successor, William R. Tolbert (1971–1980), when reforms directed toward addressing the problems afflicting Liberia led many to believe that the country had a bright future.

Though Tubman was part of the Americo-Liberian elite and was a member of the True Whig Party, the political party that had dominated Liberian politics for years, he saw helping the indigenous population living in the hinterlands as part of his mission as president. Realizing that economic development was necessary if standards of living were to be raised, he announced the Open Door Policy, which involved inviting foreign companies to invest in Liberia. When he took office, Firestone was the only major foreign company with holdings in Liberia. The country's economic growth was tightly linked to one commodity – rubber. Liberia, however, also had iron ore and other natural resources that could be developed. As the investments of American, Swedish, German, and other foreign-owned firms came to fruition, iron ore in time accounted for as much as 75 percent of export earnings.[30] By the mid-1960s, there were twenty-five major

---

[29] Chalk, "Anatomy of an Investment," 31.
[30] Liebenow, *Liberia*, 59–60.

foreign companies with operations in Liberia, compared to just one – Firestone – when Tubman was first elected.[31]

Tubman was aided in his efforts by a good deal of personal charisma. Many Liberians came to affectionately refer to him as "Uncle Shad." (His full name was William Vacanarat Shadrach Tubman.) He attained a level of popularity unequaled by any other Liberian in history. His stature was such that the constitutional provision limiting the president to two terms was repealed, allowing the president to be elected to an unlimited number of four-year terms.[32]

Tubman's charisma and political instincts served him well when striking rubber plantation workers marched on the Executive Mansion in 1961 and demanded government action to correct what they alleged was discrimination in pay and promotion. He agreed to meet with representatives of the strikers, provided refreshments for them, and brought in the police band to entertain them. He promised he would look into their complaint that better jobs had been denied to qualified black employees but rejected their demand that foreign companies be asked to leave Liberia, noting that if they left Liberia the jobs they had created would leave with them. The strikers, believing that their concerns would be addressed, disbanded.[33]

Tubman remained in office until July 23, 1971, when he died from complications following surgery in a London hospital. He was succeeded by Vice President Tolbert, the descendent of a former slave from South Carolina who had become a wealthy coffee planter in Liberia. Tolbert continued the reform programs Tubman had initiated, including the Open Door Policy, but put pressure on foreign companies with operations in Liberia to make them more responsive to the needs of Liberians. In 1976, the Firestone Plantations Company accepted a new agreement with the government that made it subject to the full range of Liberian tax laws.[34]

Tolbert, however, lacked Tubman's personal charisma and was challenged both by members of the old guard, who opposed change, and groups that believed change was too slow in coming. Early on the

---

[31] Rinehart, "Historical Setting," 52. For a list of the foreign companies with operations in Liberia, see Morrow, *Liberia*, 202.
[32] Rinehart, "Historical Setting," 53
[33] *Ibid.*, 56.
[34] Rinehart, "Historical Setting," 63.

morning of April 12, 1980, a successful coup d'état by a unit of the
National Guard loyal to a group of seventeen noncommissioned officers and other enlisted personnel, who had formed what they called
the "People's Redemption Council (PRC)," toppled the Tolbert government. Led by Master Sergeant Samuel Kanyon Doe, they stormed
the Executive Mansion and killed Tolbert and twenty-seven members
of his security guard. Doe, acting on behalf of the PRC, suspended
the constitution, banned political parties, and released political pris-
oners from jail. A military tribunal tried fourteen of the most prominent members of the old regime. Several, including Speaker of the
House Richard Henries, received the death sentence and were publicly executed on a beach in Monrovia.[35]

FROM COUP D'ÉTAT TO CIVIL WAR

Notwithstanding the violent nature of the coup d'état, there was substantial support for Doe and the PRC, including from the Reagan
administration. Testifying before a congressional committee, U.S.
Assistant Secretary of State for African Affairs Richard M. Moose, while
calling the public execution of former government officials "one of
the most shocking spectacles in recent memory," expressed sympathy
for what he perceived as the goals of the PRC, asserting that Doe was
contemplating an early return to civilian rule. Once it became clear
that Doe was committed to respecting private property (American
investment in Liberia was estimated to be approximately $500
million – roughly half the foreign investment – with Firestone, which
had 10,000 employees, the largest single employer in the country) and
was willing to be a U.S. ally in the Cold War, the Reagan administration substantially increased economic aid to Liberia, notwithstanding
the violent nature of the Doe regime. Prior to the coup, U.S. aid had
never exceeded $20 million annually. By 1984, U.S. budgetary support
had grown to approximately $35 million a year with $13 million more
in developmental assistance and $15 million provided for the import
of rice from the United States. When Doe visited the United States in
1982, he was invited to meet with U.S. President Ronald Reagan at the
White House, where the two posed for an official photograph.[36]

---

[35] *Ibid.*, 69–70.
[36] Jean R. Tartter, "Government and Politics" in *Liberia: A Country Study*, 241–244.

As a first step toward making good on his promise to return the country to civilian rule, Doe announced on the first anniversary of the coup the creation of a National Constitutional Commission (which became known as "Con-Com"). Though the PRC would have veto power over specific aspects of the work of the commission, the entirely civilian commission was given wide latitude to establish procedures for broad citizen participation and for deciding what would go into the document. Apart from the fact that women were significantly underrepresented (only one of the twenty-five members was female), membership on the commission did reflect the geographical, economic, professional, and religious diversity of the country. Doe appointed highly respected and admired Dr. Amos C. Sawyer, who had been one of the more effective challengers of the Tolbert regime, to chair the commission.[37]

Though there were many bumps in the road along the way, the commission, after more than two years of work, did produce a draft that was acceptable to the PRC and to the Advisory Assembly that Doe had created to review the draft. After months of delay, the final draft was voted on in a referendum in which all citizens over the age of eighteen were eligible to vote. The constitution was approved by a substantial majority.[38]

The new constitution retained the basic structure of representative government and separation of powers delineated in the 1847 constitution but expanded the section on rights and emphasized freedom of religion, making the constitution less overtly Christian in tone. The new constitution dropped the property requirement for voting but retained the requirement that citizenship be limited to persons with African roots, stating that "in order to preserve, foster and maintain the positive Liberian culture, values, and character, only persons who are Negroes or of Negro descent shall qualify by birth or by naturalization to be citizens of Liberia" (Article 27[b]), and stipulated that "only Liberian citizens shall have the right to own real property within the Republic" (Article 22[a]).[39]

---

[37] Liebenow, *Liberia*, 217–218.
[38] *Ibid.*, 221–222.
[39] The full text of the Liberian Constitution of 1984 can be accessed at http://onliberia.org/con_1984_2.htm#ChIII.

In the election of 1985 – the first election under the new constitution – Doe ran for president as the candidate of National Democratic
Party of Liberia (NDPL). Amidst allegations of vote fraud and after
a lengthy delay in announcing the outcome of the election, Doe was
officially named the winner with 50.9 percent of the votes in the four-
way race for president. On January 6, 1986, he was inaugurated as the
first president under the 1984 constitution.[10]

Though the inauguration of the first president under the new
constitution should have marked a significant milestone in the quest
for democracy, allegations of vote fraud and manipulation of the
results cast a long shadow over the outcome of the 1985 election.
Controversy continued to surround Doe as he was accused of corruption and human rights abuses and of favoring members of his own
tribe (Krahn).[11] J. Gus Liebenow, who earlier had been optimistic
about the prospects for a return to democracy, wrote:

Unfortunately, by the end of the fourth year of PRC rule, the desire of Doe and
the PRC to entrench itself permanently in office had become all too apparent. The flawed electoral process, the escalating violations of human rights
and press freedom, and the transparent efforts to reestablish a one-party
state undermined the legitimacy of the new government which took office 6
January 1986. The fledgling experiment in Liberian democracy, which was
reflected in the popularly supported constitution of the Second Republic,
became a victim of infanticide. It was strangled almost at the moment of leaving the nest by the very man who had once given so many Liberian citizens
hope that their aspirations for liberty were about to be realized – the usurper
president, Samuel K. Doe.[12]

The stage was set for civil war, which was not long in coming. On
December 24, 1989 – less than four years after Doe had assumed the
presidency under the new constitution – a small band of rebels led
by Charles Taylor invaded Liberia from Côte d'Ivoire (Ivory Coast).
Fighting under the banner of the National Patriotic Front of Liberia
(NPFL), they gained the support of many Liberians and within six
months were at the outskirts of Monrovia. One of Africa's bloodiest

[10] Liebenow, *Liberia*, 293–297.
[11] U.S. Department of State Bureau of African Affairs, "Background Notes: Liberia"
    at http://www.state.gov/r/pa/ei/bgn/6618.htm (last accessed August 29, 2008).
[12] Liebenow, *Liberia*, 7.

civil wars – a civil war that was to last, with little interruption, for four-teen years and claim the lives of more than 200,000 Liberians while displacing a million more (of a population of less than 4 million) – had begun.[43]

Taylor, who was born outside Monrovia, was the son of a teacher descended from the freed slaves who had founded Liberia though he was not part of the Americo-Liberian elite. A student activist in the 1970s who challenged Tolbert's out-of-touch regime, he studied economics at Bentley College in Waltham, Massachusetts, return-ing to Liberia in 1980 just in time to see Doe and his fellow rebels topple the Tolbert government. He immediately ingratiated him-self with the Doe regime, in time gaining control of the govern-ment's purchasing arm. After a falling out with Doe, he again fled to the United States, taking with him $1 million allegedly embez-zled from the Liberian government. He was jailed in Massachusetts but escaped in 1985 by sawing through the bars of his jail cell. Once back in Africa, he met with Liberian dissidents and revolutionar-ies in other African countries. In Libya, he spent time in camps Colonel Muammar al-Qadaffi had established to train rebels for what al-Qadaffi hoped would be a continent-wide revolution. When Taylor crossed the border between Côte d'Ivoire and Liberia on Christmas Eve of 1989, it was with arms and money provided by Libya and with the political and financial backing of Burkina Faso and Côte d'Ivoire.[44]

Intervention by the Economic Community of West African States (ECOWAS) prevented Taylor and his band of rebels from taking Monrovia. However, an offshoot of the NPFL led by Prince Johnson captured and killed Doe on September 9, 1990.[45] BBC correspon-dent Bill Law reported, "Even by the standards of the time it was a particularly brutal slaying. Before he was killed, Doe was mutilated, his ears sliced off. Prince Johnson supervised the proceedings sitting in a chair while one of his soldiers fanned him. The whole affair was videotaped."[46]

[43] U.S. Department of State Bureau of African Affairs, "Background Notes: Liberia."
[44] Lydia Polgreen, "A Master Plan Drawn in Blood," *New York Times*, April 2, 2006.
[45] U.S. Department of State Bureau of African Affairs, "Background Notes: Liberia."
[46] Bill Law, "Meeting the Hard Man of Liberia," *BBC News*, broadcast November 4, 2006 on BBC Radio 4 at 11:30 GMT.

Former soldiers of the Armed Forces of Liberia (AFL) who had sought refuge in Sierra Leone and other neighboring countries formed the United Liberation Movement of Liberia for Democracy to fight Taylor's NPFL.[47] Liberia was engulfed in a full-scale civil war of horrendous proportions.

Under the auspices of the Economic Community of West African States (ECOWAS), a unity government headed by Dr. Amos C. Sawyer (who had chaired the commission that drafted the 1984 constitution) was formed. Taylor's NPFL and the other warring factions refused to work with the unity government and continued fighting. In time, Taylor agreed to the formation of a five-person transitional government. After hasty disarmament and demobilization of warring factions, a special election was held on July 19, 1997. Taylor and the NPFL won by a large majority – according to some because Liberians feared a return to civil war had Taylor lost.[48]

In six years of misrule, Taylor did nothing to improve the lives of Liberians. Both unemployment and illiteracy remained above 75 percent while schools, hospitals, and roads damaged by the fighting were left unrepaired. Instead, Taylor focused his efforts on trying to help an insurgent group in neighboring Sierra Leona unseat the government there. His misrule led to the resumption of military activity by groups opposing him.[49]

On June 4, 2003, peace talks among the warring parties facilitated by the Economic Community of West African States (ECOWAS) were convened in Ghana. That same day, the chief prosecutor of the Special Court for Sierra Leone announced the opening of a sealed indictment dated March 7, 2003, charging Taylor with "bearing the greatest responsibility" for atrocities in Sierra Leone that had occurred since November 1996. In July of that year, the government of Liberia and the warring factions signed a ceasefire that all sides failed to respect. Bitter fighting reached Monrovia, creating a huge humanitarian crisis.[50] A rebel group led by Sekou Conneh, whose drugged fighters were filmed holding up a human heart, attacked the capital three times in battles so devastating Liberians came to refer

---

[47] U.S. Department of State Bureau of African Affairs, "Background Notes: Liberia."
[48] *Ibid.*
[49] *Ibid.*
[50] *Ibid.*

to them as World War I, World War II, and World War III. The group's indiscriminate shelling of the capital resulted in so many deaths that Liberians started piling up the bodies in front of the United States Embassy as a plea for help.[51]

Under intense pressure from the United States and other countries, Taylor resigned on August 11, 2003, and went into exile in Nigeria, which paved the way for the deployment of a 3,600 member peacekeeping force under the auspices of the Economic Community of West African States (ECOWAS). A week after Taylor's resignation, representatives from the Liberian government, rebel groups and various political parties signed a comprehensive peace agreement that provided a framework for a two-year National Transitional Government headed by business leader Gyude Bryant. The United Nations took over security operations in October of 2003, subsuming the ECOWAS-sponsored peacekeeping force into the United Nations Mission in Liberia (UNMIL), a force that in time numbered 12,000 troops and 1,148 police officers.[52]

Presidential and legislative elections on October 11, 2005, and the subsequent presidential run-off on November 8, 2005, have been described by outside observers as "the most free, fair, and peaceful elections in Liberia's history." In the presidential run-off, Ellen Johnson Sirleaf, who served as finance minister in the Tolbert administration prior to resigning because of policy disagreements, defeated international soccer star George Weah 59.4% to 40.6% to become the first female African head of state. She formed a government of technocrats drawn from among Liberia's various ethnic groups and included expatriates who returned to help rebuild Liberia after the devastation of the civil war. The political situation has remained stable since the 2005 elections.[53]

HUMAN RIGHTS IN LIBERIA TODAY

The Liberian Constitution of 1984, which remains the operative constitution, includes a strongly stated chapter on rights. Article 11, the

---

[51] Associated Press, "Ex-Rebel Leader Deflects Questions about Atrocities in Liberia," *New York Times*, August 28, 2008.
[52] U.S. Department of State Bureau of African Affairs, "Background Notes: Liberia."
[53] *Ibid.*

first article in the chapter on rights, begins by noting, "All persons are born equally free and independent and have certain natural, inherent and inalienable rights, among which are the right of enjoying and defending life and liberty, of pursuing and maintain the security of the person and of acquiring, possessing and protecting property, subject to such qualifications as provided for in this Constitution." (As noted previously, the Constitution limits citizenship to persons "who are Negroes or of Negro descent" [Article 27] and ownership of real property to Liberian citizens [Article 22].) Article 11 further notes that "all persons, irrespective of ethnic background, race, sex, creed, place of origin or political opinion, are entitled to the fundamental rights and freedoms of the individual, subject to such qualifications as provided for in this Constitution" and that "all persons are equal before the law and are therefore entitled to the equal protection of the law."

Article 12 states, "No person shall be held in slavery or forced labor within the Republic, nor shall any citizen of Liberia nor any person resident therein deal in slaves or subject any other person to forced labor...." Article 14 asserts, "All persons shall be entitled to freedom of thought, conscience and religion.... The article adds, "No religious denomination or sect shall have any exclusive privilege or preference over any other, but all shall be treated alike.... Consistent with the principle of separation of religion and state, the Republic shall establish no state religion."

Article 15 guarantees freedom of expression and adds that "access to state owned media shall not be denied because of any disagreement with or dislike of the ideas express[ed]." Other articles guarantee "privacy of person, family, home or correspondence except by order of a court of competent jurisdiction" (Article 16), "equal opportunity for work and employment regardless of sex, creed, religion, ethnic background, place of origin or political affiliation" and "equal pay for equal work" (Article 18), and due process in judicial proceedings (Article 20). Article 21 states, "No person charged, arrested, restricted, detained or otherwise held in confinement shall be subject to torture or inhumane treatment ..." and promises, "Every person arrested or detained shall be formally charged and presented before a court of competent jurisdiction within forty eight hours." The article further asserts, "The right to counsel and the rights of counsel shall be inviolable." Article 26 – the last article in the chapter on fundamental rights – concludes:

[A]nyone injured by an act of Government or any person acting under its authority, whether in property, contract, tort or otherwise, shall have the right to bring suit for appropriate redress. All such suits brought against the Government shall originate in a Claims Court; appeals from judgment of the Claims Court shall lie directly to the Supreme Court.

None of these guarantees of rights, of course, mean anything if they are ignored in practice, as they were during the Taylor presidency, which perpetrated arbitrary arrest, torture, and other abuses of basic rights. However, Harvard and University of Colorado–educated Ellen Johnson Sirleaf, the current president of Liberia, appears to be quite strongly committed to respecting and protecting human rights. One indication of her strong commitment is her decision early in her presidency to ask Nigeria to extradite her predecessor, Charles Taylor, so that he could face war crimes charges in Sierra Leone, a request she made at considerable risk to herself because there are still supporters of Taylor in Liberia, including former combatants who were part of his insurgent group during the civil war.[54] (Taylor was subsequently arrested as he tried to leave Nigeria and is now being tried by the Special Court for Sierra Leone, a special court set up jointly by the government of Sierra Leone and the United Nations; because of concerns about security, the venue of the trial was moved to The Hague, Netherlands.[55]) Johnson Sirleaf's commitment to human rights is further evidenced by her decision to establish a Truth and Reconciliation Commission to look into the human rights abuses that occurred during the civil war. The 2008 Amnesty International report on Liberia states, "The human rights situation improved throughout [2007], although challenges remained with regard to the administration of justice. Prisons were overcrowded, with the majority awaiting trial." It further notes, "The fight against corruption remained a priority for Ellen Johnson-Sirleaf's government. Trials of former members

---

[54] Warren Hoge, "Liberian Seeks Extradition of Predecessor for Atrocities Trial," *New York Times*, March 18, 2006.

[55] The proceedings of the trial can be accessed on the website of the Special Court for Sierra Leona at http://www.sc-sl.org/Taylor.html.

of the National Transitional Government charged with theft were ongoing."[56]

Though the report notes improvement, it also notes problems, including problems related to women's rights:

Despite the passing of a new law on rape in December 2005 providing a clearer definition of rape and more stringent punishments, a high incidence of rape against women and girls continued. There was an increase in the number of rape cases tried in circuit courts and 2007 saw the first successful conviction for rape since the end of the conflict. However, relevant portions of the ... law were not uniformly applied by court officials with the majority of the cases being settled out of court.[57]

The report also notes interference with freedom of the press. One case involved police closing down an independent newspaper when it published photos of a high-level government official in bed with two women. The Supreme Court of Liberia attempted to lift the ban but the government maintained the ban for a couple of months by instructing printing houses not to print the paper. In a more serious case of interference with freedom of the press, journalist Othello Guzean, who was employed by the government-owned radio network, was suspended indefinitely after airing an interview with an opposition leader, which the director of the radio network concluded was unacceptable and in contravention of the network's editorial policy.[58]

The 2009 report on Liberia released by the U.S. Department of State Bureau of Democracy, Human Rights, and Labor, notes that "civilian authorities generally maintained effective control of security forces" but adds:

Mob violence and land disputes resulted in deaths, and ritualistic killings occurred. Police abused, harassed, and intimidated detainees and citizens. Prison conditions remained harsh, and arbitrary arrest and detention occurred. Judicial inefficiency and corruption contributed to lengthy pretrial detention and denial of due process. Some incidents of trial by ordeal were reported. The government restricted the press. Corruption and impunity were endemic through all levels of government. Violence against women,

---

[56] Amnesty International, *2008 Report on Liberia* at http://thereport.amnesty.org/ eng/regions/africa/liberia (last accessed August 29, 2008).

[57] *Ibid.*

[58] *Ibid.*

including rape, was a problem, and domestic violence was widespread. Some ethnic groups continued to practice female genital mutilation (FGM). Child abuse and sexual violence against children were problems, and a few cases of human trafficking were reported. Racial and ethnic discrimination continued, and instances of child labor were reported, especially in the informal sector.[59]

And so, though the situation has improved significantly from the terrible days of the Doe and Taylor regimes, there is still work to be done in the area of human rights.

In an address to a joint session of the Liberian National Legislature on August 13, 2009, U.S. Secretary of State Hillary Rodham Clinton noted that "in just three years, there are encouraging signs of progress" even though the people of Liberia have been "climbing up [a] mountain that sometimes looks as if there is no end in sight." Clinton noted:

There are forces at work trying to undermine the progress and fuel old tensions and feuds. Many Liberian people still need jobs, electricity, housing, and education. Law enforcement is still inadequate, and after years of war and lawlessness, institutions have been left crippled, unable to function properly or serve the public efficiently or effectively.[60]

Clinton encouraged Liberians to hold on to the progress that has been made and "continue up the mountain together because there is no guarantee that the progress remains." She added, "Change is inevitable; progress is not." The United States, she assured Liberians, "stand[s] ready to help you in partnership and friendship."[61]

FIRESTONE IN LIBERIA TODAY

Though Firestone's Guthrie and Sinoe plantations and other Firestone facilities in Liberia were devastated during the civil war, the company, which was purchased by Japan-based Bridgestone Corporation in

---

[59] U.S. Department of State Bureau of Democracy, Human Rights, and Labor, *2009 Human Rights Report: Liberia* (March 11, 2010) at http://www.state.gov/g/drl/rls/hrrpt/2009/af/135961.htm (last accessed May 2, 2010).

[60] Hillary Rodham Clinton, "Address to Joint Session of Liberian National Legislature" at http://www.state.gov/secretary/rm/2009a/08/127872.htm (last accessed August 21, 2009).

[61] *Ibid.*

1988,[62] continues to have operations in Liberia. Now named Firestone Natural Rubber Company, the company provides jobs for more than 7,000 Liberians in a country in which unemployment remains high.[63] Following months of negotiations, Firestone and the Liberian government signed a new concession agreement in February 2008. The new agreement extends Firestone's concession in Liberia to 2041 while increasing the level at which the company will be taxed and mandating increased commitments by the company to housing and education. According to the agreement, Firestone will be taxed on its net taxable income at a rate not to exceed 30 percent, with the increased tax applied retroactively to Firestone's 2007 net taxable income, resulting in an increase of $2.5 million in government revenues for 2007. The agreement further calls for the company to pay a 2 percent tax on gross income, with the rate reduced to 1 percent in years in which the company does not turn a profit. In the area of housing, the agreement calls for the company to construct 2,300 new houses to meet the company's improved housing standard by December 31, 2010, with the company agreeing to provide one house for each employee entitled to housing by 2015. The agreement requires the company to provide $165,000 in financial assistance to Harbel Multilateral High School over a three-year period from 2008 to 2011 and $115,000 per year in scholarships for students on various levels through 2015, at which time the amount is to increase to $150,000 annually. In the area of employment, Firestone agreed to give preference to qualified Liberians for all skilled and management-level jobs with at least 30 percent of the ten most senior management positions to be held by Liberians within five years and at least 50 percent within ten years of the effective date of the agreement. At the signing ceremony, Liberian Agriculture Minister Dr. Chris Toe stated that the agreement was in the best interest both of the people of Liberia and of Firestone while Firestone's President and Managing Director Charles Stuart characterized the agreement as a milestone in revitalizing Liberia's rubber sector.[64]

[62] "About Bridgestone Americas" at http://www.firestone.com/about_bg_index.asp (last accessed September 2, 2008).
[63] Firestone Natural Rubber Company, "Community Involvement – Jobs" at http://www.firestonenaturalrubber.com/jobs.htm.
[64] "Liberia; Country, Firestone Sign 36-Year Agreement," *Africa News*, February 25, 2008.

Notwithstanding the new concession agreement, Firestone remains the center of a storm of controversy. The Stop Firestone Coalition, a group comprised of both U.S. and Liberia–based organizations,[65] maintains a website that has been sharply critical of Firestone's labor practices in Liberia. Referring to a report that ran on CNN, an article on their website charges:

> CNN ... calculated that one worker would have to spend 21 hours a day working to fill his quota [of trees to be tapped]. If a worker does not fill his quota, he loses 50% of his pay, resulting in only $1.59 a day. This is why the families have been forced to bring their children to work. They must enslave their own children, alongside themselves, or watch them starve. This is the choice Firestone has forced Liberian plantation workers to make.[66]

The Stop Firestone Coalition adds, "The broad spectrum of human rights abuses is clear. Firestone has used the forced labor of thousands to profit few."[67]

In November of 2005, International Rights Advocates, which is the successor to the litigation department of the International Labor Rights Fund (ILRF), filed a class action suit in the United States District Court for the Southern District of Indiana, Indianapolis Division, on behalf of adults and children working and living on Firestone plantations in Liberia. The suit charged that Firestone and affiliated companies forced workers to meet impossible quotas and benefited from the use of unlawful child labor.[68] Attorneys for Firestone entered a motion to dismiss the case. The district court granted the motion to dismiss all claims except the claim filed on behalf of children alleging that their working conditions violated international law.[69] Commenting on the decision, International Rights Advocates noted, "On June 26, 2007, in a truly groundbreaking decision, the judge denied Firestone's motion to dismiss and allowed this case to move forward to trial on child labor claims. This ruling represents the first-ever decision allowing a

---

[65] The list of participating organizations can be accessed at http://www.stopfirestone. org/about/coalition/.

[66] *Ibid.*

[67] *Ibid.*

[68] *Roe v. Bridgestone Corp.*, 2008 WL 2732192 (S.D.Ind. 2008). The case is currently in the United States District Court for the Southern District of Indiana, Indianapolis Division (Case No.: 1:06-cv-00627-DFH-JMS).

[69] *Roe v. Bridgestone Corp.*, 492 F. Supp. 2d 988 (S.D. Ind. 2007).

claim for child labor under the Alien Tort Statue."[70] (Chapter 9 of this volume will discuss in greater detail use the Alien Tort Claims Act as a tool for putting pressure on multinational corporations to respect human rights.) A subsequent decision by the United States District Court for the Southern District of Indiana, Indianapolis Division, however, complicated matters greatly for the plaintiffs. In a decision filed March 4, 2009, the court denied the plaintiffs' motion for class certification, which would have enabled the case to proceed as a class action on behalf of all children who might have been employed by or otherwise adversely affected by Firestone. The court concluded that "individual inquiries would be required to determine which children performed which tasks at what ages, for not all labor performed by all of these individuals, regardless of age, would be actionable."[71] This means that plaintiffs will have to pursue claims against Firestone individually, which is much more financially onerous, particularly for those with little income or other financial resources.[72]

Firestone responds to criticism by noting that it is investing more than $100 million on projects to help Liberia rebuild after the devastating civil war, projects that include new housing, schools and healthcare facilities.[73] The company states:

With Firestone Natural Rubber Company's strong support, the Liberian people have created the country's natural rubber industry. Yet the future of this business – and the future of Liberia – depends on its people. Through jobs, education, health care services and environmental stewardship, Firestone Natural Rubber Company is making a significant difference in the lives of Liberians, today and tomorrow.[74]

---

[70] International Rights Advocates, "Cases: Bridgestone-Firestone" at http://iradvocaters.org/bfcase.html (last accessed September 2, 2008).

[71] *Roe v. Bridgestone Corp.* 257 F.R.D. 159 ((S.D. Ind. 2009).

[72] If International Rights Advocates' financial resources are not adequate to pursue these cases individually, many of the plaintiffs – perhaps all of them – will have to find lawyers who would be willing to take on their cases on a contingency fee basis, if the litigation is to proceed. When lawyers take on cases on a contingency fee basis, plaintiffs are not required to pay those representing on a fee-for-service basis but, if the litigation is successful, the lawyers receive a specified portion of the settlement.

[73] "Firestone and Liberia – About Firestone Natural Rubber Company" at http://www.firestonenaturalrubber.com/about_fnrc.htm (accessed 2 September 2008).

[74] "Firestone and Liberia – Community Involvement" at http://www.firestonenaturalrubbercompany.com/community_involvement.htm (last accessed September 2, 2008).

The company adds, "By providing jobs, education opportunities, housing, critical infrastructure and health care services to Liberians, Firestone Natural Rubber Company is living up to its core values: respect and trust for its customers, teammates and the communities in which the company operates."[75]

In the area of education, the company reports that it operates and covers the entire cost of a twenty-three-school system, including a high school, with more than 15,000 children enrolled in this school system. The company also offers scholarships for advanced education at home and abroad.[76] In the area of health care, the company reports that it spends approximately $2 million a year to operate its medical programs in Liberia, with as many as 9,000 patient visits each month at its medical facilities. The company works with the Liberian Ministry of Health to control HIV/AIDS, tuberculosis, and malaria and partners with UNICEF and the Ministry of Health to store and administer vaccines to protect Liberians from various infectious diseases.[77]

As for Firestone employees, the company asserts that they "earn salaries typically much higher than their fellow Liberians" and "receive free housing, free medical care, free education for their children, subsidized food, paid vacation, a pension upon retirement and other employment benefits." The company states that children "are protected by strict child labor policies." It adds, "Firestone does not hire or employ anyone under 18, and has a zero-tolerance policy against bringing children to a work site."[78]

In short, the facts are disputed with respect to Firestone's employment practices and, in the case of allegations concerning the use of child labor, await adjudication in a court of law. However, a 2008 labor agreement signed with the Firestone Agricultural Workers Union of Liberia (FAWUL), the union that represents Firestone's workers, has been widely applauded. The contract increases wages for rubber

---

[75] "Firestone and Liberia – Community Impact" at http://www.firestonenaturalrubbercompany.com/community_impact.htm (last accessed September 2, 2008).

[76] "Firestone and Liberia – Education" at http://www.firestonenaturalrubber.com/eduction.htm. (last accessed September 2, 2008).

[77] "Firestone and Liberia – Health Care" at http://www.firestonenaturalrubber.com/health_care.htm. (last accessed September 2, 2008).

[78] "Firestone and Liberia – Jobs" at http://www.firestonenaturalrubber.com/jobs.htm. (last accessed September 2, 2008).

tappers by 24 percent over three years retroactive to January of 2007, reduces the daily rubber tree quota for tappers by 20 percent (150 trees), and provides for transportation for bringing latex to weigh stations.[79] "We were able to sit down at the table with management as equals and to negotiate an agreement that provides our members with hard-won respect and dignity," FAWUL President Austin Natee stated.[80] Charles Stuart, Firestone's general manager in Liberia, said that Firestone welcomes the agreement and will implement all of its provisions.[81] A spokeswoman for Firestone stated, "Along with the renegotiation of our Liberian concession agreement earlier this year, we feel that this new labor contract is a very positive moment in history for us."[82]

The labor agreement, though, has not ended criticism of Firestone's operations in Liberia. International Rights Advocates is continuing litigation on behalf of children of Firestone workers in Liberia.[83]

SUMMING IT ALL UP

Where does all of this leave us? While Firestone's record in Liberia is not without blemish, we believe that Firestone should be given a chance to show what it can do under the terms of the new concession agreement and the new labor agreement. To withdraw from Liberia would be disastrous for the more than 7,000 workers employed by Firestone, who would be left without jobs at a time when unemployment in Liberia exceeds 75 percent. It would also be disastrous for a country trying to rebuild after the massive destruction of the fourteen-year civil war.

At the same time, this is not to suggest that Firestone should be given free rein in Liberia to do whatever the company might be inclined to do. Careful monitoring by the government and by labor

[79] "USW Congratulates Liberian Rubber Workers on Landmark Labor Agreement" in *USW News*, August 7, 2008.

[80] Quoted in *ibid.*

[81] Ansu Konneh, "Firestone Plantation in Liberia Signs Wage Accord with Workers" at http://www.stopfirestone.org/2008/08/firestone-plantation-in-liberia-signs-wage-accord-with-its-workers-bloomberg (last accessed September 2, 2008).

[82] Quoted by Miles Moore in "Unions Hail BFS Rubber Plantation Labor Agreement," *Rubber & Plastics News*, August 25, 2008.

[83] *Ibid.*

organizations can help ensure that Firestone will make good on the commitments it has made in the agreements it has signed. Pressure from outside groups such as the Stop Firestone Coalition can also be a force for constructive change, not because Firestone is likely to accede to all of their demands but rather because gadfly organizations, though irritating to management, sometimes perform a useful function by motivating managers to improve their companies' social performance in order to blunt public criticism. As in the case of Starbucks and the trademarking of high-quality Ethiopian coffee (a controversy that will be discussed in the next chapter), a public relations offensive that gains the attention of corporate managers is sometimes the most practical way of effecting social change.

The story of Firestone in Liberia is far from over. The years to come will determine whether Firestone ends up being a key player in a new era of freedom and democracy or, conversely, an impediment to progress.

6

Free Trade, Fair Trade, and Coffee Farmers in Ethiopia

Adam Smith (1723–1790) never visited Ethiopia. The closest he got to Africa was Toulouse in southern France, where he spent eighteen months of boredom serving as a tutor for a young member of the nobility – boredom that was partially alleviated when he spent his spare time working on a manuscript that was in time to become *An Inquiry into the Nature and Causes of the Wealth of Nations*. But were he to visit Ethiopia today, he would see much that validates theories he set forth in *Wealth of Nations*, a ground-breaking work published in 1776, the same year the U.S. Declaration of Independence was signed. Smith envisioned a nation of small shopkeepers and producers with prices determined by the laws of supply and demand in a competitive market economy. The coffee trade in Ethiopia approximates the world that Smith envisioned with 95 percent of Ethiopian coffee produced by small farmers.[1]

Coffee was cultivated in Ethiopia as early as 600 AD, first as a medicine, then as a beverage. The beverage made from the roasted beans was introduced from Arabia to Turkey in 1554, from Turkey to Italy in 1615, and then to other European countries. In 1727, coffee reached Brazil, which is now the world's largest producer, in 1727.[2]

---

[1] "Ethiopian Coffee Farmers Lead the Way with First Rainforest Alliance Certification in Africa," Rainforest Alliance at http://www.rainforest-alliance.org/news.cfm?id=africa_certification (last accessed January 23, 2008).

[2] *Ibid.*

But though Brazil and other countries in Latin America today account for much of world coffee production, coffee remains tremendously important for the agriculturally based economy of Ethiopia, where it accounts for more than 60 percent of the country's foreign exchange earnings and provides a means of livelihood for over 15 million people in a country with a population of 78 million.[3] The foreign exchange earnings from coffee are crucial in Ethiopia, a country in which more than 75 percent of the population lives on less than $1 a day, making it one of the poorest countries in the world.[4]

Coffee Arabica, the most widely grown variety of coffee today, originated in Ethiopia, where the cool, shady forests of the highlands provide an ideal environment for growing this variety.[5] The coffee grown by Ethiopian farmers today is good coffee – some of the best grown anywhere in the world. None of this, however, protected Ethiopian farmers from economic disaster when a glut of coffee on the world market sent coffee prices plunging, reaching one-hundred year lows when adjusted for inflation.[6]

Many did just what Smith said should happen if prices for one commodity drop to the point that it is no longer profitable to produce it – they switched to growing other crops that were more profitable.[7]

---

[3] Sustainable Tree Crops Program, "Ethiopia: Coffee History, Production, Economy Facts" at http://www.treecrops.org/country/ethiopia_coffee.asp (last accessed January 23, 2008).

[4] Make Trade Fair, "Coffee in Ethiopia" at http://www.maketradefair.com/en/index.php?file=starbucks_01.html (last accessed March 24, 2008).

[5] *Ibid.*

[6] Bryan Lewin, Daniele Giovannucci, and Panos Varangis, *Coffee Markets: New Paradigms in Global Supply and Demand* (Washington, DC: International Bank for Reconstruction and Development, 2004), 19. Contrary to what classic economic theory would suggest, plunging prices have not resulted in decreases in coffee production. In fact, worldwide coffee production has increased even as prices have decreased. Lewin, Giovannucci, and Varangis report that most of the increased production has occurred in Brazil and Vietnam, which, for various reasons, have best been able to manage production costs (63–65).

[7] In *An Inquiry into the Nature and Causes of the Wealth of Nations*, Adam Smith writes, "The market price of any particular commodity ... can seldom continue long below its natural prices. Whatever part of it was paid below the natural rate, the persons whose interest it affected would immediately feel the loss, and would immediately withdraw either so much land, or so much labour, or so much stock, from being employed about it...." (*An Inquiry into the Nature and Causes of the Wealth of Nations*, [Oxford: Clarendon Press, 1976], 79 [I, vii, 30].) Smith did not assume, however, that the land and labor withdrawn from producing a commodity for which the price

But here the story of coffee farmers in Ethiopia and Smith's vision what is best for society as a whole begin to diverge. The crop to which many Ethiopian farmers switched – an estimated 75 percent of coffee farmers in the highlands of Hararghe alone – was khat, a narcotic that can fetch as much as $200 a pound in Great Britain and in the United States, where it is illegal.[8] In short, contrary to what Smith believed to be the case, switching to alternate crops does not necessarily contribute to human well-being.

A TRADE AGREEMENT?

Some have suggested that a trade agreement beneficial to Ethiopian coffee farmers and others in less-developed countries might be the solution. That, however, is far easier said than done. The round of talks by representatives of countries that are members of the World Trade Organization (WTO) that began in Doha, Qatar, in 2001 collapsed in 2008,[9] though there are reports that U.S. President Barack Obama hopes to get them going again.[10] The dispute became a three-way stand-off involving the United States, the European Union (EU), and a group of developing nations led by Brazil and India. U.S. and EU agricultural subsidies, which enable American and European farmers to sell their products at prices below the break-even point for farmers in less-developed countries who receive no subsidies, proved to be a major stumbling block in the discussions.[11] Farmers in the United States and Western Europe are exceedingly reluctant to give

had dropped below the point that it would be profitable would remain idle. Rather, he believed that it would be shifted to producing some other commodity.

[8] Global Exchange, "Fair Trade Farmers in Ethiopia" at http://www.globalexchange. org/campaigns/fairtrade/coffee/EthiopiaFlyer.pdf (last accessed March 14, 2008). See also William Wallis, "Farmers of Ethiopia Turn to Khat as World Coffee Prices Tumble," *Financial Times*, December 8, 2003. Wallis notes that Oxfam predicts that within ten years khat will overtake coffee as Ethiopia's leading export if coffee prices do not recover.

[9] Stephen Castle and Mark Landler, "After 7 Years, Talks Collapse on World Trade," *New York Times*, July 30, 2008, A1.

[10] Reuters, "U.S. Serious About Getting Doha Round Trade Deal: EU," *New York Times*, October 26, 2009.

[11] Mark Landler, "A Gloomy WTO Chief Says Time Is Brief for Saving Talks," *New York Times*, May 5, 2006. See also Elizabeth Becker, "WTO Moves to Revive Talks on Farm Subsidies," *New York Times*, June 2, 2004; Carter Dougherty, "Once Again, Trade Effort Stumbles on Subsidies, *New York Times*, June 22, 2007; and Associated Press, "WTO to Look at U.S. Subsidies," December 18, 2007.

up import quotas and government subsidies and the governments of the United States and Western European countries are exceedingly reluctant to take the political risks of infuriating farmers by bargaining away import quotas and subsidies, even though so doing could go a long ways toward alleviating poverty in less-developed countries.

All of this is probably a moot point insofar as Ethiopian coffee farmers are concerned. None of the wealthy nations that heavily subsidize their agricultural sectors is a significant producer of coffee. Hence, even if wealthy countries were willing to give up all subsidies to their farmers, so doing would have little, if any, impact on Ethiopian coffee farmers.

INTERNATIONAL COFFEE AGREEMENTS (ICAS)

The International Coffee Organization (ICO), which was organized in London in 1963 under the auspices of the United Nations, is the main intergovernmental organization for coffee, bringing together producing and consuming countries. It has administered seven successive International Coffee Agreements (ICAs).[12]

The economic clauses of ICAs helped keep coffee prices stable at predetermined levels by using export quotas to control the exports of individual countries (something Adam Smith would not have liked). For awhile, this worked reasonably well. But in time, the system began to come apart at the seams. Coffee was diverted to importing countries that were not ICO members, thereby sidestepping the quotas. Some producers circumvented the quotas by rebagging their coffee offshore. In 1989, the program collapsed when a number of countries withdrew from the organization.[13]

Various efforts have been made to resuscitate the system. The most recent effort is in the form of the *International Coffee Agreement 2007*, the seventh agreement adopted by the organization. The 2007 agreement takes a decidedly free-market approach, stating in Article 24:

> (2) Members recognize that there are at present in effect measures which may to a greater or lesser extent hinder the increase in consumption of coffee, in particular:

[12] International Coffee Organization, "About Us" at http://www.ico.org/mission.asp (last accessed March 25, 2008).
[13] Lewin, Giovannucci, and Varangis, *Coffee Markets*, 24.

    (a) import arrangements applicable to coffee, including pref-
erential and other tariffs, quotas, operations of government monopolies and official purchasing agencies, and
other administrative rules and commercial practices;

    (b) export arrangements as regards direct or indirect subsi-
dies and other administrative rules and commercial practices; and

    (c) internal trade conditions and domestic and regional
legal and administrative provisions which may affect
consumption.

(3) Having regard to the objective stated above and to the provisions of paragraph (4) of this Article, Members shall endea-
vour to pursue tariff reductions on coffee or to take other
action to remove obstacles to increased consumption.

(4) Taking into account their mutual interest, Members undertake
to seek ways and means by which the obstacles to increased
trade and consumption referred to in paragraph (2) of this
Article may be progressively reduced and eventually, whenever
possible, eliminated, or by which the effects of such obstacles
may be substantially diminished.[14]

It remains to be seen whether the ICO efforts to increase coffee prices
by increasing consumption are more effective than failed efforts to
revitalize the organization in the years following the collapse of the
system in 1989.

SEARCHING FOR SOLUTIONS

To recapitulate, a WTO trade agreement favorable to Ethiopian coffee farmers is unlikely to be reached while the prospects for success
for the *International Coffee Agreement 2007* are far from certain. Insofar
as coffee farmers in Ethiopia are concerned, where does this leave
us? Basically there are three options: (1) simply ignore the plight of
Ethiopian coffee farmers while singing the praise of Adam Smith and

---

[14] International Coffee Organization, *International Coffee Agreement 2007* (September
2007) at http://dev.ico.org/documents/ica2007e.pdf (last accessed March 25,
2008).

a competitive world economy; (2) encourage and support cooperatives, trademarking, and other efforts to strengthen the market position of Ethiopian coffee farmers in a competitive world economy; or
(3) appeal to the moral sentiments of consumers to encourage them
to purchase coffee that provides a better return to coffee farmers
in Ethiopia and elsewhere. The first option cannot be defended by
anyone with even a modicum of human decency and, accordingly,
will not be discussed further in this chapter. The second and third
options, however, merit serious consideration and will be examined
in detail in the pages that follow.

STRENGTHENING MARKET POSITION

We begin by noting a very basic market reality. In any economic trans-
action, whichever party is more powerful is in a stronger position to
dictate or otherwise determine prices. If it is a seller's market with
far more potential customers than goods available to be sold, sellers
can ask for – and get – higher prices for their products. On the other
hand, if it is a buyer's market with far more sellers than buyers (as is
the case with respect to coffee today), prices take a hit.

So far what we have is just good old-fashioned Adam Smith free
market economics. What might appear to be an economic truism,
however, leaves an important question unanswered: Are there ways
of increasing the return to producers apart from changing the economic equations by increasing demand or decreasing supply? As a
matter of fact there are. If done in an effective manner, cooperative
marketing arrangements and trademarking (the two can be done in
combination) can give producers a better return.

Some examples from the world of health care illustrate what is at
stake here. As already noted, when there is a significant power disparity between the providers and purchasers, the party with the power
can, in substantial measure, dictate prices. Because of Medicare, the
federal government in the United States is such a powerful player in
the field of health care that it can dictate prices to hospitals – and
does via the diagnosis-related group (DRG) system by which Medicare
simply informs hospitals what they will pay for Medicare-covered
patients with various types of ailments. In like manner, hospitals are
so powerful in relation to private individuals that they simply inform

private pay patients what the charges are, with the private pay individual having little, if any, say in the matter. In short, a private individual attempting to negotiate a discounted rate with a hospital – or a hospital attempting to negotiate a higher level of reimbursement from the federal government – is unlikely to succeed.

The pricing equations start changing, however, when private insurance companies and other major purchasers of health care enter into negotiations with hospitals and other healthcare providers to secure special pricing agreements. When there is not a great power disparity between the buyer of health care and the seller of health care, negotiated prices are possible.

It is for precisely this reason that coffee farmers in Ethiopia have banded together in cooperatives such as the Oromia Coffee Farmers Cooperative Union[15] and the Sidama Coffee Farmers Cooperative Union.[16] Tadessa Meskela, the general manager of the Oromia Coffee Farmers Cooperative Union, and Tsegaye Anebo, who heads up the Sidama Coffee Farmers Cooperative Union, work tirelessly to find buyers willing to pay a fair market price for the coffee produced by the farmers they represent.

Simply banding together to form a cooperative, to be sure, does not in and of itself guarantee higher prices for the crops produced by members of that particular cooperative. It does, however, make it easier to negotiate more favorable prices.

Once again the world of health care provides an illustrative example. Prior to the 1980s, most hospitals, visiting nurses associations, and other healthcare providers were free-standing institutions. However, when health maintenance organizations (HMOs) and other purchasers of health care started negotiating pricing agreements with healthcare providers, many hospitals, visiting nurses organizations, and other health care providers started banding together (or were bought out) to form regional health systems. The reason for this consolidation is that HMOs and other purchasers of health care preferred one-stop shopping where they could purchase a wide range of

---

[15] For an overview of the Oromia Coffee Farmers Cooperative Union, see "About Us" on their website at http://oromiacoffeeunion.org/aboutus.html.
[16] For an overview of the Sidama Farmers Cooperative Union, see the home page of their website at http://www.sidacoop.com/.

health services, rather than having to negotiate pricing agreements with myriad institutions and organizations.

Something similar to this is happening with respect to the coffee business in Ethiopia. Forming cooperatives places coffee farmers in Ethiopia in a stronger position to negotiate better prices for the coffee beans they produce. The significance of this comes into perspective when coffee production in Ethiopia is compared to that in Brazil, where the low-lying areas of many of the major coffee growing regions are more hospitable to mechanized forms of production than are the highlands of Ethiopia – mechanization that has led to large plantations where production far exceeds that of small farmers in Ethiopia and elsewhere.[17] Cooperatives such as the Oromia Coffee Farmers Cooperative Union and the Sidama Coffee Farmers Cooperative Union enable Ethiopian coffee farmers, by banding together, to deal directly with coffee buyers, thereby cutting out the middleman, and giving them greater parity with large plantations in Brazil and other coffee-producing countries. This is particularly beneficial when dealing with large purchasers of coffee such as Starbucks, Nestlé, and Sara Lee.

TRADEMARKING

Placing small coffee farmers in Ethiopia in a stronger market position by forming cooperatives and cutting out the middleman is only part of what is happening. Because coffee grown in the Harar, Yirgacheffe, and Sidamo areas is of exceptional quality, the Ethiopian Intellectual Property Office is spearheading an effort to trademark coffee of exceptional quality.[18] Under their leadership, the Ethopian Coffee Trademarking and Licensing Initiative was introduced in 2004. The Ethiopian Fine Coffee Stakeholder Committee, with representation from cooperatives, private exporters, the Ethiopian Intellectual Property Office, and other government offices, has assumed management responsibility for the initiative.[19]

---

[17] Brian Martell, "They Grow an Awful Lot of Coffee in Brazil" at http://heritage-coffee.com/CoffeeInBrazil.htm (last accessed March 17, 2008).

[18] Matthew Clark, "In Trademarking Its Coffee, Ethiopia Seeks Fair Trade," *Christian Science Monitor*, November 9, 2007.

[19] Ethiopian Coffee Network, "About the Trademarking and Licensing Initiative" at http://ethiopiancoffeenetwork.com/about.shtml (last accessed February 14, 2008).

The Ethiopian Coffee Trademarking and Licensing Initiative is based on a very simple premise: Quality sells. Connoisseurs of fine coffee, fine wine, and fine cars are often willing to pay top dollar for top-quality products. Sometimes those desiring top-quality products come to their own judgments about what constitutes quality and which products possess this quality. Sometimes they depend on reviews by other connoisseurs. In many cases, however, those desiring top-quality products look to the name brand or to certification, be it Volvo or Porsche in the world of automobiles or the Gallo Nero (Black Rooster) seal of quality for chianti classico wine.

The experience of the Gallo Nero Chianti Classico Consortium is instructive. The sangiovese grape that is used to make chianti wine has been grown for hundreds of years in the Chianti region of Tuscany in central Italy, located between Florence on the north and Siena on the south. (Like bordeaux, burgundy and a number of other French wines, chianti wine is named after the region in which it is grown, rather than after the grape used to produce it.) In Chianti, soil conditions, plentiful sunshine, and temperatures that vary little in the course of the day during the growing season combine to make the region the perfect place to grow sangiovese grapes. Chianti classico wine ("classico" is an official designation that means "the first" or "the original") is produced in the central portion of the region in vineyards on the sides of the hills surrounding Greve in Chianti, one of the most picturesque market towns in all of Italy.[20]

As chianti wines grew in popularity, vintners and bottlers in the area surrounding Greve became concerned when they discovered that wines of inferior quality were being marketed as chianti wines, including some wines that were not produced in Chianti. On May 14, 1924, thirty-three producers met in Radda in Chianti and formed a consortium to protect the integrity of their product and promote the wine they produced. They chose as their trademark the Gallo Nero (Black Rooster), the historic symbol of the old Chianti Military League.[21]

---

[20] Chianti Classico, "The Territory" at http://www.chianticlassico.com/english/il-territorio.htm (last accessed March 21, 2008).
[21] Chianti Classico, "The Black Rooster Consortium" at http://www.chianticlassico.com/english/il-consorzio.htm (last accessed March 21, 2008).

For more than half a century, the consortium engaged in long and difficult legal and political battles to secure recognition and protection for their trademark and the wine they produced. In time, they prevailed. Today, the Chianti Classico Consortium, which now has more than 600 members (about half of them bottlers), is a prominent presence in the world of wine, and the black rooster is a widely recognized symbol of quality. The consortium has a test laboratory to make certain that the wine that bottlers wish to market with the black rooster trademark meets their standards of quality. They have inspection and legal departments and a marketing and communication office.[22] All of this adds up to a classic story of business success. A snapshot of the economic benefits of the black rooster symbol of quality for members of the consortium can be gained by browsing through the Italian wine section of a wine shop and noting the price differential between bottles of chianti wine that carry the symbol of the black rooster and those that do not.

Whether the product is wine, coffee, or anything else, there are several necessary components of a successful trademarking program:

- There must be sponsoring organization such as a consortium, a cooperative or a major business entity.
- They must have a high-quality product to sell.
- There must be quality controls such as testing laboratories to monitor and ensure the quality of the product.
- They must receive trademark protection from the government to prevent other business entities from using their trademark to market competing or inferior products.
- For optimal success, they must have an effective marketing program, including public relations and advertising programs directed toward increasing consumer awareness of the trademark and the quality it represents.

Though programs to trademark and promote Ethiopian coffee of superior quality are still in their early stages, officials in the Ethiopian Intellectual Property Office and leaders of various coffee farmers cooperatives are keenly aware of what needs to be done. Dessalegn Jena,

---

[22] *Ibid.*

assistant general manager of the Oromia Coffee Farmers Cooperative Union, emphatically states that simply registering a trademark is not enough. "The government needs to give special emphasis to ensuring the quality of coffee to maintain the reputation for specialty coffees," he observes, adding that the government must crack down on anyone falsely labeling beans or mixing inferior beans into bags of premium beans. Most important of all, he notes, the specialty coffees must be skillfully marketed in Europe and in the United States.[23]

The payoff for Ethiopian coffee farmers could be substantial. Getachew Mengistie, the head of the Ethiopian Intellectual Property Office, states, "I'm very certain that five to ten years down the line, specialty farmers will make much more than they make now.... They could make 75 percent to 100 percent more."[24]

Payoffs of that magnitude, though, are still far in the future. The Ethiopian Fine Coffee Stakeholder Committee is making progress, however, in making a reality the dream that gave rise to the Ethiopian Coffee Trademarking and Licensing Initiative. With trademarks already secured in twenty-eight countries, they are building a network of licensed distributors throughout the world.[25] The work of the committee is made easier in one respect – consumers are already willing to pay top dollar for high-quality Ethiopian coffee. In the United States, Harar and Sidamo specialty coffees have been retailing for more than $20 a pound. The problem is, however, that coffee farmers in Ethiopia receive only 5 to 6 percent of that amount. In substantial measure, the trademarking and licensing initiative is directed toward increasing the portion of the retail price of specialty coffees that goes to the Ethiopian farmers who raise the coffee beans.[26]

The trademarking and licensing initiative has been aided by organizations such as Oxfam International, which played a key role in persuading Starbucks to sign a historic fair-trade agreement with Ethiopia that recognizes Ethiopia's right to control the use of its Harar, Sidamo, and Yirgacheffe specialty coffee brands.[27] Ending a bitter dispute over

[23] Quoted by Clark in "In Trademarking Its Coffee, Ethiopia Seeks Fair Trade."
[24] Quoted in *ibid.*
[25] Ethiopian Coffee Network, "About the Trademarking and Licensing Initiative."
[26] *Ibid.*
[27] Oxfam International, "Starbucks Signs Historic Agreement with Ethiopia" at http://www.maketradefair.com/en/index.php?file=starbucks_main.html (last accessed

trademarks that turned into a public relations problem for Starbucks, the company's chairman, Howard D. Schultz, announced after meeting with Ethiopian Prime Minister Meles Zenawi, that Starbucks would open a center in Ethiopia to help coffee farmers improve the profitability of their crops. He stated, "We feel very strongly that the long-term success of our company is directly linked to the long-term success of not only the Ethiopian coffee farmer, but all the coffee farmers around the world."[28] Unfortunately, Starbucks put the plans on hold because of the world-wide recession that began in 2008.[29]

Even with the setbacks that have occurred, Getachew Mengistie, the head of the Ethiopian Intellectual Property Office, sees mutual benefit resulting from trademarking specialty varieties of coffee. He observes:

When farmers can grow and prosper by not only improving production and quality but also by building up the value of their intellectual property portfolios, then everybody in the coffee industry – including partners in retail and distribution as well as consumers – reap benefits. Moreover, in a case like Ethiopia's, the importance of doing this cannot be overstated: Stronger negotiating power could enable millions of coffee farmers and traders to prosper and invest in the future of these fine coffees.[30]

APPEALING TO MORAL SENTIMENTS

Trademarking high-quality products, be they specialty coffees, wine, or anything else, is essentially a practical business decision intended to increase the returns for producers by strengthening market position in a competitive market economy. The benefits of trademarking, of course, accrue primarily to those who produce and market the

March 25, 2008). See also Oxfam America, "Starbucks Agrees to Honor its Commitments to Ethiopian Coffee Farmers" at http://www.oxfamamerica.org/whatwedo/campaigns/coffee/starbucks.

[28] "Ending Dispute, Starbucks Is to Help Ethiopian Farmers," *New York Times*, November 29, 2007.

[29] Jason McLure, "Starbucks Delays Ethiopian Research Center, Capital Says" at http://www.bloomberg.com/apps/news?pid=20601012&sid=a4xgM2P4Ug78 (last accessed October 31, 2009).

[30] Quoted by Ethiopian Coffee Network in "What People Are Saying about the Initiative" at http://www.ethiopiancoffeenetwork.com/media/shtml (last accessed February 24, 2008).

product that is trademarked. In short, trademarking specialty coffees will do little, if anything, for the Ethiopian coffee farmers whose coffee beans do not meet the criteria for trademark certification.

There are, however, other types of certification – types of certification that appeal to the moral sentiments of consumers – that offer benefits to a wider range of producers. In 2006, the Rainforest Alliance, an organization dedicated to preserving rainforests, certified a group of 678 coffee farmers in Ethiopia after having determined that they meet the alliance's strict set of environmental and social standards, which include ecosystem and wildlife conservation, reducing the use of agrochemicals, and providing better working and living conditions for workers.[31] Similarly, as noted in Chapter 2, various fair trade organizations, many of them affiliated with Fairtrade Labelling Organizations International (FLO), certify coffee, the purchase of which provides what they view as a fair return to coffee farmers.

This brings us back to Adam Smith, who, seventeen years before *Wealth of Nations* while holding the chair of moral philosophy at the University of Glasgow, published a lesser known work entitled *The Theory of Moral Sentiments*, which, unfortunately, is rarely read today. In this insightful book, Smith wrestles with the question of how people, who, he believes, are motivated by self-interest and desire for self-preservation, can make moral judgments, including moral judgments about their own behavior. Chapter 1 of Section I begins, "How selfish soever man may be supposed, there are evidently some principles in his nature, which interest him in the fortune of others, and render their happiness necessary to him, though he derives nothing from it, except the pleasure of seeing it."[32]

And what enables this empathy? Smith observes, "As we have no immediate experience of what other men feel, we can form no idea of the manner in which they are affected, but by conceiving what we ourselves should feel in the like situation."[33] Thus, gaining awareness

---

[31] Rainforest Alliance, "Ethiopian Coffee Farmers Lead the Way with First Rainforest Alliance Certification in Africa" at http://rainforest-alliance.org/news.cfm?id=africa_certification (last accessed January 23, 2008).

[32] Adam Smith, *The Theory of Moral Sentiments*, with an introduction by E.G. West (Indianapolis: Liberty Classics, 1976), 47 (I, i).

[33] *Ibid.*

of what it would be like to be in someone else's shoes is the key ingredient in what Smith labels "fellow-feeling." He writes:

> By the imagination we place ourselves in [someone else's] situation, we conceive ourselves enduring all the same torments, we enter as it were into his body, and become in some measure the same person with him, and thence form some idea of his sensations, and even feel something which, though weaker in degree, is not altogether unlike them.[34]

He adds, "Neither is it those circumstances only, which create pain or sorrow, that call forth our fellow-feeling.... Our joy for the deliverance of those heroes of tragedy or romance who interest us, is as sincere as our grief for their distress, and our fellow-feeling with their misery is not more real than that with their happiness."[35] In short, as we come to empathize with others, this empathy can be either in the form of compassion when they experience suffering or rejoicing when they experience happiness.

The human tendency to be motivated by self-interest is taken by Smith as a given. However, the human capacity for fellow-feeling serves as a counterbalance to self-interest, which, if left unchecked, exhibits itself in greed and selfishness detrimental to others. The human capacity for reason, Smith suggests, enables us to rise above mere self-interest and, moved by fellow-feeling for others, take courses of action and create social institutions that are beneficial to others, as well as to ourselves – to function, as it were, as an impartial spectator. Smith writes:

> To disturb [our neighbor's] happiness merely because it stands in the way of our own, to take from him what is of real use to him merely because it may be of equal or of more use to us, or to indulge, in this manner, at the expense of other people, the natural preference which every man has for his own happiness over that of other people, is what no impartial spectator can go along with."[36]

Smith suggests that "to feel much for others, and little for ourselves, that to restrain our selfish, and to indulge our benevolent, affections, constitutes the perfection of human nature; and can alone produce

---

[34] *Ibid.*, 48 (I, i).
[35] *Ibid.*, 49 (I, i).
[36] *Ibid.*, 161 (II, ii).

among mankind that harmony of sentiments and passions in which consists their whole grace and propriety."[37]

We leave to others the question of whether the theories Smith advances in *The Theory of Moral Sentiments* are consistent with or at odds with the theories he advances in *Wealth of Nations* (though we do note the celebrated metaphor of the invisible hand first appeared in *The Theory of Moral Sentiments*, albeit in a somewhat different context than in *Wealth of Nations*[38]). We do believe, however, that Smith's theory of human nature is, in substantial measure, correct and that it lends credence to efforts of organizations such as Oxfam International to improve the economic condition of coffee farmers in Ethiopia and elsewhere by appealing to the moral sentiments of consumers.

To be sure, the fellow-feeling of which Smith speaks is not without limitations. In the course of history, countless perpetrators of horrific atrocities appear to have extinguished any sense of fellow feeling with respect to their victims. To illustrate this point, one only need look at the Spanish Inquisition in the fifteenth and sixteenth centuries and the French Wars of Religion in the sixteenth century (events of which Smith was presumably aware) or, in more recent times, the Holocaust or genocide in Rwanda.

At the same time, as is illustrated the massive humanitarian response to the tsunamis triggered by an undersea earthquake near Indonesia in December of 2004 – tsunamis that took the lives of more than 200,000 men, women, and children in eleven different countries and left nearly eight times that many homeless – there is tremendous potential for responding to the needs of others in times of crisis. And so, at least in some cases, the fellow-feeling of which Smith speaks can be a powerful motivating factor.

---

[37] *Ibid.*, 71–72 (I, v).

[38] In *The Theory of Moral Sentiments*, Smith suggests that when dividing "the produce of all their improvements," the rich "are led by an invisible hand to make nearly the same distribution which would have been made had the earth been divided into equal portions among all its inhabitants…" (304 [IV, 4]), a statement that, when judged on empirical grounds, is patently false. In *The Wealth of Nations*, Smith states that "by directing that industry in such a manner as its produce may be of the greatest value, [an individual] intends only his own gain, and he is, in this, as in many other cases, led by an invisible hand to promote an end which was no part of his intention.… By pursuing his own his own interest he frequently promotes that of the society more effectually than when he really intends to promote it" (456 [IV, ii, 9]).

It is also a sentiment that can be fostered. The massive media coverage of the 2004 tsunamis seared the consciences of people throughout the world. In other cases, such as the plight of coffee farmers in Ethiopia, there is little public awareness of the suffering that they endure or what might be done to alleviate this suffering. It is for this reason that directors Marc Francis and Nick Francis put together *Black Gold: A Film about Coffee and Trade,* a film featuring Tadesse Meskela, which documents the plight of Ethiopian coffee farmers.[39] It is for this reason that Oxfam and other organizations present programs and distribute brochures to increase awareness of how the coffee trade works and what might be done to secure a greater return for coffee farmers in Ethiopia and elsewhere. And it is for this reason that churches, synagogues, and other organizations make available for sale to their members coffee that provides what they view as a fair return to the farmers who raised the coffee beans of which it is made. In short, when coupled with efforts to raise awareness of the plight of others, the fellow-feeling of which Smith speaks can motivate people to look beyond their own self-interest (which would be served by buying coffee at the lowest possible price) and spend the portion of their budget devoted to consumption on products that provide a fair return to those who produced them.

SUMMING IT ALL UP

In conclusion, we note that (1) an unregulated market economy such as that idealized by Smith can be detrimental to the well-being of coffee farmers in Ethiopia and elsewhere, (2) cooperatives and trademarking can strengthen the market position of Ethiopian coffee farmers, and (3) appealing to moral sentiments such as the fellow-feeling of which Smith writes can encourage consumers to purchase products such as fair trade coffee that provides a better return to those who produce these products. None of this is a panacea for the hardship experienced by coffee farmers in Ethiopia and elsewhere. Forming cooperatives, trademarking, and appealing to the moral sentiments of consumers can, however, improve Ethiopian coffee

---

[39] Additional information about "Black Gold: A Film about Coffee and Trade" can be accessed at http://www.blackgoldmovie.com.

farmers' lot in life, which is a good and sufficient reason for pursuing these options.

Commenting on the impact of fair trade efforts on Ethiopian coffee farmers, Asnake Bekele, general manager of the Sidamo Coffee Farmers Cooperative Union, observes, "Things are better. They're definitely better. But there is still a very long way to go."[40] The fact that things are getting better is reflected in the fact that, as reported by Solomon Tilahun, a marketing expert at Ethiopia's Agriculture Ministry, coffee production in Ethiopia is expected to increase by as much as 20 percent in the next five years.[41] Perhaps khat will not end up winning out after all.[42]

---

[40] Quoted by Stephanie Nolen in "In Ethiopia, Fair Trade for Bean Farmers Is Slowly Raising Incomes in One of the World's Poorest Countries," *The Globe and Mail* (Canada), May 19, 2006.

[41] Quoted in "Ethiopia: Country Sees 20 Pct Coffee Crop Rise in 5 Years; Harvest Seen Up 10 Pct. At 16.5 Mln Tonnes," *The Daily Monitor*, February 17, 2008.

[42] This chapter is a slightly revised version of an article that appeared in *The Global Studies Journal*, Vol. 1 (2008).

7

Maquiladoras

Exploitation, Economic Opportunity, or Both?

The factories in Mexico commonly known as "maquiladoras" are assumed by many to be a by-product of the North American Free Trade Agreement (NAFTA). Such, however, is not the case, though, as will be noted in this chapter, NAFTA did contribute to rapid expansion of maquiladoras – and to the controversy surrounding maquiladoras. In part, the controversy surrounding maquiladoras stems from a belief that maquiladoras have cost many U.S. workers their jobs as U.S. companies shifted production to low-wage factories south of the border in an effort to gain a competitive advantage in an increasingly competitive global economy. And in part, the controversy surrounding maquiladoras involves widespread allegations about substandard wages, unhealthy working conditions, and other exploitative practices.

In 1965 – three decades before NAFTA – the government of Mexico established the maquiladora program as part of that country's Border Industrialization Program (BIP), a program instituted to develop employment opportunities for Mexican workers displaced by the 1964 termination of the Bracero Program, a guest worker program that had been introduced in 1942 to deal with critical World War II labor shortages in the United States in the agricultural and rail sectors. Under the terms of the maquiladora program, foreign-owned companies were allowed to import temporarily raw materials and components duty free for processing or assembly by Mexican workers with the resulting products to be exported, primarily to the

United States.[1] ("Maquiladora" is a term derived from the Spanish word "maquilar," which means "to assemble."[2])

In the course of the years, the term "maquiladora" has come to be rather loosely used to refer to any foreign-owned subsidiary in any Latin American country established to produce goods for export while taking advantage of low wage rates.[3] A more precise use of the term, however, limits it to plants registered with the government of Mexico under the provisions of the Border Industrialization Program (BIP).[4] We prefer the more precise definition.

The first maquiladoras established during the 1960s were primarily U.S.-affiliated assembly operations taking advantage of Mexico's low labor costs. By the 1980s, U.S. companies were joined by Japanese and European companies competing for sales to U.S. consumers. In an article entitled "Plants in Mexico help Japan Sell to U.S." that ran in the *New York Times* in 1987 (seven years prior to NAFTA), Larry Rohter observed, "Mexico's duty-free assembly industry, originally conceived as a program to link manufacturers in the United States and Mexico, is increasingly being regarded by Japan and other countries as a way to further their penetration of the American market while avoiding trade squabbles."[5]

Today, two-thirds of maquiladoras are affiliated with U.S. companies, with Japanese, Dutch, German, Canadian, Korean, Chinese, Swedish, Finnish, French, and Australian companies operating most

[1] General Accounting Office (GAO), *International Trade: Mexico's Maquiladora Decline Affects U.S.-Mexico Border Communities and Trade; Recovery Depends in Part on Mexico's Actions* (July 2003) at http://www.gao.gov/new.items/d03891.pdf (last accessed September 29, 2008), 5.
[2] *Spanish Dictionary* at http://www.spanishdict.com/translate/maquilar (last accessed October 1, 2008). *Maquilar* also means "to measure and take the miller's dues for grinding corn."
[3] See, e.g., Ralph Armbruster-Sandoval, "Globalization and Transnational Labor Organizing: the Honduran Maquiladora Industry and the Kimi Campaign," *Social Science History* 27:4 (Winter 2003), 551–576; Agnes R. Quisumbing, Kelly Hallman, and Marie T. Ruel, "Maquiladoras and Market Mamas: Women's Work and Childcare in Guatemala City and Accra," *Journal of Development Studies*, 43:3 (April 2007), 420–255; and Jennifer Bickam Mendez, *From the Revolution to the Maquiladoras: Gender, Labor, and Globalization in Nicaragua* (Durham, NC, and London: Duke University Press, 2005).
[4] General Accounting Office, *Mexico's Maquiladora Decline*, 5–6.
[5] Larry Rohter, "Plants in Mexico help Japan Sell to U.S.," *New York Times*, May 26, 1987.

of the remaining one-third. Five of the top 100 maquiladora employers are companies owned by wealthy Mexican investors who see economic opportunity in serving the U.S. market. Among the U.S. companies involved in maquiladora operations are General Electric, Whirlpool, Motorola, Honeywell, Bose, Mattel, and numerous other well-known companies.[6]

Not all of the maquiladoras affiliated with U.S. companies are directly owned. Some involve a complex subcontracting arrangement known as the *plan de albergue* (shelter plan). The U.S. company wishing to establish a maquiladora contracts with the U.S. branch of a company offering shelter services. The U.S. branch of the shelter operator then contracts with its Mexican branch, which handles the legal aspects of the enterprise and provides other services. The shelter plan arrangement enables U.S. companies to avoid legal involvement in Mexico while retaining most of the advantages of direct control, among them quality control and delivery specifications.[7] One of the more prominent shelter plan companies is Collectron International Management, Inc., which through its Mexican subsidiaries Sonitronies, S.A. de C.V., and Sonoros S Plan has helped more than 180 companies set up and operate maquiladoras. Under Collectron's shelter plan, the investment of the companies it assists is limited to machinery and equipment, materials, transfer of technology, and on-site plant management.[8] Services that Collectron and its Mexican subsidiaries provide include assistance in site selection, securing all required Mexican permits, interface with Mexican government agencies, assistance in complying with Mexican environmental requirements, recruiting the labor workforce and technical and managerial personnel, payroll processing and accounting services, and providing warehouse space.[9] Thus U.S. and other foreign-owned companies can enjoy all of the

[6] Maquila Portal, "100 Top Maquilas" at http://www.maquilaportal.com/cgi-bin/top100/top100.pl (last accessed October 30, 2009). The statistics were last updated on January 31, 2006.
[7] Altha J. Cravey, *Women and Work in Mexico's Maquiladoras* (Lanham, MD: Rowman & Littlefield Publishers, Inc., 1998), 78–79.
[8] Collectron International Management, Inc., "About Us" at http://www.play4brew.com/site/about.html (last accessed October 10, 2008).
[9] Collectron International Management, Inc., "Shelter Plan Services" at http://www.play4brew.com/site/shelter.html (last accessed October 10, 2008).

benefits of using maquiladoras to lower their production costs without the hassle of having to deal with local officials and agencies.

In the course of the years, maquiladoras have changed in other ways as well, with many of them hiring highly skilled technicians of various types, along with unskilled assembly-line workers. For example, Delphi Automotive Systems established a highly sophisticated research and development center in Ciudad Juárez that in time came to employ hundreds of highly skilled engineers and technicians.[10] By 2006, Delphi Corporation (the company shortened its name in 2002 to reflect diversification into components for appliances and electronics) had more than 60,000 employees at fifty-one maquiladora plants.[11]

Delphi's research and development center is typical of third-generation maquiladoras. First-generation maquiladora plants (which are the plants most social critics have in mind) are labor-intensive assembly operations employing unskilled workers, many of them young women, at wages at or near the lowest levels allowed by Mexico's minimum wage laws. Second-generation maquiladoras are oriented less toward assembly and more toward manufacturing processes. They employ more technicians and engineers and make use of robotics and automation. Third-generation maquiladoras focus on research, design, and development, relying on highly skilled employees such as highly specialized engineers and technicians.[12]

While a few maquiladoras are located in interior regions of the country, most are located close to the U.S.-Mexico border, which is to be expected because the Mexican government introduced the maquiladora program as part of the Border Industrialization Program (BIP). Cities with substantial numbers of maquiladoras include Tijuana in Baja California, Nogales in Sonora, Ciudad Juárez in Chihuahua, and Reynosa and Matamoros in Tamaulipas.[13]

[10] General Accounting Office, *Mexico's Maquiladora Decline*, 5–6.
[11] Maquila Portal, "100 Top Maquilas." All has not been smooth sailing for Delphi Corporation, however. In 2005 the company was forced to file for Chapter 11 bankruptcy and is undergoing reorganization.
[12] Collectron International Management, Inc., "The Maquiladora Program" at http://www.play4brew.com/site/maquiladora.html (last accessed October 9, 2008).
[13] General Accounting Office, *Mexico's Maquiladora Decline*, 12–14, and U.S. Consulate, Nogales, Mexico, "History and General Information" at http://nogales.usconsulate.gov/history.html (last accessed September 25, 2008).

As noted previously, maquiladoras are not the by-product of NAFTA, the free trade agreement U.S. President George H.W. Bush, Mexican President Carlos Salinas de Gortari, and Canadian Prime Minister Brian Mulroney signed on December 17, 1992 (though it did not go into effect until January 1, 1994, following approval by both houses of Congress with President Bill Clinton signing NAFTA into law on December 8, 1993.)[14] NAFTA did, however, have an impact on maquiladoras. It required the elimination by 2008 of tariffs and other barriers to trade between the United States and Mexico. It also required Mexico to modify certain provisions of the maquiladora program, among them the provision allowing duty-free imports of components from non-NAFTA countries. NAFTA also helped facilitate production sharing, whereby some of the parts are manufactured and assembled in the United States with other aspects of the assembly process, including in many cases, final assembly, occurring in Mexico.[15]

From January 1993 (a year before NAFTA went into effect) to October 2000, maquiladora production increased by 197 percent while overall manufacturing production in Mexico increased by only 58 percent. Maquiladora employment increased from 446,436 jobs in 1990 to 1,347,803 jobs in October 2000,[16] adding nearly 900,000 jobs to the Mexican economy and in time accounting for approximately 4 percent of total employment in Mexico and approximately 20 percent of employment in manufacturing.[17] More than 200,000 of the new jobs created were in the electronics industry, the largest maquiladora employer.[18] This robust growth, it should be added, was not solely the result of NAFTA. The booming U.S. economy during the 1990s

---

[14] U.S. President George H.W. Bush (who had been defeated in his reelection bid), Mexican President Carlos Salinas de Gortari, and Canadian Prime Minister Brian Mulroney signed the historic North American Free Trade Agreement (NAFTA) December 17, 1992. The U.S. House of Representatives approved NAFTA by a vote of 234–200 on November 17, 1993, with the Senate voting 60–38 for approval on November 20, 1993. President Bill Clinton signed NAFTA into law on December 8, 1993. The trade agreement took effect January 1, 1994 ("North American Free Trade Agreement [NAFTA]" at http://www.infoplease.com/ipa/A0104566.html [last accessed October 2, 2008]).

[15] General Accounting Office, *Mexico's Maquiladora Decline*, 6–7.

[16] *Ibid.*, 68.

[17] *Ibid*, 14.

[18] *Ibid.*, 15.

significantly increased consumer demand for products manufactured in maquiladoras. Another significant factor was the 1994 devaluation of the peso, which resulted in reduced labor costs because of a substantial reduction in dollar-denominated Mexican wages.[19] The continued depreciation of the peso throughout the remainder of the 1990s led to greater exports. However, this was a mixed blessing for the people of Mexico because the devaluation of the peso also resulted in a decline in real income, hurting both the poorest segments of the population and the emerging middle class.[20]

Prior to NAFTA, maquiladoras were limited to selling up to 50 percent of their previous year's exports in Mexico's domestic market. NAFTA increased the percentage of the previous year's export production that could be sold in Mexico's market. Most maquiladoras, however, continue to export the bulk of their production to the U.S. market.[21]

DECLINE . . .

Maquiladora employment continued to grow until October 2000. Then the roof fell in. From late 2000 to early 2002, nearly 300,000 maquiladora jobs disappeared, with some industries experiencing greater declines than others. The electronics industry experienced one of the greatest declines in maquiladora employment, losing more than 112,000 jobs in two years, a decline of 31 percent. The job losses in the electronics industry alone accounted for nearly 40 percent of the decline in maquiladora employment. Textiles and apparel also suffered steep decline, with employment levels falling by 26 percent. The decline in the automobile and auto parts sector was far less severe.

The decline was not equally spread across the towns and cities in which maquiladoras were located. Ciudad Juárez and Tijuana, the two largest border cities, both experienced significant declines in

---

[19] Federal Reserve Bank of Dallas, El Paso Branch, "The Maquiladora Industry in Historical Perspective," *Business Frontier*, Issue 4 (1998) at http://www.dallasfed.org/research/busfront/bus9804.html (last accessed September 25, 2008).

[20] M. Angeles Villareal, "U.S.-Mexico Economic Relations: Trends, Issues, and Implications," *Congressional Research Service* (May 25, 2005), CRS-13.

[21] Villarreal, "U.S.-Mexico Economic Relations," CRS-8.

maquiladora employment, accounting for more than half of the total jobs lost in the border region.[22] (The film *Maquilapolis*, which will be discussed in greater detail later in this chapter, documents the plight of workers who lost their jobs at a Sanyo plant in Tijuana.) Nogales, Sonora, experienced one of the sharpest declines in maquiladora employment, with 44 percent of workers employed by maquiladoras in Nogales losing their jobs.[23] Other areas were less drastically affected.

What accounted for the loss of jobs? While a cyclical downturn in the U.S. economy, which reduced the demand for goods produced in maquiladoras, accounted for some of the maquiladora job loss, far more significant were decisions by U.S. and other foreign-owned companies to shift production to China and other low-wage countries, either by direct investment or by outsourcing. This is reflected in U.S. import statistics during the period of decline. Mexico lost U.S. market share in 47 of 152 major U.S. import categories while China gained U.S. market share in 35 of these 47 import categories, among them toys, furniture, electrical household appliances, television and video equipment and parts, and apparel and textiles.[24] A study published in 2007 suggests that the major variables affecting the level of maquiladora employment include the level of U.S. industrial activity, real wage rates, the real exchange rate of the peso, and the number of maquiladora plants in operation.[25]

... AND RECOVERY

But then, just as suddenly as the period of decline set in, many maquiladoras bounced back. For some sectors, the period of decline was relatively brief. For example, the period of decline in the automobile and auto parts industry lasted less than a year before growth of employment resumed.[26] In other cases, recovery took two to three

---

[22] General Accounting Office, *Mexico's Maquiladora Decline*, 17–19.
[23] *Ibid*, 20.
[24] *Ibid.*, 27, 63–65.
[25] Jesús Cañas, Thomas M. Fullterton, Jr., and Wm. Doyle Smith, "Maquiladora Employment Dynamics in Nuevo Laredo," *Growth and Change*, 38:1 (March 2007), 23–38.
[26] *Ibid.*, 18–19.

years. By 2004, newspapers were carrying headlines such as "Mexico's Factories on the Mend,"[27] "Made in Maquilas – Again; A Stronger U.S. Economy and Cheaper Peso Bring Export Factories Back to Life,"[28] "Machine Sales Booming in Maquiladora Area,"[29] and "A Boom Along the Border." In the article with latter headline that ran in the *New York Times* with a Tijuana dateline, Elisabeth Malkin observed:

> Across Tijuana's vast industrial parks, the export assembly plants known as maquiladoras are thriving, posting giant 'help wanted' signs. In June, an industry group estimated that the Tijuana plants needed to fill some 15,000 jobs.... [T]he boom is being repeated all along the border.
>
> It is a sharp change. Three years ago, as American consumer demand shriveled and plants shut or moved to China, maquiladoras lost 280,000 jobs. In Tijuana, more than 60,000 jobs evaporated. But this year the tide is turning. Maquiladora exports rose 22.4 percent in June, driving a more general export surge for Mexico. The nation expects economic growth of 4 percent this year, the strongest since 2000.[30]

Malkin added, "Investment poured into Mexico after the North American Free Trade Agreement took hold in 1994.... But by 2001, the maquiladora industry was shocked to discover how vulnerable it was to swings of the American economy and to Asian competition."[31]

An upturn in the U.S. economy contributed the recovery of maquiladora industries in Mexico. There was far more to the story, however. Jorge Carillo, a researcher at *El Colegio de las Frontera Norte* in Tijuana, observes, "Those who stayed have had to restructure to diminish costs and raise competitiveness. They had to reduce the work force and do more with less. Factors like technology, innovation, and delivery are all critical. Now the ones who stayed are starting to grow."[32] (As will be noted in greater detail later in this chapter, downsizing, restructuring, and technological innovation in maquiladora industries parallels

---

[27] Tim Gaynor, "Mexico's Factories on the Mend," *Toronto Star*, June 13, 2004.
[28] Geri Smith, "Made in the Maquilas – Again; A Stronger U.S. Economy and Cheaper Peso Bring Export Factories Back to Life," *Business Week* 3896 (August 16, 2004), 45.
[29] Stephen Downer, "Machine Sales Booming in Maquiladora Area," *Plastics News*, 4 (December 2006), 17.
[30] Elisabeth Malkin, "A Boom Along the Border," *New York Times*, August 26, 2004.
[31] *Ibid.*
[32] Quoted in *ibid.*

what was happening in the U.S. industrial sector during the same period of time, changes that resulted in increased productivity with fewer workers.) Such being the case, it is not surprising that maquiladora employment has not returned to the October 2000 level; by 2008, employment was 1,191,250,[33] compared to 1,347,803 in October 2000.[34]

TRANSPORTATION COSTS

Transportation costs are a key factor in the economic equations that determine plant locations. Huge increases in energy costs resulting in much higher transportation costs changed the economic landscape with respect to plant location. By 2008, the cost of shipping a forty-foot container from Shanghai to the United States had risen to $8,000, compared with $3,000 just a few years earlier. To save on fuel costs, many of the huge ships that transport containers from Shanghai, Hong Kong, and other ports in Asia to the United States have reduced their top speed by nearly 20 percent, significantly slowing down shipping times.[35] In an article that ran in the *New York Times*, correspondent Larry Rohter notes, "Globe-spanning supply chains – Brazilian iron ore turned into Chinese steel used to make washing machines shipped to Long Beach, California, and then trucked to appliance stores in Chicago – makes less sense today than they did a few years ago."[36] With transportation costs going up and shipping times increasing, locating production facilities right across the border, rather than

---

[33] Maquila Portal, "Manufacture in Mexico" at http://maquilaportal.com/cgi-bin/public/index.pl (last accessed October 1, 2008).

[34] General Accounting Office, *Mexico's Maquiladora Decline*, 68.

[35] Larry Rohter, "Shipping Costs Start to Crimp Globalization," *New York Times*, August 3, 2008, Section A, 1. This also makes more attractive a return of production facilities to the United States to produce goods for the U.S. market. Rohter cites the example of Tesla Motors, a pioneer in electric-powered cars. When mapping out a production strategy for a luxury roadster for the U.S. market, the company planned to manufacture the 1,000 battery packs in Thailand, ship them to the United Kingdom for installation and then bring the mostly assembled cars to the United States. But the company changed its mind because of high transportation costs and instead decided to make the batteries and assemble the cars near its home base in California, eliminating 5,000 miles from the shipping bill for each vehicle.

[36] *Ibid.*

overseas, became more attractive. Cesar Lopez, president of the Tijuana Maquiladora Industry Export Association, observes, "It's not convenient to produce large items ... and weighty and bulky goods far [from market] on account of the transport costs."[37]

FAST DELIVERY

Maquiladoras also enjoy a competitive advantage in areas such as certain types of electronics in which fast delivery is important – a competitive advantage that increased as higher fuel costs resulted in greater shipping times from overseas suppliers. With many U.S. factories improving their efficiency and lowering their production costs by implementing just-in-time inventory control (rather than, as was traditionally done, warehousing large quantities of components for assembly and production), the proximity of maquiladoras has become even more important. Judith Valdés, a trade specialist at U.S. Commercial Service's office in Tijuana, observes, "Most of the manufacturing plants along the [Mexican side of the] border have no warehouses. Their production and supply is just-in-time. Production is going directly into trucks and being transported into the United States. This is one of the elements that make the border region so attractive."[38]

A NEW ERA

Competition from China and other Asian countries has forced many maquiladoras to shift away from the cheap, low-skilled assembly work that previously had been their mainstay toward higher value-added forms of production.[39] Federico Lepe, who served as the deputy secretary for foreign trade and investment in Jalisco, a western state that has emerged as Mexico's Silicon Valley, observes, "We needed to transform ourselves from being a perspiration industry to an inspiration industry."[40] The result has been a growth

---

[37] Quoted in Gaynor, "Mexico's Factories on the Mend."
[38] Quoted in Downer, "Machine Sales Booming in Maquiladora Area."
[39] "China Forces Mexico To Climb Value-Added Chain," *South China Morning Post*, 25 (January 2005), Business Post, 4.
[40] Quoted in Joseph Contreras, "Economy: What China Threat?; Mexico's Manufacturing Slump Was the Result of Its Own Problems, not Rising Competition from the East," *Newsweek International*, May 15, 2006.

of second and third-generation maquiladoras that employ greater numbers of engineers and highly skilled technicians. In an article entitled "Manufacturing in Sonora Goes High-Tech: Fuel Costs, China Worries Boost Border City in Sonora" that ran in the *Arizona Daily Star* on April 24, 2008, Gabriela Rico reports that the maquiladora industry has succeeded in attracting aerospace, medical, and military suppliers to Nogales. Among these are Arrow Electronics, Inc., which produces connector assemblies for commercial airplanes and military helicopters and tanks, and Edwards Vaccum Ltd., a British company specializing in high-performance vacuum pumps with 120 employees at its Sonora maquiladora, including twenty-three engineers earning between $15,000 and $38,000 a year.[41] Jesus Montoya, executive director of the Maquiladora Association of Sonora, notes that these high-tech jobs are the key to Nogales' success. "We don't need people who work only with their hands, but [also] with their heads," he observes. "The days of sewing dresses and handbags have disappeared."[42]

AN UNCERTAIN FUTURE

Yet the future is far from certain. There is an old saying that suggests that "when the United States sneezes, Latin America catches pneumonia." While the recession that started with 2008 international credit crisis has been difficult for the United States, it has been devastating for Mexico. In 2008, unemployment in Mexico rose to an all-time high,[43] a trend that continued in 2009, which brought even higher unemployment rates[44] as the economy continued to contract.[45] Though the government of Mexico no longer compiles separate employment statistics for maquiladoras, it is a fair assumption that maquiladora job losses account for a significant portion of

[41] Gabriela Rico, "Manufacturing in Sonora Goes High-Tech: Fuel Costs, China Worries Boost Border City in Sonora," *Arizona Daily Star*, April 24, 2008.

[42] Quoted in *ibid.*

[43] Ixel Yutzil González, "Unemployment in Mexico in 2008 Rose to an Historic High," at http://mexidata.info/id2164.html (last accessed October 30, 2009).

[44] Trading Economics, "Mexico Unemployment Rate" at http://www.tradingeconomics.com/Economics/Unemployment-rate.aspx?symbol=MXN (last accessed October 30, 2009).

[45] "The Mexican Economy: Following Closely in Its Neighbor's Footsteps" at http://www.wharton.universia.net/index.cfm?fa=viewArticle&id=1725&language=english (last accessed October 30, 2009).

rising unemployment rates. Job losses have been particularly severe in the northern states, where most maquiladoras are located – job losses that would have been even more severe had not a number of employers struck deals with unions to retain workers by cutting the hours they were able to work.[46]

The contraction of the U.S. economy, of course, was a major reason that maquiladoras, most of which serve the U.S. market, saw significant declines in employment. There is, however, more to the story. Even as world demand for consumer products declined, China was able to secure a larger piece of the shrinking pie by cutting prices – price reductions that were made possible by slashing the wages of the workers who produce these products,[47] many of whom are, as noted in Chapter 4, rural-to-urban migrants who suffer greatly from discrimination and harsh working conditions. China's larger piece of the shrinking pie is illustrated by the fact that during the first seven months of 2009, U.S. knit apparel imports from China increased by 10 percent while U.S. imports from Mexico and other Latin American countries plunged.[48]

In short, the wildly swinging changes in the level of maquiladora employment in recent years underscore a very basic fact of life for maquiladora workers: Job security is exceedingly difficult to attain. Indeed, for the vast majority of maquiladora workers, there is no such thing as job security.

NAFTA: SOME ADDITIONAL OBSERVATIONS

While the focus of this chapter is on maquiladoras rather than on NAFTA, some additional observations about NAFTA are in order before proceeding to address the question posed in the title of this chapter – namely, the question of whether maquiladoras involve exploitation, economic opportunity, or both.

On the American political scene, few issues have been as controversial – and continue to be as controversial – as NAFTA. In the second

---

[46] Recession Hurting Maquila Industry" at http://www.spislandbreeze.com/articles/recession-6041-reynosa-industry.html (last accessed October 30, 2009).

[47] David Barboza, "In Recession, China Solidifies Its Lead in Global Trade," *New York Times*, October 14, 2009, B1.

[48] *Ibid.*

television debate in 1992 between George H.W. Bush, Bill Clinton, and H. Ross Perot, the latter, who had grave reservations about NAFTA (which had not yet been adopted), warned of a "giant sucking sound going south" with U.S. jobs being siphoned off to factories located in Mexico.[49] That concern was shared by others, both before and after NAFTA redefined the economic landscape of North America. In a piece that ran in the *New York Times* December 13, 1987 (six years before NAFTA), John J. LaFalce, a Democratic member of Congress who represented the 32nd District of New York, stated, "Much of the blame for America's loss of critical manufacturing capacity must go to transnational firms that claim no allegiance to country or government. Rather, they fly a flag of convenience in their quest for market penetration and cost minimization." He added that by encouraging American manufacturers to invest in maquiladoras, "we are providing [American companies] with an incentive to become more competitive at the expense of our workers...."[50] Two decades later while competing for labor votes in the spirited contest for the 2008 Democratic nomination for president, Sen. Barack Obama accused Sen. Hillary Clinton of supporting NAFTA. (Sen. Clinton was First Lady when her husband, President Bill Clinton, signed NAFTA into law.) Sen. Clinton responded by claiming that she raised a "yellow caution flag" on NAFTA. Gerry McEntee, president of the American Federation of State, County, and Municipal Employees (AFSCME), supported her claim, reporting that the day that NAFTA was approved, she called him and said, "We lost."[51]

Labor union opposition to NAFTA is underscored in a 2001 statement by the United Auto Workers (UAW) entitled "NAFTA's Hidden Costs: Trade Agreement Results in Job Losses, Growing Inequality." The statement pulls no punches:

The North American Free Trade Agreement (NAFTA) eliminated 766,000 actual and potential U.S. jobs between 1994 and 2000 because of the rapid growth in the net U.S. export deficit with Mexico and Canada. The loss of

[49] "The 1992 Campaign; Transcript of 2d TV Debate Between Bush, Clinton and Perot," *New York Times*, October 16, 1992.
[50] John J. LaFalce, "Masquiladoras Cost American Jobs," *New York Times*, December 13, 1987.
[51] Katharine Q. Seelye, "Clinton Says She Raised 'Yellow Caution Flag' on NAFTA," *New York Times*, April 1, 2008.

these real and potential jobs is just the most visible tip of NAFTA's impact on the U.S. economy. In fact, NAFTA has also contributed to rising income inequality, suppressed real wages for production workers, weakened collective bargaining powers and ability to organize unions, and reduced fringe benefits.[52]

A statement issued by the Office of the United States Trade Representative in March 2008 paints a very different picture. Responding to the charge that NAFTA has cost U.S. jobs, the statement observes, "U.S. employment rose from 110.8 million people in 1993 to 137.6 million in 2007, an increase of 24 percent. The average unemployment rate was 5.1 percent in the period 1994–2007, compared to 7.1 percent during the period 1980–1993." As for the allegation that NAFTA has hurt America's manufacturing base, the document states, "U.S. manufacturing output rose by 58 percent between 1993 and 2006, as compared to 42 percent between 1980 and 1993. Manufacturing exports in 2007 reached an all time high with a value of $982 billion." In response to the allegation that NAFTA has suppressed U.S. wages, the document states, "U.S. business sector real hourly compensation rose by 1.5 percent each year between 1993 and 2007, for a total of 23.6 percent over the full period. During 1979–1993, the annual rate of real hourly compensation rose by 0.7 percent each year, or 11 percent over the full 14-year period."[53]

Two very different views. Which view most accurately depicts the impact of NAFTA on employment in the United States? To answer that question, we need to take a closer look at what has happened in the U.S. industrial sector in the last half-century. In the post-World War II years, the United States, which was the only major industrial country to survive the war without damage to its factories and infrastructure, was in the driver's seat. U.S. companies could pretty much do whatever they wished to do, as long as their domestic competitors did likewise. This resulted in practices such as pattern bargaining. When it came time to negotiate new labor contracts, unions would

---

[52] United Auto Workers, "NAFTA's Hidden Costs: Trade Agreement Results in Job Losses, Growing Inequality," *Region 8 Review* (July/August 2001) at http://www.uaw.org/solidarity/rnews/r8/01/riq2_2.html (last accessed October 2, 2008).

[53] Office of the United States Trade Representative, *NAFTA – Myth vs. Facts* (March 2008) at http://www.ustr.gov/assets/Document_Library/Fact_Sheets/2008/asset_upload_file855_14540.pdf (last accessed October 3, 2008).

target one company in a particular industrial sector, with the implicit understanding that whatever the targeted company agreed to in terms of compensation would be accepted as the pattern for the new labor agreement by other companies in that sector. For example, if the United Auto Workers (UAW) targeted Ford, it was understood that General Motors and Chrysler would accept whatever Ford agreed to do. The advantage of this implicit understanding was that if the union decided that it was necessary to go on strike to get what it wanted from the targeted company, production would continue without interruption at the other companies in that particular sector. To maintain as much equity as possible, unions rotated targeted companies from contract to contract. Thus, if Ford was the targeted company one year, it would be General Motors or Chrysler the next time around, with the remaining company being targeted the time after that.[54]

This somewhat cozy arrangement facilitated increases in compensation levels during the post-World War II years. However, it did little to encourage increases in productivity. As long as the playing field was level with respect to U.S. companies in a particular industrial sector, increasing productivity was not high on the list of priorities for either labor or management. As a result, growth in productivity stagnated. From 1909 until 1947, productivity in the private business sector increased an average of 2.5 percent a year. The period from 1947 to 1965 was even better, with productivity increasing an average of 3 percent a year. But then growth in productivity slowed down substantially. From 1965 to 1973, productivity in the private business sector increased only an average of 2.1 percent a year. The slowdown in productivity growth was even greater between 1973 and 1978 with productivity increasing only 1.6 percent a year. In 1978, the increase in productivity was only 1.1 percent.[55]

Increases in compensation levels combined with slowdown in the growth of productivity set the stage for hard times in the U.S. industrial sector in the late 1970s and the 1980s when European and

---

[54] The UAW broke with the tradition of pattern bargaining in 2005 when it agreed to help Ford and General Motors reduce health benefit costs by shifting some costs to workers but refused to grant Chrysler the same deal (Nick Bunkley, "U.A.W. Opens Contract Talks with Detroit, *New York Times*, 21 July 2007).

[55] William Serrin, "Decline in Productivity in U.S. Spurs Intense Debate and Study," *New York Times*, October 29, 1979.

Japanese companies, which by then had recovered from the devastation of World War II and had built modern factories that were far more efficient than the older factories still being used in the United States, started flooding the U.S. market with high-quality products at prices U.S. producers were hard-pressed to meet, resulting in loss of market share for U.S. producers.

Down but not out, U.S. producers responded by implementing measures to improve productivity. These included enhancing employees' skills by improving training programs, reducing warehousing costs by adopting computer-monitored just-in-time inventory control systems that enabled parts to be delivered to assembly plants as needed, investing in laser-guided fabricating machines that produced higher-quality parts in less time, and expanding the use of robots for welding, painting, and many other tasks. Changes in productivity were quite dramatic. After languishing at an average annual rate of increase of 1.8 percent from 1987 to 1990, average annual productivity gains in the manufacturing sector shot up to 3.4 percent from 1990 to 1995 and to an even more robust 4.6 percent for 1995 before easing a bit to 3.7 percent for 2000 to 2007.[56] This robust growth in productivity is reflected by the fact that in 2007, American workers were the most productive in the world (though China and much of the rest of Asia were starting to catch up, with productivity gains exceeding those of American workers).[57] Because of significant growth in productivity, labor costs per unit of production in the United States decreased by 0.5 percent, even as hourly compensation in manufacturing increased by 3.5 percent. [58]

---

[56] U.S. Department of Labor Bureau of Labor Statistics, "Productivity and Costs: Productivity Change in the Manufacturing Sector, 1987–2007" at http://www.bls.gov/lpc/prodybar.htm (last accessed October 3, 2008).

[57] Reuters, "U.S. Leads Productivity Ranking; China Gains," *New York Times*, September 4, 2007.

[58] U.S. Department of Labor Bureau of Labor Statistics, "International Comparisons of Manufacturing Productivity and Unit Labor Cost Trends, 2007" at http://www.bls.gov/news.release/prod4.nro.htm (last accessed October 3, 2008). Contrary to what many outside the business world assume to be the case, wage and salary levels, while having an impact on production costs, are not absolutely determinative. The key factor is labor costs per unit of production, which are in substantial measure determined by productivity. For example, if workers in Factory A are paid twice as much as workers in Factory B but are three times as productive as workers in Factory B, the labor costs per unit of production are lower for Factory A than for Factory B.

But these increases in productivity came with a cost. When manufacturers discovered that they could produce more with fewer workers, jobs began to disappear. In an interview published in the *New York Times* in 2005, Diane C. Swonk, chief economist at Mesirow Financial in Chicago, observed:

> You can more than explain the loss of jobs in manufacturing by increased productivity growth, not outsourcing or anything else.... We're producing a record number of vehicles in this country with fewer people. We've got foreign producers investing in the U.S. successfully, but with fewer people per vehicle than their Detroit-based counterparts.... The only way we can expect to see [General Motors and other U.S. auto companies] survive is to continue to gain productivity growth, which means a loss of jobs."[59]

And indeed the loss of jobs in the U.S. manufacturing sector was substantial. As reported by the the U.S. Department of Labor Bureau of Labor Statistics, employment in manufacturing declined from 18,932,000 in 1978 to 13,884,000 in 2007 – a loss of more than 5 million manufacturing jobs over a period of 30 years.[60]

The decline in employment in manufacturing, it might be added, began several years before NAFTA. In the fourteen years before NAFTA took effect, more than 2 million manufacturing jobs disappeared – an average of 143, 867 jobs a year. The fourteen years after NAFTA took effect saw the loss of nearly 3 million jobs – an average of 206,427 jobs a year.[61] Labor leaders are quick to blame NAFTA for the greater job loss after the trade agreement was implemented. However, the increase in the number of jobs lost in manufacturing roughly coincides with greater increases in productivity. Though often overlooked, there is a link, as Swonk correctly notes, between productivity gains and job loss in the manufacturing sector. If it is possible to produce more with fewer workers, it should surprise no one that the result is a loss of jobs if total sales do not increase commensurate with increases in productivity – something it has been

---

[59] Quoted by William J. Holstein in "Job Insecurity from the Chief Down," *New York Times*, March 27, 2005.

[60] U.S. Department of Labor Bureau of Labor Statistics, "Employment, Hours, and Earnings from the Current Employment Statistics Survey" at http://data.bls.gov/PDQ/servlet/SurveyOutputSersvlet (last accessed October 4, 2008).

[61] *Ibid.*

difficult for U.S. companies to accomplish in an intensely competitive global economy.

Swonk overstates the case, though, when she suggests that job losses in the manufacturing sector can be attributed in their entirety to increases in productivity.[62] Some of the job losses result from decisions by U.S. manufacturers to shift production facilities to Mexico or overseas. Maytag is a case in point. For years, Maytag was the largest employer in Galesburg, Illinois, a prairie town in western Illinois that was the birthplace of poet and author Carl Sandburg, and some years earlier – on October 7, 1858, to be exact – was the site of the fifth Lincoln-Douglas Debate. The sprawling Maytag plant in Galesburg made refrigerators. The company first threatened to leave Galesburg in 1994, the year NAFTA came into effect. In an effort to keep the plant in Galesburg, the state of Illinois gave Maytag $7.5 million in grants and loans for training and improvements. The city increased its sales tax by one-quarter percent, raising $3 million to assist Maytag. The machinists' union local representing Maytag workers accepted concessions the company said it needed to remain competitive. These included more mandatory overtime and a stricter policy on sick days.[63]

All of this was for naught. In 2002, Maytag announced plans to close its Galesburg plant, where wages at that time averaged $15.14

---

[62] A contrasting view is stated by Robert E. Scott, a senior international economist with the Economic Policy Institute in Washington. He argues, "Some have mistakenly blamed productivity growth or slow demand for manufactured goods for manufacturing job losses in Pennsylvania and nationally, arguing that the sector's decline is inevitable. This is wrong. Manufacturing has always enjoyed fast productivity growth, and demand for its goods remains strong. What has changed in the past decade is that a much larger share of goods purchased by U.S. consumers are now imported, and jobs displaced by these imports have not been replaced by export-supported jobs (Robert E. Scott, "Pennsylvania Stagnation: Is Nafta the Culprit?" *New York Times*, April 15, 2008). While Swonk is mistaken in suggesting that the loss of manufacturing jobs can be explained in its entirety by increases in productivity, Scott is mistaken in suggesting that productivity growth is not a factor. If because of productivity growth, fewer workers can produce more of whatever is being produced, it stands to reason that productivity increases will result in the loss of manufacturing jobs unless sales can increase commensurate with productivity gains. Scott is also mistaken in suggesting that manufacturing has always enjoyed fast productivity growth. The facts suggest otherwise, particularly with respect to the late 1960s and the 1970s.

[63] Steven Greenhouse, "City Feels Early Effects of Plant Closing in 2004," *New York Times*, December 26, 2002.

an hour, and shift refrigerator production to its plant in Reynosa, Mexico, where they would pay an average wage of approximately $2 an hour.[64] Two years later, the company closed the Galesburg plant, where Maytag had been making refrigerators for more than fifty years, leaving its 1,600 employees without jobs.[65] Among those losing their jobs was John Ester, who had worked in the huge factory for twenty-six years (to whom reference was made in the prologue to this volume). At the time that plans to close the plant were announced in 2002, William Beer, president of Maytag's appliance division, stated, "We deeply regret that we couldn't identify a cost-effective solution that would allow us to continue long-term production of refrigerators in Galesburg." He added, "Maytag's plans are designed to produce refrigerators more economically and therefore more profitably. [The company conducted] a study of competitive business strategy, and we don't believe it is possible for the production of side-by-side and top-mount refrigerators in Galesburg to become competitively viable."[66]

Maytag executives refused to answer questions about whether the Galesburg plant was profitable, leading many in the community to conclude that it was not losing money. Dave Brevard, vice president of the machinists' local that represented Maytag workers, commented, "It's not that Maytag can't still make money in the United States, it's that they can't make enough money.... It's all about corporate greed."[67]

The experience of Maytag employees in Galesburg, Illinois, is by no means unique. In a piece entitled "Free Trade Accord at Age

[64] *Ibid.*

[65] Timothy Egan, "Anger over Tax Cuts as Jobs Leave Towns," *New York Times*, October 20, 2004.

[66] Quoted in Greenhouse, "City Feels Early Effects of Plant Closing in 2004."

[67] Quoted in *ibid*. In the spring of 2006, Whirlpool acquired Maytag. Less than six weeks after acquiring Maytag, Whirlpool announced plans to eliminate 4,500 jobs of a workforce of 80,000 with the cuts partially offset by the addition of 1,500 jobs at two Ohio plants (Associated Press, "Whirlpool to Eliminate Jobs of 4,500," May 11, 2006). Facilities that Whirlpool shut down include the former Maytag headquarters and production facilities in Newton, Iowa, which is where Fred L. Maytag founded the company that bore his name more than a century ago (Louis Uchitelle, "Is There (Middle Class) Life after Maytag?" *New York Times*, August 26, 2007). Whirlpool continues to operate several plants in Mexico, where in 2006 it was the nineteenth largest maquiladora employer (Maquila Portal, "100 Top Maquilas").

10: The Growing Pains Are Clear" that ran in the *New York Times* as the tenth anniversary of NAFTA approached, Elizabeth Becker, Clifford Krauss, and Tim Weiner report the following with respect to Goshen, Indiana:

Indiana, like the rest of the United States, has enjoyed a growth of exports under NAFTA. But Goshen is also like thousands of towns across the nation that have seen jobs and health benefits disappear with the accord.... Half of Elkhart County [in which Goshen is located] depends on manufacturing. Once dozens of locally owned factories across the state churned out parts for all sorts of products, electronics, pharmaceuticals, furniture, pianos, and especially the automotive industry. Even before NAFTA those jobs were facing growing pressure from emerging low-wage competitors abroad. Since NAFTA took hold, hundreds more jobs have gone south to Mexico, transplanted by big corporations that bought out local firms.[68]

THE ETHICS OF PLANT RELOCATION

We leave to others the question of how much of the loss of manufacturing jobs in the United States can be attributed to NAFTA. Suffice it to say that NAFTA has been a factor though by no means the only factor. Our focus here is on the ethical dimensions of plant relocation. In Chapter 2, we suggested that business organizations and all other organizations and individuals have concentric circles of responsibility, with greater responsibilities to near neighbors than to distant neighbors. The basic argument here is that because some rights, including rights of entitlement, are relational in nature – that is, they stem from contractual relationships or from other relationships such as the employer-employee relationship – the responsibilities related to these rights are greater with respect to the other parties involved in these relationships. Applied more specifically to the world of business, this means that the responsibility of business to provide employment is greater with respect to current employees than it is with respect to those with whom the company does not have, and never has had, a business relationship. Thus, it is plausible to argue that Maytag, prior to closing its plant in Galesburg, Illinois, had a greater

[68] Elizabeth Becker, Clifford Krauss, and Tim Weiner, "Free Trade Accord at Age 10: The Growing Pains Are Clear," *New York Times*, December 27, 2003.

obligation to maintain the jobs of actual employees then working in the Galesburg plant, than to provide jobs for potential employees in Reynosa, Mexico, or elsewhere.

This is, however, not an obligation without limits. Here, as elsewhere, the Kantian dictum that the ought implies the can comes into play. If the economic realities are such that it is not feasible for a company to continue operating a high-cost plant, the obligation to provide continued employment for those working at that plant no longer applies, though there might well be ancillary obligations such as providing outplacement services if the plant is closed. In such situations, companies would be well-advised to make financial information available to their employees to provide documentation of the economic factors that necessitate closing a plant and shifting production elsewhere. Transparency, something that Maytag failed to provide, is very important in these situations.

We stop short of suggesting that companies ought to keep plants open as long as they are not losing money. As noted in Chapter 3, business organizations have responsibilities, not just to employees, but also to shareholders and other investors (as well as to other constituencies). This means that companies need to maintain a sufficient level of profitability to provide a fair return to investors, a consideration that is driven not just by ethical considerations but also by market realities related to raising the capital needed for investing in research and development, new equipment and other areas essential to maintaining the viability of the company. Thus, in some situations there might well be ethically acceptable reasons for shifting production to another venue, even if an existing plant is not losing money. However, we are quick to add that these reasons come into play only after current employees are given every opportunity, and assisted in every way possible, to improve productivity to the level that the existing facility is sufficiently profitable to justify continuing its operation.

What we have argued in the preceding paragraph does not translate into a rationale for maximizing profits. As noted in Chapter 3, maintaining profitability ought to be viewed as a means to other ends, not as the ultimate goal or objective. The key here is maintaining appropriate levels of profitability, rather than simply trying to make as much money as possible. There is a difference between corporate responsibility and corporate greed. Maintaining appropriate levels of profitability is consistent with – indeed, is part of – the former but at odds with the latter. We recognize that there might be differences of opinion as to how appropriate levels of profitability might be defined. A plausible working definition, however, is to suggest that appropriate levels of profitability are those levels of profitability that must be maintained if a company is to serve effectively the various constituencies noted in Chapter 3 – shareholders and other investors, customers, employees, suppliers, and the communities in which company-owned facilities are located.

In discussions of the ethics of relocating plants to low-wage areas, it is very easy to focus on just one of the constituent groups, be it employees or shareholders and other investors, while overlooking other constituent groups such as consumers, who can benefit from lower prices for refrigerators and other consumer goods – lower prices that are made possible by plant relocation that reduces production costs. This, of course, ought not be the only factor considered. It is, however, yet another factor to weigh in the balance.[69] It might be added that, as noted previously, NAFTA has helped facilitate production sharing, whereby some of the parts are manufactured and assembled in the United States with other aspects of the assembly process, including in many cases, final assembly, occurring in Mexico. Thus, there are some advantages to U.S. workers if companies forced by economic factors to relocate production facilities move them to Mexico, rather than overseas, because Mexico's proximity facilitates production sharing, thus retaining for U.S. workers at least some of the jobs related to the production of refrigerators, automobiles, or whatever else is being produced. Maquiladoras also provide an export market for U.S. companies. Fernando Sandoval of Bordertec, Inc., and a consultant for

---

[69] In the case of plant relocation to Mexico or Canada, there are also tax advantages as a result of NAFTA and CFTA (the U.S.-Canada Free Trade Agreement). The Office of the United States Trade Representative estimates that had NAFTA and CFTA not been in effect, duties paid on 1999 U.S. imports would have been $14.2 billion higher, which would have been passed on to U.S. consumers in the form of higher prices. Not paying duties on imports covered by these trade agreement breaks down to a price reduction of $210 for an average household of four (Office of the United States Trade Representative, *NAFTA – An Annual Tax Cut and Income Gain for American Families* [March 2008] at http://www.ustr.gov/ assets/Document_Library/Fact_Sheets/2008/asset_upload_file855_14540.pdf [last accessed October 3, 2008]).

the U.S. Department of Commerce estimated that prior to the beginning of the 2008 recession, the 243 maquiladoras in Sonora alone imported from the United States approximately $2 billion worth of components and raw materials each year.[70]

To summarize, relocating production facilities to low-wage countries simply as a means of maximizing profits cannot be justified on moral grounds. However, in some situations, market conditions might necessitate plant relocation in order to maintain financial viability and serve customers effectively in an intensely competitive global economy. Companies contemplating such courses of action, though, owe it to their employees to explore possibilities for maintaining economic viability without relocating production facilities, leaving relocation only as the last resort after everything else has failed. Moreover, when relocation ends up being the only viable option, companies owe it to their employees to provide them with ample information to make it clear that relocation is the only viable option. And it is incumbent on companies to provide outplacement services and other assistance to employees who lose their jobs as a result of a plant closing down.

EXPLOITATION

We return to the question posed in the title of this chapter, namely, the question of whether maquiladoras provide economic opportunities for Mexican workers or exploit them – or some combination of both. As noted earlier in this chapter, maquiladoras have provided more than a million jobs for Mexican workers. Thus, it is relatively easy to argue that maquiladoras provide economic opportunities for Mexican workers. Accordingly, it is not a matter to which we need to devote additional attention.

The question of whether exploitation occurs, however, is a more difficult matter. Before looking at that question in greater detail, we need to be as precise as possible in defining what we mean by exploitation. As noted in Chapter 3, the second formulation of Immanuel Kant's categorical imperative provides a useful starting point for addressing a wide range of ethical issues, including those

---

[70] Quoted in Joe Pangburn, "Exports to Mexico's Maquiladoras Can Provide a Large profit Bump to Bottom Line," *Inside Tucson Business*, September 12, 2008.

related to globalization. In the *Groundwork of the Metaphysic of Morals*, Kant admonishes, "For, all rational beings stand under the *law* that each of them is to treat himself and all others *never merely as means* but always *at the same time as ends in themselves*."[71] Using this precept as a reference point, we can define exploitation as treating other people merely as means to accomplish whatever we might be attempting to accomplish, without at the same time also treating them as ends in themselves. While discussions of exploitation often focus on the way that the less advantaged members of society are treated – and appropriately so, for they are often the victims of exploitation – exploitation can involve treating anyone merely as a means, rather than as an end. For example, it is plausible to argue that companies that pay their employees substantial salaries but expect them to work huge amounts of overtime to the detriment of family and the health and well-being of the employees themselves and then dump them if downsizing is financially advantageous to the company that is exploiting their employees.

Our concern here, however, is primarily with the low-wage employees who make up the bulk of the workforce of many maquiladoras. Are they being exploited? There is substantial evidence that suggests that in many cases they are.

A documentary by filmmakers Vicki Funari and Sergio de la Torre entitled *Maquilapolis* (the title means "City of Factories") that premiered on PBS October 10, 2006, tells the story of maquiladora workers in Tijuana, located just across the border from San Diego. Playing central roles in the film are two people adversely affected by maquiladoras – Carmen Durán and Lourdes Luján – who, armed with cameras, provided an inside look at the world of maquiladoras. Durán, a single mother of three, earned just $6 a day working the graveyard shift at the Sanyo factory in Tijuana – significantly less than the $11 a day touted by the maquiladora system's promoters. The $6 a day was not enough to get decent housing for her family. They were forced to live in a dirt-floor shack built of discarded garage doors brought across the border from San Diego. The shack is located in a part of the city where sewage and frayed electric wires run down the middle

---

[71] Immanuel Kant, *Groundwork of the Metaphysic of Morals*, tr. Mary Gregor (Cambridge, UK: Cambridge University Press, 1998), 41 (4:433).

of streets, notwithstanding the government's promises to provide municipal services. With no other employment options, she stayed on at the factory for six years despite the harsh conditions – harsh conditions that she believes caused the kidney problems and anemia from which she suffers. Then Sanyo decided to move production to Indonesia, and Durán and her coworkers lost their jobs when the company shut down its Tijuana plant. The situation was made worse by the fact that the company reneged on the severance pay required by Mexican law. Angered by this betrayal, Durán, joined by coworkers who rallied to her cause, filed a claim with the labor board.[72]

Luján's situation is even more precarious. She lives in a part of Tijuana that not only has ordinary sewage running down the streets but also a toxic mixture of chemicals from factories on the mesa above their homes. The factories take advantage of every rainfall, however slight, to send an extra torrent of chemical-laden water down through the neighborhood. Not surprisingly, those living in the neighborhood experience an epidemic of skin rashes, respiratory problems, birth defects, and other health problems. Like Durán, Luján decides to take action. She helps organize the Chilpancingo Collective for Environmental Justice to fight for a cleanup of the environmental problems plaguing her neighborhood, including a toxic waste dump left behind by a departing battery-recycling factory.[73]

Maquilapolis, however, is not just a film about human rights abuses. Ultimately *Maquilapolis* is a story of triumph, even though it is not complete success. Durán and her coworkers win their case. The labor board forces Sanyo to give their former employees severance pay, which in Durán's case amounts to $2,500 – enough to put a floor under the feet of her children though she is still left without a job. Luján and the Chilpancingo Collective for Environmental Justice succeed in forcing both the U.S. and Mexican governments to recognize the need for environmental cleanup and to begin creating an environmental cleanup fund, though the film ends with uncertainty as to whether that will actually materialize.[74]

---

[72] "Maquilapolis: About the Film" at http://www.pbs.org/pov/pov2006/maquilapolis/about.html (last accessed September 26, 2008).
[73] *Ibid.*
[74] "Maquilapolis: About the Film."

Are the hardships and human rights abuses suffered by Durán and Luján unique experiences? Unfortunately they are not. In an article that ran in *Tucson Weekly*, J.E. Rally paints the following picture:

On the parched hills of Nogales, Sonora, live the recipients of the maquila industry's supposed $29-billion-a-year prosperity. In Colonia Los Encinos, a community of some 2,000 makeshift shelters, Yolanda Estrada and her extended family won electricity and intermittent running water after a squatter's sit-in grabbed headlines and then official attention. [Estrada and her extended family] share a cramped three-room palette and cardboard house...."[75]

In an article with the headline "Chasing Mexico's Dream Into Squalor" published in the *New York Times*, Ginger Thomson reports:

All along the border, the land, the water and the air are thick with industrial and human waste. The National Water Commission reports that the towns and cities, strapped for funds, can adequately treat less than 35 percent of the sewage generated daily. About 12 percent of the people living on the border have no reliable access to clean water. Nearly a third live in homes that are not connected to sewage systems. Only about half the streets are paved.[76]

Thomson describes the experiences of Nora Lydia Urias Pérez, a twenty-nine-year-old single mother who left her home in Veracruz, where she was struggling to pay for the basic necessities for her daughter and herself on the $5 a day she was able to earn working in seasonal agricultural jobs, to go to Nogales, where she hoped to find a job that paid more. Within a week after arriving in Nogales, she found a job in a maquiladora making Swingline staplers, a job that paid nearly $10 a day. Finding a place to live, however, was difficult. She considered sharing an apartment with ten others but decided instead to move to a shantytown outside of Nogales. Thomson continues:

With only a pocketknife and their strong arms, she and her father cleared the brush and boulders from a small patch of land in the tumbledown barrio. All around them were hundreds of dwellings in various stages of completion. The best ones, usually inhabited by families who had worked long enough

[75] J.E. Rally, "The Allure of Nogales' Maquilas after the Peso Crash," *Tucson Weekly*, December 5, 1996.
[76] Ginger Thompson, "Chasing Mexico's Dream Into Squalor," *New York Times*, February 11, 2001.

to save money for conventional building materials, were simple structures with walls of concrete block and tin roofs. The newest arrivals built flimsier homes, patched together from crates, old tires, and cardboard. None of the dwellings had running water. None were connected to city sewage lines. Hundreds of improvised electricity wires crisscrossed the dirt roads. The air was filled with the smells of human waste and burning garbage.[77]

Companies operating maquiladoras are quick to point out that the wages they pay are in many cases two to three times higher than the minimum wage levels required by Mexican law. However, the mandated minimum wage levels are so low that it is impossible for minimum-wage employees to support a family. Elias Islas, who because of his excellent English was able to get a better-paying job driving trucks for a maquiladora, observes that it takes six minimum-wage incomes to support one Nogales household. All four of Urias Pérez's children went to work for maquiladoras.[78] Compensation levels for maquiladora employees remain low. In September of 2008, the average hourly wage for direct labor (those working on assembly lines and holding other similar jobs) was $1.98 while technicians were paid somewhat better, receiving $5.50 an hour.[79]

ENVIRONMENTAL HAZARDS

Levels of compensation at many maquiladoras are not the only concern. Another problem is exposure to toxic substances in the workplace. Elizabeth Grossman, who has written several books and articles on environmental issues, notes that maquiladora workers in electronics industries are exposed to lead, which is highly toxic to the nervous system and kidneys, plastics that contain brominated flame retardants, which accumulate in fat cells and interfere with the endocrine system and lead to neurological problems, and adhesives that contain aldehydes, which are highly toxic compounds used in pesticides, and other toxic substances.[80] A study by Catalina Denman of *El Colegio*

---

[77] *Ibid.*
[78] *Ibid.*
[79] Maquila Portal, "Maquila Census September 2008" at http://www.maquilaportal. com/cgi-bin/public/index.pl (last accessed October 13, 2008).
[80] Point of View, "Wasting Away: An Interview with Elizabeth Grossman" at http:// www.pbs.org/pov/pov2006/maquilapolis/special_wasting.html (accessed October 8, 2008).

de Sonora in Hermosillo, Sonora, indicates that the chemical exposure and physical demands to which pregnant women were subjected
in maquiladoras led to a 14 percent incidence of low-birth-weight
babies, a rate three times higher than that of the control group of
pregnant women who worked in service occupations.[81] Some maquiladora employers reportedly deal with this problem by firing women
who are pregnant. In some cases, managers request medical exams
for female job applicants to determine if they are pregnant.[82]

The incidence of nonfatal occupational injuries and illnesses
among maquiladora workers is substantially higher than that of U.S.
workers. Infant mortality and age-adjusted mortality rates on the
Mexican side of the border, including mortality rates for cancer, are
not only higher than those in the United States but higher than those
for Mexico as a whole. Differences are even greater for the incidence
of infectious diseases such as tuberculosis, hepatitis, and typhoid
fever.[83]

DISCRIMINATION AND VIOLENCE DIRECTED
TOWARD WOMEN

Though the maquiladora program was introduced by the Mexican
government to reduce male unemployment after termination of the
bracero program, maquiladora employers rather quickly showed
a preference for hiring female workers, many of them still in their
teens, who, managers believed, would be more compliant and more

---

[81] Reported by Altha J. Cravey in *Women and Work in Mexico's Maquiladoras* (Lanham,
MD: Rowman & Littlefield Publishers, Inc., 1998), 97.

[82] Cirila Quintero-Ramírez, "The North American Free Trade Agreement and
Women," *International Feminist Journal of Politics*, 4:2 (August 2002), 252.

[83] R. Scott Frey, "The Transfer of Core-Based Hazardous Production Processes to the
Export Processing Zones of the Periphery: The Maquiladora Centers of Northern
Mexico," *Journal of World-Systems Research*, 9:2 (Summer 2003), 331. See also
Genoveva Buelna and Rumana Riffat, "Preliminary Environmental Monitoring of
Water Quality in the Rio Grande in the Laredo-Nuevo Laredo Region," *Journal
of Environmental Science and Health*, 42 (2007), 1379–1390. The study conducted
by Buelna and Riffat detected levels of oil and grease in all of the river samples
that exceeded the limits established by the government of Mexico. The study also
found concentrations of aluminum above the permissible levels of drinking water.
Concentrations of other elements for which they tested were within permissible
levels.

willing to work long hours doing tedious work for minimal compensation. In the 1970s, female workers accounted for nearly 100 percent of the maquiladora workforce. But in the 1980s and 1990s, that began to change, with the percentage of women in the workforce dropping to 55.2 percent by 2000. In part, this was because the new generations of maquiladoras require workers with training and skills that many women do not have because of gender biases in education.[84] Cirila Quntero-Ramírez, who is affiliated with El Colegio de la Frontera Norte in Tijuana, notes:

[T]he decline in female workers employed in maquiladoras may also be the result of continuing discriminatory practices [in the workplace]. For example, women are concentrated in assembly and their presence in more advanced manufacturing processes is informally prohibited."[85]

Feminist scholars and activists have been very concerned about the plight of women in maquiladoras, in particular, and in Mexican society, in general – and appropriately so, for women have been victims of sexual harassment and job discrimination in the workplace and victims of violence, including widespread domestic violence, outside the workplace. Several hundred young women have been murdered in the Ciudad Juárez area, a significant number of them employees of maquiladoras.[86] In an article entitled "Murder, Mystery and Mistreatment in Mexican Maquiladoras" published in *Women & Environments* in 2005, Allison Moffatt, who teaches at the University of Western Ontario, notes:

Since many women working in the maquila factories cannot afford to live in Juárez, they live in shanty towns on the outskirts of the city. Unfortunately, these shanty towns have no streetlights and therefore they become incredibly dark and unsafe at night. The only mode of transportation for the women workers of the maquiladoras are buses, one at the beginning of the shift and one at the end. The bus, at the end of the shift, drops women off in their

---

[84] Quintero-Ramíez, "The North American Free Trade Agreement and Women," 249–250.
[85] *Ibid.*
[86] Amnesty International, "Mexico: Ten Years of Intolerable Crimes against Women in Ciudad Juárez and Chihuahua Must End Now" (August 11, 2003) at http://www.amnesty.org/en/library/asset/AMR41/033/2003/en/dom-AMR410332003en.html (last accessed September 25, 2008).

shanty towns at approximately midnight, leaving them to risk their lives, walking the unlit streets alone.[87]

Amnesty International reports that almost one in four women in Mexico have suffered physical and/or sexual violence at the hands of an intimate partner.[88] In a publication entitled *Women's Struggle for Justice and Safety: Violence in the Family in Mexico*, Amnesty International states that though violence against women is widespread, "[f]ew cases of violence against women are reported, fewer still result in the prosecution or conviction of those responsible or restitution for victims."[89] In a publication entitled *Mexico – Laws Without Justice: Human Rights Violations and Impunity in the Public Security and Criminal Justice System*, Amnesty International charges that Mexican authorities have been exceedingly negligent in dealing with the perpetrators of these and other crimes.[90] Virtually all of the murders in the Ciudad Juárez area remain unsolved.

The *Comisión Nacional de los Derechos Humanos* (CNDH), which is Mexico's national commission on human rights, is by and large ineffective in dealing with these and other human rights issues in Mexico. In a report assessing CNDH, Human Rights Watch observes, "The CNDH routinely abandons the human rights cases it documents

---

[87] Allison Moffatt, "Murder, Mystery and Mistreatment in Mexican Maquiladoras: It Is Never Too Late To Make a Difference," *Women & Environments* (Spring/Summer 2005), 20.

[88] Amnesty International, "Facts and Figures – Mexico: Women's Struggle for Safety and Justice" (August 1, 2008) at http://www.amnesty.org/en/for-media/press-releases/facts-and-figures-mexico-women (last accessed September 25, 2008). Though women comprise a significant portion of the maquiladora workforce, Leslie C. Gates reports in "The Strategic Uses of Gender in Household Negotiations: Women Workers on Mexico's Northern Border," *Bulletin of Latin American Research* 21:4 (2002) that employment does not always increase women's power in the household.

[89] Amnesty International, *Women's Struggle for Justice and Safety: Violence in the Family in Mexico* (August 2008), 5.

[90] Amnesty International, *Mexico – Laws Without Justice: Human Rights Violations and Impunity in the Public Security and Criminal Justice System* at http://www.amnesty.org/en/library/asset/AMR41/002/2007/en/dom-AMR410022007en.html (last accessed September 25, 2008). See also, U.S. Department of State Office of the Coordinator for International Women's Issues, "Director Denounces Gender-Based Violence and Recognizes Mexico's International Women of Courage" (July 2008) at http://www.state.gov/g/wi/archives/108130.htm (last accessed September 25, 2008).

before they are resolved. After documenting violations and issuing recommendations for redressing them, CNDH officials choose not to monitor implementation of these recommendations to ensure the abuses are remedied."[91]

LABOR UNIONS

Organizing democratic unions to represent maquiladora workers has proven to be very difficult. A number of maquiladora employers have signed labor agreements with the Confederación de Trabajadores de México (CMT), the largest confederation of labor unions in Mexico. Many regard CMT as little more than a "company union" that protects maquiladora employers from other unions and grassroots organizing. Some managers refer to these agreements as "desk drawer" contracts because they are often put in a desk drawer and forgotten.[92]

Efforts to organize democratic unions that will more aggressively represent workers have been met with violence. Martha Ojeda, who was involved in efforts to secure more democratic union representation, recounts her experience:

In my hometown of Nuevo Laredo, Tamaulipas, you cannot get a job in a maquiladora if you're not affiliated to the CTM (the official Confederation of Mexican Workers). In 1994, I was working in the Sony Co. maquiladora, where we tried to democratize our CTM-affiliated union by holding elections. We acted entirely within our union's bylaws. However, the CTM committed an electoral fraud, and blocked our efforts. We had no alternative but to create an independent union. We had a walkout, and tried to have our union registered. Unfortunately the company and the government sent in police to break the strike. They beat up the workers, and several ended up in the hospital with severe injuries.[93]

The experience of Ojeda and her associates is by no means unique. Other union organizers who have been subjected to violence include

---

[91] Human Rights Watch, *Mexico's National Human Rights Commission: A Critical Assessment* at http://hrw.org/reports/2008/mexico0208/1.htm (last accessed September 25, 2008).

[92] Cravey, *Women and Work in Mexico's Maquiladoras*, 85.

[93] Information Services Latin America, "Coalition for Justice in the Maquiladoras: an Interview with Martha Ojeda" at http://isla.igc.org/Features/Border/mex2.html (last accessed October 10, 2008).

Isidoro Pío Ortiz, who, Amnesty International reports, was abducted on May 15, 2007, beaten and threatened with death by members of a rival trade union. According to reports received by Amnesty International, Pío Ortiz was standing in front of the food processing plant where he worked handing out information leaflets about the newer union of which he is a member. Members of the union that Pío Ortiz's union was challenging grabbed him, forced him into a van and, while the van was being driven around the area for approximately half an hour, beat him and told him that they would kill him if he did not stop supporting the newer union.[94]

In other cases, those attempting to organize independent unions are simply fired. Among those is Martin Zacatzi Tequextle, who worked at a textile factory in southern Mexico making Tommy Hilfiger, Calvin Klein, Levi's, and Guess jeans. Tequextle was fired when he started organizing workers to demand better working conditions.[95] While Mexican courts have held that it is unconstitutional to fire workers because they are trying to organize unions, in practice this happens with some frequency. Many of the contracts signed with CMT and other unions that essentially function as company unions include an exclusion clause that gives the union the right to instruct the employer to fire workers the union wishes to have fired.[96]

Though rare, efforts to organize independent unions are occasionally successful. One of these rare successes occurred at the Kukdong (now Mexmode) garment factory in Atlixco, a picturesque town in the state of Puebla a few kilometers south of the city of the same name. In 2001, unionized workers forced their maquiladora employer to provide better working conditions.[97] The workers were aided in their

[94] Amnesty International, "Mexico: Fear for Safety" (June 4, 2007) at http://www.amnesty.org/en/library/info/AMR41/024/2007/en (last accessed October 16, 2008).
[95] Susan Ferriss, "Workers Say Rights Denied as Firms Threaten to Pull Out," *Cox News Service*, October 30, 2003.
[96] UE International, "Organizing in Mexico: It's Tough, Often Brutal and It Means Taking on the State" at http://www.ueinternational.org/Mexico_info/Mex_org.html (last accessed October 10, 2008).
[97] Ginger Thompson, "Mexican Labor Protest Gets Results," *New York Times*, October 3, 2001. See also Jeremy Blasi, *Kukdong: A Case of Effective Labor Standards Enforcement* at http://henningcenter.berkeley.edu/gateway/kukdong.html (last accessed December 1, 2008) and Centro de Apoyo al Trabajador, *La Lucha Suigue: Stories*

struggle by groups such as the AFL-CIO's Solidarity Center in Mexico City and antisweatshop groups such as United Students Against Sweatshops. The latter was particularly effective in bringing pressure to bear on Nike, which was Kudong's principle corporate customer. In an article entitled "Bringing the Local Back In: Trajectory of Contention and the Union Struggle at Kukdong/Mexmode" that appeared in *Social Movement Studies* in 2007, Graham Knight and Don Wells observe with respect to the success of Kukdong workers, "The two levels of struggle, the transnational and the local, were mutually empowering; each level was a necessary but, by itself, insufficient condition for the success."[98]

MORE ENLIGHTENED EMPLOYMENT PRACTICES

As the foregoing suggests, the list of maquiladora abuses is a long one. It would be a mistake, however, to paint all maquiladoras with the same brushstroke. There are maquiladoras, many of which are second and third generation maquiladoras, that reportedly follow more enlightened employment practices by providing their workers with better compensation and clean, safe workplace environments. As noted earlier in this chapter, second-generation maquiladoras are oriented less toward assembly and more toward manufacturing processes, employing more technicians and engineers and making use of robotics and automation while third-generation maquiladoras are oriented toward research, design, and development, relying on highly skilled employees such as highly specialized engineers and technicians.

There are problems here as well, though not necessarily problems that are the fault of the second and third generation maquiladoras. As maquiladoras have shifted from assembly operations involving unskilled workers to more capital-intensive operations that require workers with higher technology skills levels, they often have had difficulties finding workers with these skills. Raul Carbajal, president

---

from the People of the Kukdong Factory at http://henningcenter.berkeley.edu/gateway/pdf/kukdong.pdf (last accessed December 1, 2008).

[98] Graham Knight and Don Wells, "Bringing the Local Back In: Trajectory of Contention and the Union Struggle at Kukdong/Mexmode," *Social Movement Studies*, 6, no. 1 (May 2007), 98.

of the Nogales Chamber of Commerce, observes that the city's most pressing economic problem is finding skilled workers to fill these positions. He reports that 40 percent of the migrants who come to the area looking for jobs cannot pass a state test of basic technology work skills and literacy required for employment.[99]

The problem is exacerbated by the fact that many Mexican schoolchildren drop out of school without developing the skills needed for these better jobs. Among them is Estrada's daughter, Bobby, who, though she was legally underage, dropped out of school when she was fourteen and went to work at a maquiladora. Her mother supported her decision. The costs of uniforms and books were becoming prohibitive. Bobby and her mother were also concerned about the increase in gang activity at the school she was attending.[100]

The more enlightened maquiladora managers do not limit their efforts to the workplace. Like their U.S. counterparts, many work hard to improve quality of life in the communities in which their plants are located. Among these is Tom Higgins, who served as president of the S.L. Waber de Mexico plant in Nogales, Sonora, a plant that manufactures surge suppressors and voltage regulators. Higgins helped pioneer a collaborative program between his industry and the Mexican government to provide decent housing for low-income maquiladora employees. The result was the construction of several hundred worker-owned, single-family, two-bedroom homes. Several maquiladoras agreed to help their employees with the down payments for these homes.[101] Though falling far short of providing decent housing for all maquiladora employees, the housing program is at least a step in the right direction.

A CONTRASTING VIEW

As preceding pages suggest, criticism of maquiladoras, which many view as sweatshops, is widespread. There is, however, a contrasting

---

[99] Riccardi, "On the Border, in a Fix," *Los Angeles Times,* July 19, 2006.
[100] Rally, "The Allure of Nogales' Maquilas after the Peso Crash."
[101] Miriam Davidson, "Maquiladora Workers Get Homes of Their Own," *APF Reporter,* 18, no. 3 (1997).

view. In a 1997 panel discussion at Harvard University, Harvard economist Jeffrey D. Sachs commented, "My concern is not that there are
too many sweatshops but that there are too few."[102] Sachs was being
slightly facetious. He was not suggesting that child labor, forced labor,
and other human rights abuses ought to be overlooked. He is strongly
opposed to such practices. Rather, he was suggesting that many poorer
nations have no hope better than plants that merely pay subsistence
wages. "Those are precisely the jobs that were the steppingstone for
Singapore and Hong Kong," he commented, "and those are the jobs
that have to come to Africa to get them out of their backbreaking
rural poverty."[103]

In a piece that ran in the *New York Times* June 6, 2006, entitled "In
Praise of the Maligned Sweatshops," columnist Nicholas D. Kristof
wrote, "We in the West mostly despise sweatshops as exploiters of
the poor, while the poor themselves tend to see sweatshops as opportunities." He notes:

[C]ompanies like Nike, itself once a target of sweatshop critics, tend not to
have highly labor-intensive factories in the very poorest countries, but rather
more capital-intensive factories (in which machines do more of the work)
in better-off nations like Malaysia or Indonesia. And the real losers are the
world's poorest people."[104]

And indeed when multinational corporations cut their ties with
sweatshops, the victims can be the very same people opponents of
sweatshops say they want to help. For example, when Wal-Mart can-
celed its contract with the factory in Honduras where teenage girls
were working seventy-five hours a week for minimal wages to make
the Kathie Lee Gifford line of clothing, the girls lost their jobs – and
blamed Gifford for their misfortune.[105]

---

[102] Quoted by Allen R. Myerson in "In Principle, a Case for More 'Sweatshops,'" *New York Times*, June 22, 1997.
[103] Quoted in *ibid.*
[104] Nicholas D. Kristof, "In Praise of the Maligned Sweatshop," *New York Times*, June 6, 2006.
[105] Myerson, "In Principle, A Case for More 'Sweatshops.'" The Kathie Lee Gifford line of clothing was produced by the Global Fashion plant, located at the South Korean-run Galaxy Industrial Park in Honduras (Larry Rohter, "Hondurans in 'Sweatshops' See Opportunity," *New York Times*, July 18, 1996).

In an earlier piece entitled "Two Cheers for Sweatshops" that
Kristof coauthored with his wife, Sheryl WuDunn, while they were in
Thailand, Kristof and WuDunn wrote:

Nothing captures the difference in mind-set between East and West more
than attitudes toward sweatshops. Nike and other American companies
have been hammered in the Western press over the last decade for producing shoes, toys, and other products in grim little factories with dismal
conditions.... Yet sweatshops that seem brutal from the vantage point of an
American sitting in his living room can appear tantalizing to a Thai laborer
getting by on beetles....

 This is not to praise sweatshops. Some managers are brutal in the way they
house workers in firetraps, expose children to dangerous chemicals, deny
bathroom breaks, demand sexual favors, force people to work double shifts,
or dismiss anyone who tries to organize a union. Agitation for improved
safety conditions can be helpful, just as it was in 19th-century Europe. But
Asian workers would be aghast at the idea of American consumers boycot-
ting certain toys or clothing in protest. The simplest way to help the poorest
Asians would be to buy more from sweatshops, not less.[106]

A CASE TO BE MADE FOR SWEATSHOPS?

Are Sachs, Kristof, and WuDunn right? Is there a case to be made
for sweatshops? Part of what is at stake here depends on what one
means by "sweatshop." Does the term simply refer to a low-wage factory where workers work long hours? Or does it refer to a low-wage factory where workers work long hours exposed to toxic substances that
place their health at risk, where they are subjected to sexual harassment and other forms of harassment, and are otherwise abused in
violation of the most basic human rights? We are inclined to limit the
use of the term to the latter.

 In Chapter 3 we argued that there is a moral minimum as to what
employers can in good conscience do with respect to compensation, a moral minimum that includes a level of compensation that
will provide for a baseline standard of living, defined as having food,

[106] Nicholas D. Kristof and Sheryl WuDunn, "Two Cheers for Sweatshops," *New York Times*, September 24, 2000. Kristof and WuDunn won the Pulitzer prize in journalism for their reporting of the Tiananmen Square protests in Beijing in 1989. They were the first married couple to receive this award.

shelter, basic health care, and access to educational opportunities on at least the primary and secondary levels (with the latter, in some cases such as Firestone in Liberia, being provided by the company as a direct benefit, rather than part of the compensation package). We also argued that each employee is entitled to be treated with respect and dignity, which precludes sexual harassment and all other forms of harassment, being exposed to toxic substances, and otherwise being forced to work in a workplace that places her or his health and well-being at risk. We further argued that business organizations that are unwilling or unable to meet this moral minimum have no business being in business.

This notion of a moral minimum precludes operating or doing business with sweatshops in the more narrowly defined sense of the term. It does not, however, preclude operating or doing business with low-wage production facilities, provided that compensation levels are at least on the subsistence level and provided that employees are treated with respect and dignity, rather than being abused in any or all of the ways noted.[107] As the examples cited illustrate, maquiladoras have in numerous cases been abusive of their employees. Maquiladoras of this sort have no business being in business.

However, it is also possible for maquiladoras, while paying relatively low wages and demanding long hours of work comparable to what farmers in the United States and other countries have been accustomed to doing for generations, to treat their employees with respect and dignity while maintaining clean, safe workplaces. When this is done, there is nothing intrinsically immoral about maquiladoras. And when second and third generation maquiladoras provide higher compensation levels and better training opportunities for their employees, there is much to be said for these maquiladoras.

But what about the argument that sweatshops are an important stage on the road to economic development? That is akin to suggesting that those in less-developed countries have to go through a period

---

[107] In certain respects, the position we take is not dissimilar to that taken by Jeffrey D. Sachs. In saying that there is a need for more sweatshops, not fewer, he was using the term in the broader sense to refer to all low-wage factories. We prefer a narrower definition that limits the term to low-wage factories where employers are abusive of their employees and fail to provide work environments that are safe and free from harassment. Sachs is not supportive of those types of factories.

of abuse before there is any realistic hope of things getting better for them. One is hard-pressed to find any type of ethical rationale for that assertion.

What about the argument that refusing to do business with sweatshops victimizes the very people it is intended to help? That argument would be plausible were it the case that sweatshops were the only option for doing business in less-developed countries. Granted, Mexico is not Namibia. Indeed, when viewed from the perspective of those living in Namibia, Mexico is a wealthy country. That having been said, however, the plethora of maquiladoras in Mexico, many of which are not sweatshops, suggest that there are numerous opportunities for doing business with and in low-wage countries without dealing with sweatshops.

Target Corporation and other companies with high ethical standards demonstrate that it is possible to do business in less-developed countries without purchasing products from sweatshops. As noted in Chapter 3, Target is one of more than 300 companies that signed the National Retail Federation's (NRF's) Statement of Principles on Supplier Legal Compliance. The NRF, which is the largest retail trade association in the world, organized the "Clothes Made in Sweatshops Aren't Our Style" campaign in 1996. In 2004, NRF, in cooperation with several other organizations, was instrumental in establishing the Fair Factories Clearing House (FFC), which houses a global database of factory information and social compliance audit reports.

In short, it is possible to do business successfully, including business with producers in low-wage countries, without dealing with sweatshops that are abusive of their employees. Moreover, when Target and other retailers give preference to suppliers in low-wage countries that are not abusive of their employees, they help shift the market advantage to socially responsible suppliers and away from sweatshops abusive of their employees. To be sure, as the example of Wal-Mart and the company that produced the Kathie Lee Gifford line of clothing in Honduras illustrates, refraining from doing business with sweatshops can leave sweatshop workers without whatever marginal advantage might accrue to them. However, when Target and other retailers give preference to socially responsible suppliers in low-wage countries, these suppliers benefit in ways that enable growth and expanded employment. The bottom line is that abusing people is never justifiable on moral grounds, even if sweatshop workers are in marginally better situations than those living in abject poverty unable to find employment of any type. There are far better ways of providing employment opportunities in less-developed countries. The more enlightened approach that Target and other NRF members take is beneficial to workers in less-developed countries without being abusive of them.

SUMMING IT ALL UP

We have argued that plant relocation to low-wage countries should be a last resort after companies make every effort to maintain the economic viability of existing facilities and, by so doing, the jobs of current workers. However, in a competitive global economy, continuing the operation of existing facilities is not always possible. We have also noted that while exploitation of maquiladora workers is widespread, it is not universal. Thus, the challenge for companies forced by economic realities to shift production to low-wage countries is conducting their operations in ways that treat workers with respect and dignity in safe work environments that are free from harassment and other forms of abuse. Maquiladoras can – and frequently do – provide economic opportunities for Mexican workers. They need not, however, be abusive of those they employ or the communities in which they are located. Economic opportunity without exploitation can be – and ought to be – the goal of all companies operating maquiladoras.

PART III

THE CHALLENGE OF ENFORCEMENT

8

Possibilities and Problems

Encouraging business leaders to maintain high ethical standards and respect the rights of those whose lives are affected by what their companies do is part of the process. If, as some once believed, human nature were perfectible,[1] that is all that would need to be done. The regrettable reality, however, is that there is a darker side to human nature – a tendency toward injustice, as well as a capacity for justice. In *The Children of Light and the Children of Darkness*, a book first published more than six decades ago, Reinhold Niebuhr (1892–1971) observes that our "capacity for justice makes democracy possible" but that our "inclination to injustice makes democracy necessary."[2]

These competing tendencies are not equally distributed among all individuals. Respect for the rights and well-being of other people was far more pronounced in actor and entrepreneur Paul Newman, who, as noted in Chapter 3, believed that business could be a force for good in society, than in Bernard L. Madoff, who in an elaborate Ponzi scheme swindled tens of thousands of investors of billions of dollars.

---

[1] For example, in 1907, Walter Rauschenbusch, whose name is prominently associated with the Social Gospel movement, wrote in *Christianity and the Social Crisis* (republished in 1991 by Westminster John Knox), "The swiftness of evolution in our own country proves the immense latent perfectibility in human nature," 422.

[2] Reinhold Niebuhr, *The Children of Light and the Children of Darkness* (New York: Charles Scribner's Sons, 1944), xiii.

Conversely, the tendency toward injustice was far more pronounced in Madoff than in Newman.

If the business world were comprised entirely of Paul Newmans and there were no Bernie Madoffs, enforcement would not be a problem because those in positions of power could be counted on to do what is right. The reality, however, is otherwise, which is why legal action and other coercive measures are necessary if Madoff and others like him are to be brought to justice.

All of this can be handled in a reasonably effective manner in an economy that is primarily domestic in nature. And indeed, Madoff was brought to justice in a federal court and sentenced to 150 years in prison for his wrongdoing, time that he is now serving in federal prison.

The problem, however, is that in a global economy dominated by multinational corporations, the authority structures that can be brought to bear domestically do not have the same power beyond the territorial limits of the country of which they are a part. U.S. courts do not have the same jurisdiction in Mexico or Malaysia as they do in the United States. Similarly, the U.S. Environmental Protection Agency (EPA) and the U.S. Occupational Safety and Health Administration (OSHA) do not have the same regulatory authority with respect to factories in Tijuana and Shanghai as they do with respect to factories in Cleveland and Chicago.

In a frequently quoted passage in a book published several years before *The Children of Light and the Children of Darkness*, Niebuhr observes, "Since reason is always, to some degree, the servant of interest in a social situation, social injustice cannot be resolved by moral and rational suasion alone, as the educator and social scientist usually believes. Conflict is inevitable, and in this conflict power must be challenged by power."[3] He is right about that. There is, however, a practical problem. In this age of globalization, where might the power be found that can challenge multinational corporations engaging in practices harmful to the indigenous populations of other countries and to others living outside the country in which the multinational corporation is based?

---

3 Reinhold Niebuhr, *Moral Man and Immoral Society: A Study in Ethics and Politics* (New York: Charles Scribner's Sons, 1932), xiv–xv.

A WORLD POLITICAL AUTHORITY?

In an encyclical issued in 2009 entitled *Caritas in Veritate (Charity in Truth)*, Pope Benedict XVI asserts, "To manage the global economy; to revive economies hit by the [financial] crisis; to avoid any deterioration of the present crisis and the greater imbalances that would result; to bring about integral and timely disarmament, food security and peace; to guarantee the protection of the environment and to regulate migration; for all this, there is urgent need of a true world political authority...."[4]

Though Benedict XVI's proposal underscores a key part of the problem, in practice it is not feasible. It is exceedingly unlikely that nations would hand over to an international body the authority necessary to make what Benedict XVI proposes a reality. That would entail a significant transfer of sovereignty, which few nations, if any, are likely to be willing to do.

Moreover, even if nations were willing to transfer sovereignty to a world political authority, it is by no means a foregone conclusion that it would be wise to do so. In a letter to Bishop Mandell Creighton written in 1887, John Emerich Edward Dalberg Acton, who, given the unwieldy nature of his name, is usually referred to simply as "Lord Acton," warned, "Power tends to corrupt, and absolute power corrupts absolutely."[5] James Madison and the other visionaries who drafted the Constitution of the United States of America had the foresight to insist on checks and balances and separation of power. Human nature being what it is, a world political authority with sufficient power to control multinational corporations and do everything else that Benedict XVI would like to see done would be inherently dangerous.

Where does this leave us? Should multinational corporations intent on making as much money as they can regardless of the costs imposed on other people be given free rein to do whatever they wish

---

[4] Benedict XVI, *Caritas in Veritate* (2009), 67 at http://www.vatican.va/holy_father/ benedict_xvi/encyclicals/documents/hf_ben-xvi_enc_20090629_caritas-in-veritate_en.html (last accessed August 21, 2009). Benedict XVI's statement implicitly suggests that the United Nations does not effectively fill that role.

[5] John Emerich Edward Dalberg Acton, *Letter to Bishop Mandell Creighton* (1887). Quoted at http://www.phrases.org.uk/meanings/288200.html (last accessed August 27, 2009).

to do? Not if one is committed to an ethic that affirms human rights and calls for corporate social responsibility. Apart from the power of negative publicity and threat of boycotts, is there any power that can be used to challenge the power of multinational corporations behaving badly? In the remainder of this chapter we will present an overview of various possible ways of bringing pressure to bear on multinational corporations in an age of globalization, noting their limitations, while reserving detailed discussion of the most promising avenue of action – litigation under the provisions of the Alien Tort Claims Act (ATCA) – for the following chapter, which will examine both possibilities for such litigation and the limitations courts have placed on action taken under the provisions of ATCA.

EXTRATERRITORIALITY?

Some have argued that U.S. laws can be applied outside the territorial limits of the United States. Take, for example, *Amlon Metals, Inc. v. FMC Corporation*, a case involving a shipment of containers containing copper residue. FMC Corp., a U.S. company whose principal place of business is Chicago, shipped the containers to Wath Recycling, Ltd., and Euromet, two British companies for which Amlon Metals, a New York–based company, was the sole American agent. When the containers arrived at their destination in England, they were emitting a strong odor. British environmental authorities discovered toxic organic compounds in concentrations up to ten times higher than FMC had disclosed. In the lawsuit Amlon filed against FMC in the U.S. District Court for the Southern District of New York, Amlon argued that FMC had violated the Resource Conservation and Recovery Act (RCRA), a U.S. law.[6] The District Court, however, ruled that the provisions of the Resource Conservation and Recovery Act (RCRA) do not extend to waste located within another sovereign nation, noting that "there is little if any evidence to support plaintiff's contention that Congress desired RCRA to apply extraterritorially...."[7]

The decision that the U.S. District Court for the Southern District of New York made in *Amlon Metals, Inc. v. FMC Corp.* is consistent with

---

[6] *Amlon Metals, Inc. v. FMC Corporation*, 775 F. Supp. 668, 669 (S.D.N.Y. 1991).
[7] *Ibid.* at 25.

a decision the U.S. Supreme Court made four decades earlier in *Foley Bros. v. Filardo*, a case in which a U.S. citizen contended that the provisions of a federal law mandating that overtime be paid for work in excess of eight hours per day entitled him to overtime pay for work he had done for an American contractor on construction projects in Iraq and Iran. Reversing the decision of the New York Court of Appeals, which had decided in favor of the plaintiff, the Court ruled that U.S. wage and hour laws do not apply to work done in foreign countries. The majority of the Court determined that "in the absence of expressed congressional intention to the contrary, the [federal wage and hour law] was meant to apply only within the territorial jurisdiction of the United States."[8]

Congressional intent is an important factor in these cases. In *Equal Employment Opportunity Commission v. Arabian American Oil Co.* the U.S. Supreme Court decided against the petitioner, a naturalized U.S. citizen born in Lebanon who had worked in Saudi Arabia for four years for a company chartered in Delaware prior to being discharged by the company. He argued that he had been harassed and discharged because of his race, religion, and national origin, conduct prohibited by Title VII of the Civil Rights Act of 1964.[9] In finding against the petitioner, the Court held that absent clear evidence that Congress intended to extend Title VII's reach beyond U.S. borders, Title VII does "not apply extraterritorially to regulate employment practices of United States employers who employ United States citizens abroad."[10]

Congressional intent also played a role in the decision by the U.S. Court of Appeals for the Second District in *Leasco Data Processing Equipment Corporation v. Robert Maxwell*. In this case, congressional intent proved to be advantageous to the plaintiffs, who suffered substantial losses when, acting on the advice of Maxwell and others, they

---

[8] *Foley Bros. v. Filardo*, 336 U.S. 281, 285 (1949).
[9] 42 USCS 2000e-17)
[10] *Equal Employment Opportunity Commission v. Arabian American Oil Co.*, 499 U.S. 244 (1991). See also *United States v. Rene Martin Verdugo-Urquidez*, 499 U.S. 259 (1990), a case in which the U.S. Supreme Court ruled that U.S. constitutional protections against unreasonable search and seizure did not apply to action taken by drug enforcement agents who searched the residence in Mexico of a citizen of Mexico "with no voluntary attachment to the United States."

purchased on the London stock exchange at prices in excess of its true value stock in a British company controlled by Maxwell. The plaintiffs alleged that misrepresentation by Maxwell and the other defendants was in violation of the U.S. Securities and Exchange Act. Affirming a lower court order denying motions to dismiss for lack of subject matter and personal jurisdiction over the defendant corporation, the Court of Appeals ruled that Congress intended the relevant portion of the Securities and Exchange Act "to protect against fraud in the sale or purchase of securities whether or not these were traded on organized U.S. markets...." The court, however, also noted that "substantial misrepresentations were made in the U.S." at a meeting at a hotel in New York.[11] Such being the case, it is unclear whether the Court of Appeals would have ruled in favor of the plaintiffs had the fraudulent activity occurred entirely outside the territorial limits of the United States.

Considered together, these cases leave open the question of whether Congress, if it chose to do so, could pass legislation expressly extending environmental laws, labor laws, or other similar laws to corporate conduct occurring outside the territorial limits of the United States – or somewhat more precisely, whether laws that are explicitly extraterritorial in their intended application would hold up in a court of law. We are content to leave that tangled legal thicket to others,[12] though we do note that the doctrine of international comity, which is based on respect for the sovereignty of other nations, weighs against extraterritoriality. We will return to this matter in the next chapter.

---

[11] *Leasco Data Processing Equipment Corporation v. Robert Maxwell et al.*, 468 F.2d 1326 (2d Cir. 1972).

[12] Articles that address issues related to extraterritoriality include Lea Brilmayer and Charles Norchi, "Federal Extraterritoriality and Fifth Amendment Due Process," 105 *Harvard Law Review* 1217 (1992), Michelle Schuld, "NOTE: Small v. United States Darkens the Already Murky Waters of Statutory Interpretation," 40 *Akron Law Review* 751 (2007), Stanley E. Cox, "Why Properly Construed Due Process Limits on Personal Jurisdiction Must Always Trump Contrary Treaty Provisions," 61 *Albany Law Review* 1177 (1998), Jay Alan Bauer, "COMMENTARY: Striking the Right Balance Between the Executive's War Powers and Judicial Review," 57 *Alabama Law Review* 1081 (2006), and Sean K. Nornbeck, "COMMENT: Transnational Litigation and Personal Jurisdiction over Foreign Defendants," 59 *Albany Law Review* 1389 (1996).

TRADE SANCTIONS AND TRAVEL RESTRICTIONS?

Various U.S. presidents and Congresses have responded to human rights violations in other countries perpetrated by their governments by imposing trade sanctions on the offending countries and travel restrictions on those wishing to visit those countries. Cuba and North Korea are but two of a long list of countries that have been subjected to trade sanctions and travel restrictions.

Trade sanctions and travel restrictions, of course, are directed toward the governments of countries with poor human rights records, rather than explicitly toward multinational corporations. The objective is usually regime change, either in the form of regime replacement or by forcing the regime in power to change its policies. Insofar as multinational corporations are concerned, however, trade sanctions and travel restrictions do have the practical effect of preventing them from being accomplices to human rights violations.

But how effective are trade sanctions and travel restrictions? A Brookings Institution study on Cuba released in 2009 observes, "If one compares outcomes to stated objectives, U.S. policy toward Cuba may be the biggest failure in the history of American foreign policy."[13] Vicki Huddleston, one of the codirectors of the study, observes that "U.S. sanctions now serve more to punish the Cuban people and harm our image than harm the Cuban government."[14] She and the other participants in the study concluded that the U.S. "should adopt a policy of critical and constructive engagement, phased-in unilaterally."[15] To help facilitate a transition to a policy of constructive engagement, the group mapped out a roadmap for constructive engagement.[16]

---

[13] Brookings Institution, *U.S. Policy Toward a Cuba in Transition* at http://www.brookings.edu/projects/latin-america/US-Policy-Toward-a-Cuba-in-Transition/Summary.aspx (last accessed September 4, 2009).

[14] Vicki Huddleston, "Cuba at Fifty" at http://www.brookings.edu/opinions/2008/1231_cuba_huddleston.aspx (last accessed August 27, 2009).

[15] Brookings Institution, *A New Policy of Critical and Constructive Engagement* at http://www.brookings.edu/reports/2009/04_cuba.aspx (last accessed September 4, 2009).

[16] Though it is still early in the Obama administration, there is reason to believe that President Obama is more strongly committed to constructive engagement than was his predecessor.

In Chapter 4, we presented the case for constructive engagement with China, a country with a blemished human rights record that in many respects is similar to that of Cuba under the Castro regime. We see no compelling reasons to advocate a different policy with respect to Cuba and other countries in which the ruling regime does not have an exemplary record on human rights.

INTERNATIONAL AGREEMENTS?

Might international agreements provide a framework for bringing pressure to bear on multinational corporations engaging in practices harmful to the people living in the areas where they operate factories, mines, or other facilities? On August 14, 1983, in La Paz, Baja California, U.S. President Ronald Reagan and Mexican President Miguel de la Madrid Hurtado signed an agreement to protect and improve the environment in the border area. The agreement states, "The United Mexican States and the United States of America . . . agree to cooperate in the field of environmental protection in the border area on the basis of equality, reciprocity, and mutual benefit." The two parties to the agreement promised "to the fullest extent practical, to adopt the appropriate measures to prevent, reduce and eliminate sources of pollution in their respective territory" and to "cooperate in the solution of the environmental problems of mutual concern in the border areas. . . ."[17] Annex III to the agreement, signed in 1986, specified in greater detail provisions with respect to the transboundary shipment of hazardous wastes and hazardous substances.[18] The North American Free Trade Agreement (NAFTA), which went into force January 1, 1994, affirmed the provisions of these agreements.[19]

[17] *Agreement between the United Mexican States and the United States of America on Cooperation for the Protection and Improvement of the Environment in the Border Area,* Articles 1 and 2 at http://untreaty.un.org/unts/60001_120000/12/10/00022468 .pdf (last accessed September 8, 2009).

[18] *Annex III to the Agreement between the United Mexican States and the United States of America on Cooperation for the Protection and Improvement of the Environment in the Border Area: Agreement of Cooperation between the United States of America and the United Mexican States Regarding the Transboundary Shipments of Hazardous Wastes and Hazardous Substances* at http://www.basel.int/article11/mexico-us.pdf (last accessed September 8, 2009).

[19] *North American Free Trade Agreement,* Article 104 and Annex 104.1 at http://www.sice. oas.org/trade/nafta/chap-01.asp#An104.1 (last accessed September 8, 2009).

Have these agreements succeeded in protecting those living in the border areas from the harmful effect of hazardous wastes and other hazardous substances? As noted in the previous chapter, both studies and anecdotal evidence suggest that serious problems continue to afflict maquiladora workers and others living in these areas. Having agreements such as these in place is probably preferable to having no such international agreements. However, without the political willpower to back up their provisions, they accomplish little in practice.

SUMMING IT ALL UP

The reality is that moral persuasion alone will not ensure ethical conduct on the part of all multinational corporations. As Niebuhr correctly realized, power must be challenged by power. The problem, however, is coming up with the leverage necessary to check the immense power of huge multinational corporations. Establishing a world political authority is neither feasible nor desirable. Extending U.S. laws to the conduct of U.S. multinational corporations operating overseas is problematic. Trade sanctions and travel restrictions offer little hope, if any, of transforming the policies of countries lacking a strong commitment to human rights. International agreements such as the environmental provisions included in NAFTA tend to be ineffective.

Are we left with no recourse? Is there no power that can challenge the power of multinational corporations operating outside the territorial limits of the United States? The next chapter will examine in considerable detail one of the more promising avenues of action that might be taken – litigation under the provisions of the Alien Tort Claims Act (ATCA) – while also noting the limitations that courts have placed on suits filed under this act.

9

U.S. Multinational Corporations and the Alien Tort Claims Act

The Alien Tort Claims Act (ATCA), which allows aliens to sue for damages in U.S. courts, was part of the original Judiciary Act of 1789, a landmark statute establishing the U.S. judiciary system that was enacted during the first session of the first United States Congress. The provision pertaining to tort claims by aliens (as slightly amended) is comprised of one sentence: "The district courts shall have original jurisdiction of any civil action by an alien for a tort only, committed in violation of the law of nations or a treaty of the United States."[1]

The reasons the first U.S. Congress decided to include this provision in the Judiciary Act of 1789 are somewhat obscure. Some scholars believe that when the statute was written in 1789, it was meant to display the new nation's neutrality with respect to warring European powers. According to this theory, Congress decided to grant federal jurisdiction for tort claims brought by aliens because, as Northwestern University Law Professor Anthony D'Amato noted in an article published in the *American Journal of International Law*, state courts at the time "were notoriously biased against foreigners."[2] Others suggest that the law was enacted to persuade European countries that the United States would not become a haven for pirates.[3] But whatever the

---

[1] *Judiciary Act of 1789*, ch. 20, §9, 1 Stat.73,77 (1789). (Amended 28 U.S.C. §1350, 1982.)

[2] Anthony D'Amato, "The Alien Tort Statute and the Founding of the Constitution," *American Journal of International Law* 82 (1988): 62–63.

[3] Human Rights Watch, *Defend the Alien Tort Claims Act* at http://www.hrw.org/campaigns/atca/index.htm (last accessed October 21, 2008).

reasons for including the alien tort claim provision in the Judiciary Act of 1789, little attention was paid to it for nearly 200 years.

That, however, began to change in the 1980s with *Filártiga v. Pena-Irala*, a ground-breaking case in which the 2nd Circuit Court of Appeals determined that a former Paraguayan security official was responsible for the torture and murder of Joelito Filártiga and instructed the district court, which had initially dismissed the case, to award family members Dolly M.E. Filártiga and Joel Filártiga compensatory damages.[4] The 2nd Circuit Court of Appeals ruled that "whenever an alleged torturer is found and served with process by an alien within our borders, [the Alien Tort Claims Act] provides federal jurisdiction."[5]

Starting in the 1990s, plaintiffs began using the Alien Tort Claims Act as a means of attempting to compel multinational corporations to conduct their operations in a socially responsible manner and to secure compensatory damages if they do not.[6] Texaco faced a suit for its alleged environmental degradation of indigenous Ecuadorians' homelands.[7] Unocal Corporation had to deal with a suit brought by Burmese villagers claiming that Unocal Corporation had violated human rights while protecting their pipeline in Burma (now Myanmar).[8] Residents of the Papua New Guinea island of Bougainville sued Rio Tinto mining company, claiming that the company had damaged the island's environment to such an extent that islanders could no longer fish or use water from island rivers, and that the mining operations were so divisive in Papua New Guinea that they incited a civil war that killed and injured thousands of civilians.[9]

While a wide variety of cases alleging human rights violations have been filed under the provisions of the Alien Tort Claims Act including, as noted in Chapter 5, a case alleging that Firestone Natural Rubber Company has used child labor on its rubber plantations in Liberia,[10]

---

[4] *Filártiga v. Pena-Irala*, 630 F.2d 876 (2nd Cir. 1980).
[5] *Ibid.* at 878. The Torture Victims Protection Act of 1991 is now the substantive law in cases in which torture is alleged.
[6] Ronen Shamir, "Between Self-Regulation and the Alien Tort Claims Act: On the Contested Concept of Corporate Social Responsibility," *Law and Society Review* 38 (2004): 635, 638.
[7] *Aguinda v. Texaco, Inc.*, 303 F.3d 470 (9th Cir. 2002).
[8] *John Doe I v. Unocal Corp.*, 395 F.3d 932 (9th Cir. 2002).
[9] *Sarei v. Rio Tinto, PLC*, 456 F.3d 1069, 1116 (9th Cir. 2006).
[10] *Roe v. Bridgestone Corp.*, 492 F. Supp. 2d 988 (S.D. Ind. 2007).

this chapter will focus on cases involving environmental issues. This is for two reasons. One is to keep the discussion as focused as possible. The second and more important reason is that this is a way of calling attention to the fact that environmental issues become human rights issues when environmental degradation threatens human health and well-being. Before giving more specific attention to these cases, however, we need to examine the criteria that must be satisfied if a case is to be successfully litigated under the provisions of the Alien Tort Claims Act.

THE LAW OF NATIONS

For a U.S. district court to have original jurisdiction under the Alien Tort Claim Act, plaintiffs must produce evidence sufficient to show (1) that they are aliens, (2) that they are suing for damages, and (3) that the harm that they suffered was committed in violation of the law of nations or a treaty of the United States.[11] If there is not a treaty that covers the act in question, the "threshold question on the jurisdictional issue is whether the conduct alleged violates the law of nations."[12] A violation of the law of nations occurs only when there has been a violation by one or more persons of the standards, rules or customs that govern the relationships between states or between individuals and foreign states.[13] An international tort claim must satisfy the following guidelines:

(a) No state condones the act in question and there is a recognizable "universal" consensus of prohibition against it.
(b) There are sufficient criteria to determine whether a given action amounts to the prohibited act and thus violates the norm.
(c) The prohibition against it is steadfast and therefore binding at all times upon all actors.[14]

The law of nations, which is also known as international customary law formed by the general assent of civilized nations,[15] is comprised of

---

[11] *Sarei v. Rio Tinto*, F. Supp. 2d. at 1116.
[12] *Filártiga v. Pena-Irala*, 630 F.2d at 880.
[13] *Lopes v. Reederei Richard Schroder*, 225 F. Supp. 292 (E.D. Pa. 1963).
[14] *Forti v. Suarez-Mason*, 672 F. Supp. 1531, 1539–1540 (D. Cal. 1987); *Restatement (Third) of Foreign Relations Law of the United States: Obligation to Respect Human Rights* §§ 701–702 (1987).
[15] *Doe v. Islamic Salvation Front (FIS)*, 993 F. Supp. 3 (D.D.C. 1998).

rules and principles that govern the relations and dealings of nations and of international organizations with each other, as well as some of their relations with persons, whether natural or juridical.[16] Norms of the law of nations are also found in juridical writings on public law, in the general practice of nations, and in judicial decisions recognizing and enforcing international law.[17]

JUS COGENS NORMS

Jus cogens norms are absolute principles of international law that cannot be set aside by agreement or acquiescence and hence are the strongest norms recognized within the law of nations. They are binding on all nations and cannot be preempted by treaty.[18] The *Vienna Convention on the Law of Treaties (1969)* defines *jus cogens* norms as "peremptory norm[s] of general international law" and states, "A treaty is void if, at the time of its conclusion, it conflicts with a peremptory norm of general international law."[19] Examples include the ban on extrajudicial killing,[20] torture, murder, genocide, and slavery.[21] *Jus cogens* norms are limited in number. For example, kidnapping, while recognized by many nations as a violation of domestic law, is not among the norms considered to be *jus cogens* norms.[22]

It should be added, however, that the law of nations is not comprised solely of *jus cogens* norms. In *Siderman de Blake v. Republic of Argentina*, the 9th Circuit Court of Appeals observed that the law of nations arises out of the "general and consistent practice of states followed by them from a sense of legal obligation."[23] Three years later in *In re Estate of Ferdinand E. Marcos*, the 9th Circuit Court of Appeals stated that for an act to be a violation of international law, it need only be a violation of a norm that is "specific, universal, and obligatory."[24]

---

[16] *State of New Jersey v. State of Delaware*, 391 U.S. 361 (1934).

[17] *Doe v. Unocal Corp.*, 963 F. Supp 880 (C.C. Cal. 1997).

[18] *Alejandre v. Republic of Cuba*, 996 F. Supp. 1239 (S.D. Fla. 1997).

[19] *Vienna Convention on the Law of Treaties (1969)*, Art. 53 at http://untreaty.un.org/ilc/texts/instruments/english/conventions/1_1_1969.pdf (last accessed October 21, 2008).

[20] *Alejandre v. Republic of Cuba*, 996 F. Supp. 1239.

[21] *U.S. v. Matta-Ballesteros*, 71 F.3d 754 (9th Cir. 1995).

[22] *Ibid.*

[23] *Siderman de Blake v. Republic of Argentina*, 965 F.2d 699 (9th Cir. 1991).

[24] *In re Estate of Ferdinand E. Marcos (Human Rights Litigation)*, 25 F.3d 1467, 1475 (9th Cir. 1994). See also *Martinez v. City of Los Angeles*, 141 F.ed 1373, 1383 (9th Cir. 2001).

VIOLATIONS OF INTERNATIONAL LAW THAT
DO NOT INVOLVE STATE ACTION

Most violations of international law require state action (that is, must be perpetrated by a government to be considered violations) but some do not. Among the latter are slave trading[25] and genocide, which can result in private liability without any state action requirement.[26] In *Kadic v. Karadzic*, the 2nd Circuit Court of Appeals held that rape, torture, and summary execution as crimes of war or as part of genocide are actionable under the Alien Tort Claim Act regardless of whether they involve state action.[27] The U.S. District Court for the Southern District of New York had dismissed the case that victims of atrocities committed in Bosnia brought against Radovan Karadzic, the former president of the self-proclaimed Bosnian-Serb Republic (sometimes referred to as "Srpska"), concluding that the lack of state action meant that it could not be adjudicated under the Alien Tort Claims Act.[28] The 2nd Circuit Court of Appeals, however, reversed the district court's decision, stating, "We do not agree that the law of nations, as understood in the modern era, confines its reach to state action. Instead, we hold that certain forms of conduct violate the law of nations whether undertaken by those acting under the auspices of a state or only as private individuals."[29] The 2nd Circuit Court of Appeals decision is consistent with the *Restatement (Third) of the Foreign Relations Law of the United States (1986)*, which states, "Individuals may be held liable for offenses against international law, such as piracy, war crimes, and genocide."[30] And it is consistent with the 1795 opinion by Attorney General William Bradford in which he stated that Americans who had participated in the French plunder of a British slave colony in Sierra Leone could be sued for damages, noting that "the company or individuals who have been injured by

---

[25] *Tel-Oren v. Libyan Arab Republic*, 233 U.S. App. D.C. 384, 726 F.2d 774 (D.C. Cir. 1984).
[26] *John Doe I v. Unocal Corp.*, 395 F.3d at 945–946.
[27] *Kadic v. Karadzic*, 70 F.3d at 242–243 (2nd Cir. 1995).
[28] *Ibid.* at 237–238.
[29] *Ibid.* at 239.
[30] *Restatement (Third) of Foreign Relations Law of the United States: Customary International Law of Human Rights* § 702 (1987).

these acts of hostility have a remedy by a *civil* suit in the courts of the
United States...."[31]

EVOLUTION OF THE LAW OF NATIONS

In *Filártiga v. Pena-Irala*, the 2nd Circuit Court of Appeals states that
courts ascertaining the content of the law of nations "must interpret
international law not as it was in 1789, but as it has evolved and exists
among nations of the world today."[32] And indeed, the common law
understanding of the law of nations has changed significantly in the
course of the years.

In *Sosa v. Alvarez-Machain*, a case decided by the U.S. Supreme
Court in 2004, Associate Justice David Souter, who delivered the
opinion of the Court, notes that at the time the Alien Tort Claim Act
was passed by Congress in 1789, the law of nations was commonly
understood as being comprised of two principal elements. The first
element consisted of the general norms governing the behavior of
nations with each other. This aspect of international law, he suggests,
involved the executive and legislative domains but not the judicial.
The second element of international law, which he describes as the
"more pedestrian element," did fall within the judicial domain. This
consisted of "a body of judge-made law regulating the conduct of individuals situated outside domestic boundaries and consequently carrying an international savor."[33] This is the part of international law
to which Sir William Blackstone (1723–1780) makes reference in his
Commentaries on the Laws of England when he observes:

Thus in mercantile questions, such as bills of exchange and the like; in all
marine causes, relating to freight, average, demurrage, insurances, bottomry,
and others of a similar nature; the lawmerchant, which is a branch of the
law of nations, is regularly and constantly adhered to. So too in all disputes
relating to prizes, to shipwrecks, to hostages, and ransom bills, there is no
other rule of decision but this great universal law, collected from the history

---

[31] 1 Op. Att'y Gen. 57, 59 (1795). Bradford was uncertain if criminal charges could be
brought against those involved in the plunder of the French colony.
[32] *Filártiga v. Pena-Irala*, 630 F.2d at 881.
[33] *Sosa v. Alvarez-Machain*, 542 U.S. at 714–715 (2004).

and usage and such writers of all nations and languages as are generally approved and allowed of.[34]

Blackstone goes on to note that there is a sphere in which these rules binding on individuals overlap with norms of state relationships. He mentions three specific offenses against the law of nations that are addressed by English criminal law: violation of safe conducts, infringement on the rights of ambassadors, and piracy.[35]

In time, courts came to view a greater number of offenses as being prohibited by the law of nations. In *Filártiga v. Pena-Irala*, the 2nd Circuit Court of Appeals stated:

In light of the universal condemnation of torture in numerous international agreements, and the renunciation of torture as an instrument of official policy by virtually all of the nations of the world (in principle if not in practice), we find that an act of torture committed by a state official against one held in detention violates established norms of the international law of human rights, and hence the law of nations.[36]

The 2nd Circuit Court of Appeals observed, "For purposes of civil liability, the torturer has become – like the pirate and slave trader before him – *hostis humani generic*, an enemy to all mankind."[37]

The evolution of international law is reflected in other cases as well. As noted earlier in this chapter, in *Kadic v. Karadzic*, the 2nd Circuit Court of Appeals held that rape, torture, and summary execution carried out through crimes of war or as part of genocide are actionable under the Alien Tort Claim Act. As noted in Chapter 5, in a case involving Firestone Natural Rubber Company's Liberian operations, the U.S. District Court for the Southern District of Indiana, Indianapolis Division, ruled that claims involving child labor are actionable under the Alien Tort Claims Act.[38] And in 2007 in *Khulamani v. Barclay Nat'l Bank Ltd.*, a case filed on behalf of victims of apartheid in South Africa alleging that they had been harmed by

---

[34] William Blackstone, *Commentaries on the Laws of England, Book the Fourth-Chapter the Fifth: Of Offences Against the Law of Nations* (1969), 68 at http://avalon.law.yale.edu/18th_century/blackstone_bk4ch5.asp (last accessed October 23, 2008).

[35] *Ibid.*

[36] *Filártiga v. Pena-Irala*, 630 F.2d at 880.

[37] *Ibid.* at 890.

[38] *Roe v. Bridgestone Corp.*, 492 F. Supp. 2d 988 (S.D. Ind. 2007).

multinational corporations' compliance with apartheid policies during the era of apartheid, the 2nd Circuit Court of Appeals ruled that the district court erred in holding that such claims are not actionable under the Alien Tort Claims Act.[39] The case was appealed to the U.S. Supreme Court, which declined to hear the case, thus letting the judgment of the circuit court of appeals stand.[40]

The evolution of international law, however, has not been without limits. In *Sosa v. Alvarez-Machain*,[41] the U.S. Supreme Court reversed the decision of the 9th Circuit Court of Appeals in a case involving Humberto Alvarez-Machain, a Mexican physician who won a $25,000 award in an Alien Tort Claims Act case filed in the U.S. District Court for the Central District of California against Jose Sosa, a member of a group of Mexican nationals who allegedly abducted Alvarez-Machain at the request of the U.S. Drug Enforcement Administration (DEA), which wished to have Alvarez-Machain brought to the United States to stand trial for allegedly torturing and killing a DEA official investigating a Mexican drug cartel.[42] The verdict was upheld by the 9th Circuit Court of Appeals. As noted previously, kidnapping does not meet the standard of *jus cogens*. The 9th Circuit Court of Appeals explicitly rejected the defendant's contention that a violation must meet the *jus cogens* standard to violate the law of nations,[43] a finding consistent with the court's ruling in *Martinez v. City of Los Angeles* that arbitrary arrest and detention are actionable under the Alien Tort Claims Act, even though the norms prohibiting such acts do not

---

[39] *Khulumani v. Barclay Nat'l Bank Ltd.*, 504 F.3d 254 (2nd Cir. N.Y., 2007).

[40] *American Isuzu Motors v. Ntsebera*, 128 S. Ct. 2424 (2008). The case as appealed to the U.S. Supreme Court was a consolidation of ten lawsuits filed against a long list of U.S. corporations alleging injury resulting from the apartheid policies in effect in South Africa from 1946 to 1994. The government of South Africa, which is committed to a policy of reconciliation, strongly opposes the litigation. The recusal of four of the justices serving on the Supreme Court because they own stock in various of the companies being sued left the court without the quorum of six of the nine justices necessary to conduct business, which precluded hearing the case, thus automatically letting the lower court decision stand (Linda Greenhouse, "Justices' Conflicts Halt Apartheid Appeal," *New York Times*, May 13, 2008. See also Warren Richey, "U.S. High Court Allows Apartheid Claims against Multinationals," *Christian Science Monitor*, May 13, 2008.)

[41] *Sosa v. Alvarez-Machain*, 542 U.S. 692.

[42] *Alvarez-Machain v. United States*, 1999 U.S. Dist. LEXI 23304 (D.Cal. 1999).

[43] *Alvarez-Machain v. United States*, 266 F.3d 1045, 1050 (9th Cir. 2001).

rise to the level of *jus cogens* norms[44] and with its ruling in *In re Estate of Ferdinand E. Marcos (Human Rights Litigation)*, where it held that the violation need only be of a norm that is "specific, universal, and obligatory."[45]

Reversing the decision of the 9th Circuit Court of Appeals, the U.S. Supreme Court in *Sosa v. Alvarez-Machain* took a more cautious approach. Delivering the opinion of the Court, Justice Souter stated, "We have no congressional mandate to seek out and define new and debatable violations of the law of nations, and modern indications of congressional understanding of the judicial role in the field have not affirmatively encouraged greater judicial creativity."[46] He added, "These reasons argue for great caution in adapting the law of nations to private rights."[47] However, while discouraging judicial creativity, Justice Souter did not call for a return to the narrow definition of common law specified by Blackstone. He wrote:

We assume … that no development in the two centuries from the enactment of [the Alien Tort Claims Act] to the birth of the modern lines of cases beginning with *Filártiga v. Pena-Irala* … has categorically precluded federal courts from recognizing a claim under the law of nations as an element of common law; Congress has not in any relevant way amended [the Alien Tort Claims Act] or limited civil common law power by another statute.[48]

Thus *Sosa v. Alvarez-Machain* did not overturn *Filártiga v. Pena-Irala*.

In an article entitled "Human Rights in U.S. Courts: Alien Tort Claims Act Litigation after *Sosa v. Alvarez-Machain*" that was published in the July 2007 issue of *Human Rights Review,* Jeffrey Davis observes, "After *Sosa*, most courts continue to agree that claims based on torture, extra-judicial killing and other violent human rights offenses are actionable under [the Alien Tort Claims Act]. In doing so, they often rely on the *Sosa* court's endorsement of the Second Circuit's decision in *Filártiga*...."[49]

---

[44] *Martinez v. City of Los Angeles*, 141 F.ed 1373, 1383 (9th Cir. 2001).
[45] *In re Estate of Ferdinand E. Marcos (Human Rights Litigation)*, 25 F.3d at 1475.
[46] *Sosa v. Alvarez-Machain*, 542 U.S. at 728.
[47] *Ibid.*
[48] *Ibid.* at 724–725.
[49] Jeffrey Davis, "Human Rights in U.S. Courts: Alien Tort Claims Act Litigation after *Sosa v. Alvarez-Machian*," *Human Rights Review* (July 2007), 362.

In short, there are limits as to what claims are actionable under the Alien Tort Claims Act. Claims that are not actionable include those that allege fraud,[50] libel,[51] corporate waste,[52] tortious conversion of property,[53] recovery of the proceeds of a life insurance policy,[54] restraining the testing of nuclear weapons,[55] and restraining the picketing of a foreign vessel.[56] At the same time, both the scope and content of international law have evolved since Congress enacted the Alien Tort Claims Act in 1789. As the 2nd Circuit Court of Appeals noted in *Filártiga v. Pena-Irala*, international law as it exists among nations of the world today is not the same as it was in 1789.

GROUNDS FOR DISMISSAL

There are several grounds on which federal courts can decline to exercise jurisdiction over claims made under the Alien Tort Claims Act. Reasons for dismissal include *forum non conveniens*,[57] international comity,[58] failure to join a necessary party,[59] lack of subject matter jurisdiction,[60] violations of the sovereignty of other nations under the act of state doctrine, which "precludes [U.S.] courts from inquiry into the validity of the public acts which a recognized foreign sovereign power committed within its own territory,"[61] and the political question doctrine, which, dating back to *Marbury v. Madison*,[62] holds

---

[50] *IIT v. Vancap, Ltd.*, 519 F.2d 1001 (2nd Cir. 1975).

[51] *DeWit v. KLM Royal Dutch Airlines, N.V.*, 570 F. Supp. 613 (S.D.N.Y. 1983).

[52] *IIT v. Vancap, Ltd.*, 519 F.2d 1001

[53] *Cohen v. Hartman*, 490 F. Supp. 517 (S.D. Fla. 1980).

[54] *Valanga v. Metropolitan Life Ins. Co.*, 259 F. supp. 324 (E.D. Pa. 1966).

[55] *Pauling v. McElroy*, 164 F. Supp. 390 (D. D.C. 1958).

[56] *Khedivial Line, S.A.E. v. Seafarers' International Union*, 278 F.2d 49 (2nd Cir. 1960).

[57] *De Sairigne v. Gould*, 83 F. Supp. 270 (S.D.N.Y. 1949).

[58] *Sequihua v. Texaco*, 847 F. Supp. 61 (S.D. Tex. 1994).

[59] *Alomang v. Freeport-McMioran, Inc.*, No. 96–2139, 1996 U.S. Dist. LEXIS 15908 at *6 (E.D. La. Oct. 18, 1996).

[60] *Sarei v. Rio Tinto, PLC*, 221 F. Supp. 2d at 1116.

[61] *Banco Nacional de Cuba v. Sabbatino*, 376 U.S. 398, 401 (1964). See also Branch and Marooney, "Corporate Liability under the Alien Tort Claims Act: United States Court Jurisdiction over Torts," 11.

[62] *Marbury v. Madison*, 5 U.S. 137 (1803). While Marbury v. Madison is often remembered as the benchmark case that established the right of judicial review of laws to determine whether they are consistent with the U.S. Constitution, it also specified limits on judicial authority. Delivering the opinion of the Court, Chief Justice John Marshall wrote, "The province of the court is, solely, to decide on the rights of

that certain issues that are highly political should not be decided by courts but should rather be left to the legislative and executive branches. Each of these possible grounds for dismissal merits more detailed comment.

Forum Non Conveniens

The doctrine of *forum non conveniens* allows a U.S. court to decline jurisdiction over a case when the plaintiff has an adequate alternate forum and the court finds that the case may be decided more conveniently, yet fairly, in this alternate forum.[63] This doctrine is meant to protect the defendant from being compelled to defend herself or himself in an unfair and inconvenient forum and to protect the public from being compelled to hear a case for which it has no interest.[64] Courts use a balancing test to determine whether *forum non conveniens* should be applied to a particular case. This balancing test is not administered to determine the relative interests of a U.S. forum versus the foreign forum, but rather is meant to determine whether the defendant will suffer undue hardship as a result of defending himself or herself in a given forum.[65] In *Piper Aircraft Co. v. Reyno*, the U.S. Supreme Court reaffirmed a set of factors based on the private interests of the litigants and the public interests affecting the forum in question. The factors for private interests of the litigants include (1) ease of access to proof, (2) ability to compel unwilling witnesses to attend hearings, and the cost of obtaining witnesses, (3) when appropriate, the ability

individuals, not to enquire how the executive, or executive officers, perform duties in which they have a discretion. Questions, in their nature political, or which are, by the constitution and laws, submitted to the executive, can never be made in this court" (*ibid.* at 170). In the course of the years, precisely what this means has been the topic of considerable debate. For an engaging overview of this debate, see David E. Marion, "Judicial Faithfulness or Wandering Indulgence? Original Intentions and the History of Marbury v. Madison," *Alabama Law Review* 57 (Summer 2006), 1041–1080.

[63] *Gulf Oil Corp. v. Gilbert*, 330 U.S. 501; *Semanishin v. Metropolitan Life Ins. Co.*, 46 N.J. 531 (1966); *Plum v. Tampax, Inc.*, 402 Pa. 616 (1961); *Rothluebbers v. Obee*, 668 N.W.2d 313 (S.D. 2003).

[64] *In re Smith Barney, Inc.*, 975 S.W. 2d 593 (Tex. 1998).

[65] *Candlewood Timber Group, LLC, v. Pan American Energy, LLC*, 859 A.2d 989 (Del. 2004), cert. denied, 125 S. Ct. 1314 (U.S. 2005); 20 Am. Jur. 2d Courts § 118 (2006).

to view premises in question, and (4) other issues making a trial easy, expeditious, and inexpensive. Public factors include (1) court congestion, (2) the local interest in deciding local controversies at home, (3) the avoidance of unnecessary problems in conflict of laws, or in the application of foreign law, and (4) the unfairness of burdening jurors with cases unrelated to the forum.[66]

Courts have dismissed cases for all of these reasons. For a court to dismiss a case under the doctrine of *forum non conveniens*, the defendents must first show that an adequate alternate forum exists. In *Sequihua v. Texaco, Inc.*, indigenous plaintiffs from Ecuador brought a suit against Texaco claiming that Texaco's subsidiary, TexPet, was responsible for environmental degradation that caused many residents of the Ecuadorian Amazon to experience serious illness. Texaco, however, was able to show that an adequate alternate forum existed by submitting the affidavits of two former Ecuadorian Supreme Court justices.[67]

The alternate forum need not provide the same remedy and conveniences as the U.S. forum. It need only be adequate. In weighing the private factors in *Sequihua v. Texaco, Inc.*, the district court found that (1) "all evidence and the availability of compulsory process would be present in Ecuador, not in the Southern District of Texas"; (2) "the cost of obtaining the attendance of willing witnesses would be much greater in [the Southern District of Texas] than in Ecuador . . . ."; and (3) "the view of the premises, likely in a pollution case such as this, would be possible only in Ecuador."[68]

Having found that overall the private factors weighed strongly against maintaining jurisdiction in U.S. courts, the district court then considered the public factors and found that they also weighed against keeping the case in U.S. courts. The district court concluded that (1) "the administrative difficulties flowing from court congestion favors the foreign forum"; (2) "Ecuador clearly has a local interest in having controversies regarding its air, land and water resolved at home"; (3) "this district does not have any direct interest in this case, and its citizens should not bear the burden of jury service in litigation

[66] *Piper Aircraft Co. v. Reyno*, 454 U.S. 235 (1981).
[67] *Sequihua v. Texaco, Inc.*, 847 F. Supp. 61, 64 (D. Tex. 1994).
[68] *Ibid.*

which has no relation to their community"; and (4) "dismissal would also serve to avoid unnecessary parallel litigation in Ecuador to avoid problems in conflicts of law or in the application of foreign law."[69]

The question of what constitutes an adequate alternate forum is a key issue under the doctrine of *forum non conveniens*. The U.S. Supreme Court has stated that for a forum to be inadequate it must be "so clearly inadequate to be no remedy at all."[70] The argument that the alternate forum is inadequate because it is too corrupt has not been very successful,[71] the general sentiment being: "It is not the business of our courts to assume responsibility for supervising the integrity of the judicial system of another sovereign nation."[72] In *Torres v. Southern Peru Copper Corporation*, neither the district court nor the appellate court deemed the Peruvian forum inadequate due to its corruption, noting that Peruvian courts had ruled against the defendant, Southern Peru Copper Corporation, on numerous occasions, which the U.S. district and appellate courts viewed as illustrating the ability of Peruvian courts to adjudicate these cases.[73] However, since then in *Eastman Kodak Co. v. Kavlin*,[74] the corruption argument has been successful. Kodak's argument succeeded in this case because they were able to convince the U.S. District Court for the Southern District of Florida that Bolivian courts are notoriously corrupt. Plaintiffs established this fact through numerous submissions to the district court, including a Bolivian newspaper article quoting the minister of justice saying that the Bolivian legal system was nothing more than an agency of extortion, as well as World Bank and U.S. State Department reports identifying widespread corruption in Bolivian courts. The district court found that the plaintiffs thereby established a prima facie case that the Bolivian courts would not provide an adequate alternate forum.[75]

In light of the considerations weighed in a *forum non conveniens* analysis, persuading the U.S. district court – in which a claim was filed

[69] *Ibid.*
[70] *Piper Aircraft Co. v. Reyno,* 454 U.S. at 250, 254.
[71] *Torres v. Southern Peru Copper Corp.,* 965 F. Supp. 899 (S.D. Tex.1996)
[72] *Jhirad v. Ferrandina,* 536 F.2d 478, 484–485 (2nd Cir. 1976).
[73] *Torres v. Southern Peru Copper Corp.,* 965 F. Supp. at 903.
[74] *Eastman Kodak Co. v. Kavlin,* 978 F. Supp. 1078 (S.D. Fla. 1997)
[75] *Eastman Kodak Co. v. Kavlin,* 978 F. Supp. at 1085.

under the Alien Tort Claims Act – not to dismiss the case on grounds of *forum non conveniens* can be challenging. In the environmental context, this is especially problematic for plaintiffs because the environmental harm itself is naturally going to be in the foreign country in which it occurred, the result being that a good deal of the evidence pertinent to the case will only be available in that country. There are, however, arguments that can be made against dismissal on grounds of *forum non conveniens*. Corporate headquarters, which in the case of U.S. multinational corporations are typically located in the United States, often house the documents pertaining to decisions made in regard to environmental policies and other matters of relevance to the case. In addition, the argument of *forum non conveniens* is not as convincing in the case of a multinational corporation as it may be in the case of an individual since multinational corporations by their very nature are capable of operating in numerous countries.[76]

International Comity

The doctrine of international comity is based on respect for the sovereignty of other nations.[77] Comity is not a rule of law *per se*. Instead it is a rule of practice for purposes of convenience and expediency.[78] The United States is not obligated, however, to grant deference to the laws of other nations.[79]

Comity is often used by defendants in Alien Tort Claims Act cases when the plaintiff is challenging a practice or policy of a foreign government that is not as clearly condemned by international law as is torture or genocide – practices or policies such as displacement of indigenous people for the purpose of resource exploration, or environmental claims. Such cases raise more serious issues of comity since they require a U.S. court to judge the policies of a foreign

---

[76] *Trafton v. Deacon Barclays De Zoete Wedd, Ltd.*, 1994 WL 746199, at 6 (N.D. Cal. October 21, 1994), found that the defendant was a "sophisticated entity" and that this fact weighed against its claim of *forum non conveniens*.

[77] 45 Am. Jur. 2D *International Law* § 7 (2006).

[78] *Pravin Banker Associates, Ltd. v. Banco Popular Del Peru*, 109 F.3d 850 (2d Cir. 1997); 45 Am. Jur. 2D *International Law* § 7 (2006).

[79] *In re Hackett*, 184 B.R. 656 (Bankr. D.N.Y. 1995); 45 Am. Jur. 2D *International Law* § 7 (2006).

government that are not in violation of *jus cogens* norms of international law.[80]

Failure To Join a Necessary Party

Other Alien Tort Claims Act cases have been dismissed due to an inability to join a necessary party. When a court cannot obtain personal jurisdiction over a party and that party's absence would cause serious prejudice to the case, the court may choose to dismiss the case. Often this party is a sovereign state and, therefore, unable to be joined under the Sovereign Immunities Act.[81] Under Rule 19 of the Federal Rules of Civil Procedure, courts will dismiss an action when necessary parties cannot be joined.[82] A missing party is necessary if (1) in the party's absence complete relief cannot be reached among all parties, or (2) the party claims an interest relating to the subject matter of the action. If the court decides that a party is necessary, it must then decide "whether in equity and good conscience the action should proceed among the parties before it...."[83] For example, in *Aguinda v. Texaco*, the U.S. District Court for the Southern District of New York held that the plaintiff's action against Texaco for environmental harm should be dismissed for the plaintiff's failure to join indispensable parties, namely Petroecuador and the Republic of Ecuador. The court held that the relief sought, including environmental cleanup and alteration to the oil pipelines, called for the participation of these parties because they had taken over ownership of the company in 1992.[84]

Lack of Subject Matter Jurisdiction

In Alien Tort Claims Act cases, the jurisdictional issue is almost always intertwined with the merits of the plaintiff's claim.[85] In *Kadic v.*

---

[80] See, e.g., *Sequihua v. Texaco*, 847 F. Supp. at 63; George S. Branch and Richard T. Marooney, "Corporate Liability under the Alien Tort Claims Act: United States Court Jurisdiction over Torts," 12 *Currents: International Trade L.D.*, (2003): 3, 11.

[81] 28 U.S.C.S. §§ 1603(b), 1604 (1976).

[82] Fed. R. Civ. Pro. 19.

[83] *Ibid.*

[84] *Aguinda v. Texaco*, 945 F. Supp. 625, 627 (1996 U.S. Dist. LEXIS 16884).

[85] *Sarei v. Rio Tinto*, F. Supp. 2d. at 1116.

Karadzic, the 2nd Circuit Court of Appeals states, "There is no federal subject-matter jurisdiction under the Alien Tort Act unless the complaint adequately pleads a violation of the law of nations (or a treaty of the United States)."[86] Alien Tort Claims Act cases are unusual in that a cause of action must be met before jurisdiction will be granted.[87] For this reason, claims made under the Alien Tort Claims Act will sometimes be dismissed for lack of subject matter jurisdiction if the plaintiff's allegations do not facially violate the law of nations. To evaluate plaintiffs' claims, a court must consider (1) whether they identify a specific, universal, and obligatory norm of international law, (2) whether that norm is recognized by the United States, and (3) whether the plaintiff adequately alleges its violation.[88]

Act of State Doctrine

The act of state doctrine "precludes [U.S.] courts from inquiry into the validity of the public acts which a recognized foreign sovereign power committed within its own territory."[89] In cases involving torture, genocide, and extrajudicial execution, the act of state doctrine is often insignificant because such acts are internationally condemned and are not held as acts of the state.[90] However, this doctrine is likely to be more applicable in cases involving environmental claims.[91] In environmental claims, the environmental harms in question may not violate *jus cogens* norms. Thus, whether a U.S. court may sit in judgment of another country's policy with regard to the environment within its own borders is more problematic. A country, for example, may have a policy to promote economic development over environmental conservation. National sovereignty dictates that a state has a right to make such decisions, whereas in situations involving genocide, a state does not have a sovereign right to make a "genocidal"

---

[86] *Kadic v. Karadzic,* 70 F.3d at 238.

[87] *Bigio v. Coca-Cola Co.,* 239 F.3d 440, 447 (2nd Cir. 2000).

[88] See *Unocal II,* 176 F.R.D. at 345.

[89] *Banco Nacional de Cuba v. Sabbatino,* 376 U.S. 398, 401 (1964). See also Branch and Marooney, "Corporate Liability under the Alien Tort Claims Act: United States Court Jurisdiction over Torts," 11.

[90] *Kadic v. Karadzic,* 70 F.3d at 250.

[91] Shamir, "Between Self-Regulation and the Alien Tort Claims Act," 643.

policy choice. At present, no strictly environmental law rises to the level of customary international law. Therefore, some element of human harm would likely be necessary for an environmental case to be successfully litigated under the Alien Tort Claims Act. We will return to this matter later in this chapter.

The Political Question Doctrine

The political question doctrine dates back to *Marbury v. Madison*, a decision in which the U.S. Supreme Court held that certain issues or cases considered to be highly political could not be decided by the Court because they were better suited for the legislative and executive branches.[92] In *Baker v. Carr*, the Court specified six factors that federal courts must use to determine whether the political question doctrine applies to a particular case: (1) "a textually demonstrable constitutional commitment of the issue to a coordinate department," (2) "a lack of judicially discoverable and manageable standards for resolving" the case, (3) "the impossibility of deciding without an initial policy determination of a kind clearly for nonjudicial discretion," (4) "the impossibility of a court's undertaking independent resolution without expressing lack of the respect due coordinate branches of government," (5) "an unusual need for unquestioning adherence to a political decision already made," and (6) "the potentiality of embarrassment from multifarious pronouncements by various departments on one question."[93]

But while defendants often raise the political question doctrine in Alien Tort Claims Act cases, courts have been known to reject it. In *Kadic v. Karadzic*, the Second Circuit Court of Appeals held that "universally recognized norms of international law provide judicially discoverable and manageable standards for adjudicating suits brought under the [Alien Tort Claims Act], which obviates the need to make initial policy decisions of the kind normally reserved for nonjudicial discretion."[94] The U.S. District Court for the Southern District of New York made a similar ruling in *Presbyterian Church of Sudan v. Talisman*

---

[92] *Marbury v. Madison*, 5 U.S. at 169.
[93] *Baker v. Carr*, 369 U.S. 186, 217 (1962)
[94] *Kadic v. Karadzic*, 70 F.3d at 249.

Energy, a case in which plaintiffs alleged that their villages and churches were destroyed in the areas near Talisman's oil fields. The defendant was alleged to have committed extrajudicial killings, forcible displacement, war crimes, property confiscation and destruction, kidnapping, rape, and enslavement, which, it was argued, together comprised genocide. In response to the defendant's political question defense, the district court held that norms prohibiting the acts in question are so universally recognized that they are not barred by the political question doctrine.[95] As noted in the discussion of the act of state doctrine, because environmental claims are not yet concrete in their universal recognition, the political question doctrine may be especially applicable in these cases because enforcement of such regulations could impinge on national sovereignty. We will also return to this matter later in this chapter.

THREE SUCCESSFUL CASES

In short, there are multiple grounds on which U.S. courts may dismiss claims made under the Alien Tort Claims Act. This does not mean, however, that it is not possible to litigate human rights cases successfully under the provisions of the act. We have made passing reference to three cases alleging human rights violations that have been successfully litigated – *Filártiga v. Pena-Irala*, *Kadic v. Karadzic*, and *John Doe I v. Unocal Corporation*. The first two resulted in verdicts in favor of the plaintiffs upon appeal. The third case led to an out-of-court settlement beneficial to the plaintiffs. Each of these cases merits more detailed comment.

Filártiga v. Pena-Irala

In *Filártiga v. Pena-Irala*, the son of an opponent to Paraguayan dictator Alfredo Stroessner was allegedly tortured to death by the inspector general of the police of Asunción, Paraguay. Several years later, the victim's sister and the government inspector separately came to live in the United States. After learning that the government

[95] *Presbyterian Church of Sudan v. Talisman Energy, Inc.*, 244 F. Supp. 2d 289, 298 (S.D.N.Y. 2003).

inspector was living in New York City, the alleged victim's sister and father filed a wrongful death suit under the Alien Tort Claims Act, claiming that the alleged victim had been tortured in violation of the law of nations.[96] The U.S. District Court for the Eastern District of New York dismissed the case on the grounds that it lacked jurisdiction. The 2nd Circuit Court of Appeals reversed the dismissal, ruling that there is federal jurisdiction "whenever an alleged torturer is found and served with process by an alien within our borders…."[97] The court of appeals remanded the case to the district court which, once the matter of jurisdiction was resolved, ruled, "If the courts of the United States are to adhere to the consensus of the community of humankind, any remedy they fashion must recognize that this case concerns an act so monstrous as to make its perpetrator an outlaw around the globe."[98] The district court awarded $5,175,000 to Dolly Filártiga for the torture and murder of her brother and $5,210,364 to Joel Filártiga for the torture and murder of his son.[99]

Kadic v. Karadzic

In *Kadic v. Karadzic*, a group of Croat and Muslim survivors filed a claim under the Alien Tort Claims Act against Radovan Karadzic, the president of the self-proclaimed Bosnian-Serb Republic (also referred to as "Srpska"). The plaintiffs claimed that they were victims of various human rights offenses, among them rape, forced prostitution, forced impregnation, torture, summary execution, genocide, assault and battery, sex and ethnic inequality, and wrongful death.[100] The U.S. District Court for the Southern District of New York dismissed the case for lack of subject matter jurisdiction,[101] but the 2nd Circuit Court of Appeals reversed the lower court decision and remanded the case to the district court for further findings with respect to genocide, war crimes, state action, torture, and extrajudicial killings.[102] The

[96] *Filártiga v. Pena-Irala*, 630 F.2d 876.
[97] *Ibid.*
[98] *Filártiga v. Pena-Irala*, 577 F. Supp. 860, 863 (D.N.Y. 1984).
[99] *Ibid.* at 867.
[100] *Kadic v. Karadzic*, 70 F.3d at 237.
[101] *Doe v. Karadzic*, 866 F. Supp. 734 (S.D.N.Y. 1994).
[102] *Ibid.* at 250.

district court entered an order of default on June 13, 2000. The case then proceeded to the damages phase. After hearing extensive testimony, including testimony from women who reported that Bosnian Serb soldiers raped them repeatedly while forcing their children to watch, the jury awarded $745 million ($265 million in compensatory damages and $480 million in punitive damages) to the fourteen plaintiffs, who were suing on behalf of themselves and their deceased family members.[103]

John Doe I v. Unocal Corporation

In *John Doe I v. Unocal Corporation*, a group of Burmese villagers claimed that Unocal hired Burmese army troops to secure the construction of a pipeline through the country and that the troops forced people living near the pipeline into slave labor. The pleadings in this case were appalling. Jane Doe I testified that her husband, John Doe I, was shot by soldiers in retaliation for his attempted escape from a forced labor program. She also claimed that she and her baby were then thrown into a fire, causing injuries to her and the death of the infant. Other witnesses described the summary executions of villagers who either refused to work in the forced labor programs or were simply too weak to work. Jane Doe II and Jane Doe III testified that they were raped at knife-point by Myanmar (Burmese) soldiers assigned to protect the construction of Unocal's pipeline. The plaintiffs alleged that Unocal should be held liable for these abuses.[104]

After several years of litigation, Unocal finally decided to settle the case out of court. On December 13, 2004, the parties to the dispute issued a joint statement indicating that Unocal would pay the plaintiffs an unspecified amount of money and fund programs to improve living conditions for those living in the region surrounding the pipeline "who may have suffered hardships."[105] Though the details of the

---

[103] Sean D. Murphy, *United States Practice in International Law* Vol. I: *1999–2001* (Cambridge: Cambridge University Press, 2002), 307.

[104] *John Doe I v. Unocal Corporation*, 395 F.3d 932, 940 (9th Cir. 2002). The "John Doe I" and other similar designations are, of course, pseudonyms used to protect the identity of the plaintiffs.

[105] Lisa Girion, "Unocal to Settle Rights Claims," *Los Angeles Times*, December 14, 2004.

settlement were not publicly announced, Unocal is believed to have agreed to pay about $30 million in damages to settle the case.[106]

THE BUSH ADMINISTRATION
AND THE ALIEN TORT CLAIM ACT

The administration of George W. Bush actively opposed using the Alien Tort Claim Act for human rights and environmental claims, asserting that deciding such cases must be left to the executive branch as they deal with foreign policy. For example, the State Department filed a brief in *Doe v. Exxon Mobil* stating that "the Department of State believes that adjudication of this lawsuit at this time would in fact risk a potentially serious adverse impact on significant interests of the United States, including interests related directly to the ongoing struggle against international terrorism."[107] Additionally, the letter noted that an important aspect of U.S. foreign policy is to increase opportunities for American business abroad, and that adjudication in this case involving Indonesian villagers could "prejudice the Government of Indonesia and Indonesian businesses against U.S. firms."[108]

In a brief filed in the 9th Circuit in *John Doe I v. Unocal*, Attorney General John Ashcroft argued for an overall reinterpretation of the statute. The brief asserted that the ATCA could not be used to file civil cases, that the law of nations did not include international human rights treaties, and that abuses committed outside of the United States should not be covered under the ATCA. The brief further argued that while the original intent of the law was to avoid conflicts with other countries, the present use of it could bring about the opposite result.[109]

---

[106] Paul Magnusson, "A Milestone for Human Rights," *Business Week* 3917 (January 24, 2005): 63.

[107] Quoted by Harold Hongju Koh in "Separating Myth from Reality About Corporate Responsibility Litigation," *Journal of International Economic Law* 7 (204): 263; see also Letter from William H. Taft IV to Judge Louis F. Oberdorfer, United States District Court for the District of Columbia (July 29, 2002) at http://www.humanrightsfirst.org/workers_rights/wr_indonesia/state%20exxon%20mobil.pdf

[108] *Ibid.*

[109] *See* Brief for the United States as Amicus Curiae at 3, 22, *John Doe I v. Unocal Corp.*, Nos. 00–56603, 00–56628 (9th Cir. filed May 8, 2003). See also Shamir, "Between Self-Regulation and the Alien Tort Claims Act," 653, and Richard Hermer and Martyn Day, "Helping Bush Bushwhack Justice: The Most Progressive Law on the

In *Sarei v. Rio Tinto, PLC,* the State Department filed a statement of interest (SOI) in which it argued that "[i]n our judgment, continued adjudication of the claims [made by the plaintiffs] ... would risk a potentially serious adverse impact on the peace process, and hence on the conduct of our foreign relations." The statement concluded with the observation that "[t]he Government of Papua New Guinea ... has stated its objection to these proceedings in the strongest terms" and that Papua New Guinea (PNG) "perceives the potential impact of this litigation on U.S.-PNG relations, and wider regional interests, to be 'very grave.'"[110] (The 9th Circuit Court of Appeals, however, found the State Department's Statement of Interest unpersuasive, ruling that "we cannot uphold the dismissal of this lawsuit solely on the basis of the SOI."[111])

Not enough time has passed to get a clear picture of how the Obama administration is likely to proceed on these matters. However, given the position that the Obama administration has taken on other issues, it is likely that it will be more supportive of the use of the Alien Tort Claims Act to address human rights issues, than was its predecessor.

ENVIRONMENTAL CASES FILED UNDER THE ALIEN TORT CLAIMS ACT

A number of environmental claims have been filed under the Alien Tort Claims Act. Among them are *Sequihua v. Texaco, Inc.,*[112] *Aguinda v. Texaco, Inc.,*[113] *Flores v. Southern Peru Copper Corporation,*[114] *Beanal v. Freeport-McMoran Copper and Gold, Inc.,*[115] and *Sarei v. Rio Tinto, PLC.*[116] The latter is still in court[117] and might end up being a landmark decision. The others have been unsuccessful, having been dismissed

US Statute Books Delivers Justice to Victims of Human Rights Violations. Now the Bush Regime Is Trying to Scrap It and the UK Government Is Backing Him," *Guardian* (April 27, 2004), 16.

[110] Quoted in *Sarei v. Rio Tinto, PLC,* 456 F.3d (9th Cir. 2006) at 1082–1083.

[111] *Ibid.* at 1082–1083.

[112] *Sequihua v. Texaco,* 847 F. Supp. 61 (S.D. Tex. 1994).

[113] *Aguinda v. Texaco, Inc.,* 142 F. Supp. 2d 534 (S.D.N.Y. 2001).

[114] *Flores v. Southern Peru Copper Corporation,* 253 F. Supp. 2d 510 (S.D.N.Y. 2002).

[115] *Beanal v. Freeport-McMoran Copper and Gold, Inc.,* 969 F. Supp. 362 (E.D. La. 1997).

[116] *Sarei v. Rio Tinto, PLC.,* 221 F. Supp. 2d 1116 (C.D. Cal. 2002).

[117] *Sarei v. Rio Tinto, PLC,* 499 F.3d 923 (9th Cir. 2007).

for various reasons. More detailed comments on each of these cases follow.

Sequihua v. Texaco, Inc.

In *Sequihua v. Texaco, Inc.*, a group of residents from the Ecuadorian Amazon sued Texaco, claiming that Texaco, during oil exploration in the Oriente region of Ecuador, dumped tons of toxic waste in rivers and rainforests, contaminating the environment to such an extent that 500,000 residents of the region were injured.[118] The U.S. District Court for the Southern District of Texas dismissed the case under the doctrines of international comity and *forum non conveniens*. In dismissing the case under the doctrine of comity of nations, the court noted that Ecuador regulates the challenged conduct and that the involvement of U.S. courts would interfere with Ecuador's sovereign right to control its resources. Under the doctrine of *forum non conveniens*, the court found for the defendant holding that (1) Ecuador has an adequate forum in which to try the case, (2) plaintiffs are residents of Ecuador and the defendant conducted business in Ecuador, (3) Educador provides remedies for tortious conduct and has an independent judiciary with "adequate procedural safeguards," and (4) all evidence related to the allegedly polluted land is in Ecuador.[119]

Aguinda v. Texaco, Inc.

In *Aguinda v. Texaco, Inc.*, a group of seventy-six indigenous Ecuadorians representing a class of 30,000 residents of Ecuador sued Texaco under the Alien Tort Claims Act, alleging that between 1964 and 1992 Texaco improperly disposed of waste during oil extraction in the Ecuadorian Amazon.[120] The plaintiffs complained that Texaco's alleged dumping of toxic waste in the rivers and in open pits throughout the Ecuadorian Amazon resulted in health problems for the resident of the region. Plaintiffs claimed they experienced

---

[118] *Sequihua v. Texaco, Inc.*, 847 F. Supp. at 61–62,
[119] *Ibid.* at 63–64.
[120] *Aguinda v. Texaco, Inc.*, 142 F. Supp. 2d 534 (S.D.N.Y. 2001). See also *Aguinda v. Texaco, Inc.*, 303 F.3d at 473 (2nd Cir. 2002).

"higher occurrence[s] of abortion, [and] elevated rates of fungal infection, dermatitis, headache and nausea" caused by exposure to contaminated drinking and bathing water.[121] The plaintiffs sought relief in the form of:

> [F]inancing for environmental cleanup to create access to potable water and hunting and fishing rounds; renovating or closing the Trans-Ecuadorian Pipeline; creation of an environmental monitoring fund; establishing standards to govern future Texaco oil development; creation of a medical monitoring fund; an injunction restraining Texaco from entering into activities that risk environmental or human injuries, and restitution.[122]

The U.S. District Court for the Southern District of New York dismissed the case on grounds of international comity, *forum non conveniens* and failure to join a necessary party.[123] On appeal, the 2nd Circuit Court of Appeals joined the case with *Jota v. Texaco, Inc.*, and vacated the lower court's ruling, remanding the case to the district court for reconsideration.[124] In 2001, the district court again dismissed the case on grounds of *forum non conveniens*. On the second appeal to the 2nd Circuit Court of Appeals, the court affirmed the district court's decision to dismiss the case on grounds of *forum non conveniens* provided that the defendant waived the defense of statute of limitations to allow the plaintiffs adequate time to file the case in Ecuador.[125] Texaco, however, claims that it is protected from further litigation by a contract with the government of Ecuador in which it promised to contribute $13.5 million to the proposed Oriente cleanup project.[126]

Flores v. Southern Peru Copper Corporation

In *Flores v. Southern Peru Copper Corporation*, residents of Peru sued the Southern Peru Copper Corporation in the U.S. District Court for the Southern District of New York, alleging personal injuries and property damage resulting from the defendants' copper mining and

---

[121] James Brooke, "Pollution of Water Tied to Oil in Ecuador," *New York Times* (March 22, 1994), C11.
[122] See *Jota v. Texaco, Inc.*, 157 F.3d. 153, 156 (2nd Cir. 1998).
[123] *Aguinda v. Texaco, Inc.*, 945 F. Supp. 625, 627 (S.D.N.Y. 1996).
[124] *Jota v. Texaco, Inc.*, 157 F.3d at 155.
[125] *Aguinda v. Texaco, Inc.*, 142 F. Supp. 2d 534 (S.D.N.Y. 2001).
[126] Brooke, "Pollution of Water Tied to Oil in Ecuador," C11.

refining processes near and in the city of Ilo, Peru. The plaintiffs claimed that the defendants' alleged pollution infringed the plaintiffs' "right to life" and "right to health" and that the defendants violated their "duty to assure sustainable development."[127] The district court dismissed the case for lack of subject matter jurisdiction and because the plaintiffs failed to demonstrate that high levels of environmental pollution entirely within the borders of Peru caused harm to human life, health, or development. The court found that the plaintiffs failed to show that the defendant had violated a "well-established, universally recognized" norm of international law.[128]

On appeal, the 2nd Circuit Court of Appeals affirmed the district court's decision to dismiss the case, finding that the plaintiffs did not assert a violation of international law that was sufficiently "clear and unambiguous." The appeals court examined the Universal Declaration of Human Rights and other international agreements but concluded that the "aspirations" in these documents are too amorphous to be considered binding rules of international law.[129]

Beanal v. Freeport-McMoran Copper and Gold, Inc.

In *Beanal v. Freeport-McMoran Copper and Gold, Inc.*, leaders and representatives of the Amungme people of Indonesia alleged that human rights and environmental violations perpetrated by a subsidiary of Freeport-McMoran Copper and Gold, Inc., a Delaware corporation with headquarters located in New Orleans, Louisiana, resulted in the demise of the culture of the Amungme people. Tom Beanal, "on behalf of himself and all others similarly situated," claimed that because Freeport-McMoran began operations in Indonesia, many Amungme people were displaced and relocated to areas in lowlands away from their cultural heritage in the highlands. Describing what had happened as "cultural genocide," Beanal argued:

The egregious human rights and environmental violations, which have terrorized the tribal communities of the Amungme and other Indigenous tribal people, destroyed their natural habitats and caused dislocation of

---

[127] *Flores v. Southern Peru Copper Corporation*, 414 F.3d 233, 237 (2nd Cir. 2003).
[128] *Flores v. Southern Peru Copper Corporation*, 253 F. Supp. 2d 510, 516 (S.D.N.Y. 2002).
[129] *Flores v. Southern Peru Copper Corporation*, 414 F.3d at 254.

the populations have resulted in the purposeful, deliberate, contrived and planned demise of a culture of indigenous people whose rights were never considered, whose heritage and culture were disregarded and the result of which is ultimately to lead to the cultural demise of unique pristine heritage which is socially, culturally and anthropologically irreplaceable.[130]

Beanal further alleged that the Freeport-McMoran mine hollowed out several mountains, rerouted rivers, stripped forests, and increased toxic and nontoxic materials and metals into the river system, pollution and mismanagement of waste that led to "health safety hazards and starvation" among the Amungme people.[131] The U.S. District Court for the Eastern District of Louisiana dismissed the case, referencing both *Aguinda v. Texaco, Inc.* and *Amlon Metals, Inc., v. FMC Corp.* and noting that the plaintiff "failed to articulate a violation of the international law."[132]

Sarei v. Rio Tinto, PLC

Sarei v. Rio Tinto, PLC, is the most complicated – and in many respects the most controversial – of the environmental cases filed under the Alien Tort Claims Act. It is also a case that has the potential for breaking new ground, as did *Filártiga v. Pena-Irala* in 1980. As noted earlier in this chapter, in *Sarei v. Rio Tinto, PLC*, residents of the Papua New Guinea island of Bougainville sued Rio Tinto mining company, claiming that the company had damaged the island's environment to such an extent that islanders could no longer fish or use water from island rivers, and that the mining operations were so divisive in Papua New Guinea that they incited a civil war that killed and injured thousands of civilians.[133]

The U.S. District Court for the Central District of California, which had original jurisdiction over the case, denied a motion made by the defendant to dismiss the case on grounds of *forum non conveniens*. The district court, however, concluded that all claims made by the plaintiffs

---

[130] *Beanal v. Freeport-McMoran Copper and Gold, Inc.*, 969 F. Supp. 362, 372 (E.D. La. 1997).
[131] *Ibid.* at 382, 383.
[132] *Ibid.*
[133] *Sarei v. Rio Tinto, PLC*, 456 F.3d 1069, 1116 (9th Cir. 2006).

should be dismissed on the basis of the political question doctrine,[134] which, as noted, holds that certain issues or cases considered to be highly political should not be decided by the judicial branch of government since they are better suited for the legislative and executive branches. Upon appeal, the 9th Circuit Court of Appeals reversed the lower court's dismissal of all claims on the basis of the political question doctrine while agreeing with the district court's ruling that the Alien Tort Claims Act does not require that plaintiffs exhaust all local remedies in order to file a complaint under the act.[135] On August 20, 2007, however, a majority of the nonrecused judges on the 9th Circuit Court of Appeals voted to order that the case be reheard *en banc* (that is, by the entire court) and further ruled that the opinion by the three judge panel that initially heard the case should not be cited as a precedent.[136] (Appellate courts that have a large number of judges and large caseloads often divide into three judge panels to hear cases. A majority of the circuit court of appeals judges who are in regular active service may order that a case be reheard by the entire court. This is ordinarily not done, however, unless (1) consideration by the full court is necessary to maintain uniformity of decisions, or (2) the case involves a question of exceptional importance.[137]) The 9th Circuit Court of appeals, hearing the case *en banc*, remanded the case to the district court for the limited purpose of determining whether an exhaustion requirement, which stipulates that residents of other countries should exhaust local remedies before pursuing their cases in U.S. courts, should be imposed on the foreign residents involved in the case. The court, however, added that the exhaustion requirement is not absolute. They noted, "International law – both private and public – has long anticipated that local remedies might not always be adequate and that justice may be denied if claimants are forced to exhaust before being heard in an international forum."[138] And indeed

---

[134] *Sarei v. Rio Tinto, PLC*, 221 F. Supp. 2d 1116 (C.D. Calif. 2002).

[135] *Sarei v. Rio Tinto, PLC*, 487 F.3d 1193 (9th Cir. 2007). The 9th Circuit Court of Appeals withdrew its opinion issued on August 7, 2006, and issued another opinion on April 12, 2007.

[136] *Sarei v. Rio Tinto, PLC*, 499 F.3d 923 (9th Cir. 2007).

[137] "En Banc" at http://www.techlawjournal.com/glossary/legal/enbanc.htm (last accessed November 20, 2008).

[138] *Sarei v. Rio Tinto, PLC*, 550 F.3d 822 (9th Cir. 2008). The court, however, further notes, "Though it is self-evident, it is worth remembering that in [Alien Tort Claims

that is the crux of the matter: Residents of other countries litigate in U.S. courts under the provisions of the Alien Tort Claims Act because U.S. companies go to their countries and harm them but their countries fail to protect them or provide an effective venue for addressing their grievances.

TAKING STOCK OF THE CURRENT SITUATION

To recapitulate, in the course of the years that have passed since the very first U.S. Congress enacted the Alien Tort Claims Act as part of the Judiciary Act of 1789, the norms viewed as comprising the law of nations have undergone considerable evolutionary change. There is no reason to believe that Oliver Ellsworth and the other drafters of the Judiciary Act of 1789 envisioned extrajudicial executions, torture, or genocide as acts for which victims could seek redress under the provisions of the Alien Tort Claims Act.[139] Since then, however, as reflected by decisions such as *Filártiga v. Pena-Irala* and *Kadic v. Karadzic*, U.S. courts have determined that norms prohibiting extrajudicial executions, torture or genocide can appropriately be viewed as norms of international law. In *Sosa v. Alvarez-Machain*, the U.S. Supreme Court, while warning of the dangers of judicial creativity, stated, "It would take some explaining to say now that federal courts must avert their gaze entirely from any international norm intended to protect individuals."[140]

Insofar as environmental claims filed under the Alien Tort Claims Act are concerned, the reference to "any international norm intended to protect individuals" is crucial. Because the scope of the Alien Tort Claims Act is limited to allowing victims to sue for damages for wrongs that have been done to them, it is exceedingly unlikely that litigation to protect an endangered species or to preserve coral reefs could be successful if filed under the Alien Tort Claims Act. Put in slightly different words, environmental claims must be human rights claims that involve identifiable individuals who have been harmed if claims of

Act] adjudication, the United States courts are *not* international courts. With this in mind, the appropriateness of applying prudential exhaustion to some [Alien Tort Claim Act] cases only gains force...."

[139] *Sosa v. Alvarez-Machain*, 542 U.S. at 719.

[140] *Ibid.* at 728, 730.

this sort are to have any prospects for success under the provisions of the act. As noted previously, at present no strictly environmental law rises to the level of customary international law. Therefore, some element of tangible human harm would likely be necessary for an environmental case to be successfully litigated under the Alien Tort Claims Act.

A RIGHT TO A HEALTHY ENVIRONMENT?

In an article entitled "Litigating Environmental Abuses under the Alien Tort Claims Act: A Practical Assessment" that was published in the *Virginia Journal of International Law* in 2000, Richard L. Herz, who served as counsel for the plaintiffs in *Doe v. Unocal*, argues that customary international law protects the right to a healthy environment. Commenting on the evolving nature of customary international law with the offenses actionable under the Alien Tort Claims Act (ATCA) having been expanded to include torture, genocide summary execution, and other offenses, Herz observes, "These, however, are not necessarily the only norms actionable under ATCA. Certain long-established customary norms simply have not been raised by plaintiffs or recognized by U.S. courts."[141] He goes on to argue that "the right to a healthy environment is universally recognized."[142]

Herz is correct in noting that references to a right to a healthy environment appear widely in international agreements and other

---

[141] Richard L. Herz, "Litigating Environmental Abuses under the Alien Tort Claims Act: A Practical Assessment," *Virginia Journal of International Law* 40 (Winter, 2000):558.

[142] *Ibid.*, 582. Polly Higgins, a former barrister based in London, takes a somewhat different approach. She is spearheading a campaign to persuade the United Nations to declare that mass destruction of ecosystems, which she refers to as "ecocide," is an international crime against peace, like genocide and crimes against humanity, for which those accused could be tried at the International Criminal Court (ICC). She defines ecocide as "the extensive destruction, damage to or loss of ecosystem(s) of a given territory, whether by human agency or by other causes, to such an extent that peaceful enjoyment by the inhabitants of that territory has been severely diminished" (quoted by Juliette Jowit in "British Campaigner Urges UN To Accept 'Ecocide' as International Crime," *Guardian*, April 9, 2010, at http://www.guardian.co.uk/environment/2010/apr/09/ecocide-crime-genocide-un-environmental-damage [last accessed May 6, 2010]). What happens in this regard, of course, remains to be seen.

international documents. For example, the *Declaration of the United Nations Conference on the Human Environment (Stockholm 1972)*, a document affirmed by 144 nations, states that humankind "has the fundamental right to freedom, equality and adequate conditions of life, in an environment of a quality that permits a life of dignity and well-being."[143] The *Rio Declaration on Environment and Development*, a declaration of the 1992 United Nations Conference on Environment and Development affirmed by 178 nations, states that human beings "are entitled to a healthy and productive life in harmony with nature."[144] The *African (Banjul) Charter on Human and Peoples' Rights*, adopted by the Organization of African Unity on June 27, 1981, states, "All peoples shall have the right to a general satisfactory environment favorable to their development."[145] The *Hague Declaration on the Environment*, issued in 1989, warns of the dangers of global warming and deterioration of the ozone layer and asserts that humankind has "the right to live in dignity in a viable global environment."[146] *Norms on the Responsibilities of Transnational Corporations and Other Business Enterprises with Regard to Human Rights*, a United Nations document issued in 2003, states, "Transnational corporations and other business enterprises shall carry out their activities in accordance with national laws, regulations, administrative practices and policies relating to the preservation of the environment of the countries in which they operate, as well as in accordance with relevant international agreements...."[147] In the *Additional Protocol to the American Convention on Human Rights in the Area of Economic, Social and Cultural Rights (1999)*, the Organization of American States (OAS) declares, "Everyone shall

---

[143] *Declaration of the United Nations Conference on the Human Environment* at http://www.unep.org/Documents.Multilingual/Default.asp?DocumentID=97&ArticleID=1503 (last accessed November 21, 2008).

[144] *Rio Declaration on Environment and Development (1992)* at http://www.unep.org/Documents.multilingual/Default.asp?DocumentID=78&ArticleID=1163 (last accessed November 21, 2008).

[145] *African (Banjul) Charter on Human and Peoples' Rights (1981)* at http://www1.umn.edu/humanrts/instree/z1afchar.htm (last accessed November 21, 2008).

[146] *Hague Declaration on the Environment (1989)* at http://www.nls.ac.in/CEERA/ceerafeb04/html/documents/lib_int_c1s2_hag_230300.htm (last accessed November 21, 2008).

[147] United Nations, *Norms on the Responsibilities of Transnational Corporations and other Business Enterprises with Regard to Human Rights (2003)* at http://www1.umn.edu/humanrts/links/norms-Aug2003.html (last accessed November 21, 2008).

have the right to live in a healthy environment and to have access to basic public services."[148]

Though the list of international documents that make reference to a right to a healthy environment is lengthy, the significance of these documents should not be overstated. The Stockholm and Rio declarations are statements of nonbinding principles. As such, these declarations were not intended to create legal rights and obligations.[149] To varying degrees, the same is true with respect to the other documents. As the 2nd Circuit Court of Appeals concluded in examining the Universal Declaration of Human Rights and other multinational declarations in *Flores v. Southern Peru Copper Corporation*, the declarations in documents such as these are best understood as aspirations rather than as "statements of universally-recognized legal obligations." The court added, "Accordingly, such declarations are not proper evidence of customary international law."[150] Thus, Herz overstates the case when he asserts that documents such as the ones noted "provide strong evidence that nations universally recognize the right to a healthy environment" and that this provides a basis for viewing a right to a healthy environment as being established in customary international law.[151]

A KERNEL OF CONSENSUS

Yet in all of these documents there is a kernel of consensus that might well develop into a norm of international law. In common with established norms of international law, these documents all make a very basic claim, namely that causing physical harm to other human beings violates international norms. Just as torture and genocide cause physical harm, so also environmental pollution can cause physical harm, in some cases even to the point of hastening death. As noted, in *Filártiga v. Pena-Irala*, the 2nd Circuit Court of Appeals stated:

---

[148] Organization of American States, *Additional Protocol to the American Convention on Human Rights in the Area of Economic, Social and Cultural Rights (1999)* at http://www1.umn.edu/humanrts/oasinstr/zoas10pe.htm (last accessed November 21, 2008).

[149] Circle of Rights, *The Right to a Healthy Environment* at http://www1.umn.edu/humanrts/edumat/IHRIP/circle/module15.htm (last accessed November 21, 2008).

[150] *Flores v. Southern Peru Copper Corporation*, 414 F.3d at 254.

[151] Herz, "Litigating Environmental Abuses under the Alien Tort Claims Act," 583.

In light of the universal condemnation of torture in numerous international agreements, and the renunciation of torture as an instrument of official policy by virtually all of the nations of the world (in principle if not in practice), we find that an act of torture committed by a state official against one held in detention violates established norms of the international law of human rights, and hence the law of nations.[152]

No nation of which we are aware finds acceptable poisoning people or otherwise causing physical harm to others. Perhaps in time U.S. courts will conclude that:

In light of the universal condemnation in numerous international agreements of environmental pollution that harms people, and the renunciation of environmental policies that harm people by virtually all of the nations of the world (in principle if not in practice), harm to people resulting from environmental pollution violates established norms of the international law of human rights, and hence the law of nations, and is actionable under the Alien Tort Claims Act.

This kernel of consensus and its potential for contributing to the continued evolution of norms of international law are brought into clearer focus by recalling the distinction between negative rights (rights of forbearance) and positive rights (rights of entitlement) noted in Chapter 1. Negative rights are basically rights of noninterference and are respected when those we encounter exercise restraint (forbearance) by not intervening in our lives or the lives of others or otherwise curtailing what we wish to do. In contrast, positive rights (rights of entitlement) suggest that something is owed to the holder of the right, be it a paycheck, healthcare benefits, or any of a number of other things. We further suggested that natural rights (that is, rights that are present simply by virtue of the fact that someone is a human being, in contrast to conferred rights, which are contingent on the action of others) are best understood as negative rights and that the right to live is the most basic of these rights. Respecting this most basic of all human rights involves not only refraining from courses of action that results in the death of other people but also refraining from injurious acts that adversely affect their health and well-being.

The reference that Herz and others make to a "right to a healthy environment" is problematic. As we noted in Chapter 1, positive

---

[152] *Filártiga v. Pena-Irala*, 630 F.2d at 880.

rights (rights of entitlement) carry with them the notion that other identifiable individuals have an affirmative duty to make good on that to which someone is entitled – for example, a payroll clerk whose job it is to cut a check for the worker who is entitled to compensation. To speak of rights of entitlement without going on to address the question of whose job it is to make good on this right of entitlement makes little, if any, sense. Declarations of a "right to a healthy environment" sound great. But whose job is it to make good on this claimed right of entitlement if a volcanic eruption fills the air with ashes or an earthquake destroys villages and causes flooding?

On the other hand, narrowing environmental rights claim to claims of negative rights (rights of forbearance) such as the right not to be poisoned by the irresponsible behavior of others is a claim that makes more sense and both morally and legally – a claim that has "more teeth" to it.[153] Narrowing the definition of human rights in this way makes possible the identification of norms that are specific, universal and obligatory. Just as we know of no nation that views torture, extrajudicial killing, and genocide as morally acceptable courses of action, so also we know of no nation that condones environmental pollution that poisons people, thereby adversely affecting their health and well-being and hastening their deaths. This kernel of consensus sets the stage for the next chapter in the evolution of international law, evolution that is not the result of judicial creativity but rather evolution that stems from expanded but more precise common understandings of the nature of human rights.[154]

---

[153] Of course, adjudication of violations of negative rights (rights of forbearance) can lead to a certain type of positive right (right of entitlement) in the form of entitlement to compensation for the harm someone suffered at the hand of others, as was the case in *Filártiga v. Pena-Irala* and *Kadic v. Karadzic*.

[154] In an article entitled "The U.S. Can't Be the World's Court" that ran in the *Wall Street Journal* (May 27, 2009), John B. Bellinger III suggests, "Rather than continue to leave it solely to the federal judiciary to determine what violations of international law may be heard in U.S. courts, the Obama administration should ask Congress to revise the Alien Tort Statute to provide greater specificity regarding what actions it covers" (A19). And indeed, Congress could, if it so desired, revise the statute to make it more explicit. At present, however, there is no reason to believe that this will happen in the foreseeable future. Thus, the continued evolution of the Alien Tort Claims Act is likely to result from expanded but more precise common understandings of human rights than from Congressional action.

SUMMING IT ALL UP

We have come full circle. In Chapter 1, we suggested that greater precision in the use of the language of human rights is necessary if rights claims are to be meaningful, which is essentially what the 2nd Circuit Court of Appeals concluded in examining the Universal Declaration of Human Rights and other multinational declarations in *Flores v. Southern Peru Copper Corporation*, finding them to be aspirational in nature, rather than providing specific norms that can be used in adjudicating cases in a court of law.

Some might question whether using the Alien Tort Claims Act as an instrument to encourage multinational corporations to comply with appropriate ethical standards in their international operations is at all necessary. Are there not various codes of conduct that provide ethical guidelines for multinational corporations? As noted in previous chapters, there indeed are. Among these are the United Nations Global Compact's *Ten Principles*,[155] the Caux Round Table Principles for Business,[156] the Global Sullivan Principles of Social Responsibility,[157] and the Organization for Economic Cooperation and Development (OECD) guidelines for multinational corporations.[158]

Voluntary codes of conduct can encourage multinational corporations to think beyond the bottom line and help provide guidance for operations in other countries. Such being the case, they are useful. However, they are not without their limitations. In an article entitled "Between Self-Regulation and the Alien Tort Claims Act" published in *Law and Society Review* in 2004, Ronen Shamir observes:

At their best, voluntary codes of conduct can act as a guide to corporate practice and set standards for others to follow.... At their worst, they are little

---

[155] United Nations Global Compact, *Ten Principles* (accessible at http://www.unglobalcompact.org/AboutTheGC/TheTenPrinciples/index.html).

[156] *Caux Round Table Principles for Business*, included in *American Business Values: A Global Perspective* (5th ed.) by Gerald F. Cavanagh (Upper Saddle River, NJ: Pearson/ Prentice Hall, 2006), 356–361. The Caux Round Table Principles can also be accessed at http://www.cauxroundtable.org/principles.html.

[157] *The Global Sullivan Principles of Social Responsibility* at http://globalsullivanprinciples.org/principles.htm (last accessed October 27, 2006).

[158] Organization for Economic Cooperation and Development (OECD), *Guidelines for Multinational Enterprises (2001)* at http://www.olis.oecd.org/olis/2000doc.nsf/ LinkTo/NT00002F06/$FILE/JT00115758.PDF).

more than a public relations exercise. What is needed is a set of verifiable and enforceable guidelines covering all aspects of corporate activity.[159]

It is for this reason that we suggested in our discussion of the ethics of investing in China in Chapter 4 that effective monitoring of suppliers' codes of conduct and other codes of conduct is essential.

As noted in Chapter 4, the Asia Monitor Resource Centre (AMRC), a Hong Kong-based independent nongovernment organization (NGO) that focuses on Asian labor concerns,[160] conducted a study to determine the impact of codes of conduct on foreign-owned shoe manufacturing companies in China. They discovered that notwithstanding the codes of conduct, working conditions had actually deteriorated: "All categories of the companies' codes of conduct – health and safety, freedom of association, wages and benefits, hours of work, overtime compensation, nondiscrimination, harassment and child labor – are being violated."[161]

To be sure, one study of one manufacturing sector in one country does not prove that multinational corporations in general are indifferent to the codes of conduct to which they ascribe. The study of foreign-owned shoe manufacturing companies in China, however, does serve to remind us that just because multinational corporations state for the record that they ascribe to various codes of conduct does not necessarily mean that in practice these codes of conduct govern their operations. Sometimes outside pressure is necessary to encourage multinational corporations to comply with the principles they claim to espouse. In still other cases, there is no pretense of adhering to ethical guidelines governing their operations. In all of these cases, outside pressure in the form of litigation – or even just the threat of litigation – under the provisions of the Alien Tort Claims Act can move companies in the direction of doing what is right.

Granted, this is not easily accomplished. The lobbying group CorpWatch concedes, "Using [the Alien Tort Claims Act] to hold

---

[159] Shamir, "Between Self-Regulation and the Alien Tort Claims Act," 648.
[160] Asia Monitor Resource Centre, "About Us" at http://www.amrc.org.hk/text/about (last accessed November 24, 2008).
[161] Quoted by Alan Boyd in "Global Economy: Multinationals and Accountability," *Asia Times Online*, August 19, 2003, at http://www.atimes.com/atimes/Global_Economy/EH19Djo1.html (last accessed November 24, 2008).

corporations accountable for their actions overseas is not easy. The evidence is hard to gather and gaining jurisdiction is difficult." They add, however, "Yet [the Alien Tort Claims Act] is, potentially, a crucial instrument for holding U.S. companies to the basic standards of international law. It is one of the few deterrents to abusive behavior that can help protect villagers and indigenous people from anywhere in the world."[162]

The out-of-court settlement that Unocal ultimately agreed to pay to villagers in Myanmar (Burma) in order to settle *John Doe I v. Unocal Corporation* provides an example of the use that can be made of the Alien Tort Claims Act to defend the interests of those who are harmed by multinational corporations. As international law continues to evolve, it is reasonable to expect that there will be other situations in which U.S. federal courts provide remedies in cases brought under the Alien Tort Claims Act for those in other countries who have been harmed by the activities and operations of U.S. multinational corporations – unless, of course, more enlightened corporate policies ameliorate these problems by preventing harm to others, which in all cases would be vastly preferable to litigation.

[162] Quoted by Boyd in "Global Economy: Multinationals and Accountability."

Epilogue

In this volume, we have refrained from charging, as have so many social critics, that capitalism itself is corrupt and that the marketplace is inherently immoral. We have refrained from making this charge because (a) allegations of this sort are counterproductive, and (b) they are flat out mistaken. Benedict XVI was right on target in *Caritas in Veritate (Charity in Truth)* when he suggested that the market itself is not the cause of the problems that we are facing but rather these problems are the result of the use that is made of the market when "those at the helm are motivated by purely selfish ends." He observes, "Instruments that are good in themselves can thereby be transformed into harmful ones.... Therefore it is not the instrument that must be called to account, but individuals, their moral conscience, and their personal and social responsibility."[1]

But in a competitive global economy in which many are motivated by blind pursuit of profit, is greater social responsibility in the business world even possible? Is it realistic to think that appeals to conscience and calls for higher ethical standards can in any significant way diminish the human costs that have accompanied the rapid shift to a highly competitive global economy? We are optimistic enough to believe that such is possible.

---

[1] Benedict XVI, *Caritas in Veritate* (2009), 36, 40 at http://www.vatican.va/holy_father/benedict_xvi/encyclicals/documents/hf_ben-xvi_enc_20090629_caritas-in-veritate_en.html (last accessed August 21, 2009).

The question then becomes: What might be done to foster and nurture the capacity for justice in the business world and elsewhere? Or, to put this in slightly different words, what might be done to encourage high ethical standards in business? The following guidelines are worthy of consideration:

Guideline No. 1: It is essential that we all from time to time pause and think about what we are doing, rather than just plunge blindly ahead, and that we encourage others to do likewise.

Several years ago, a young naval intelligence officer received a severe dressing down from an admiral because he failed to think about the broader implications of the surveillance mission they were on, a mission that developed in an unexpected way. The admiral called a staff meeting to discuss the situation and asked the young naval officer what he recommended doing. Noting that this was not a covert mission in which they were maintaining radio silence and that they were regularly informing fleet headquarters of their whereabouts, the young naval officer replied, "Sir, our orders are to keep these folks under surveillance," adding that if fleet headquarters wanted them to do something different, fleet headquarters would let them know.

The admiral exploded as he slammed a fist on the small table at which they were seated while emphatically stating, "We always assume TOTAL responsibility for what we do!!" He then proceeded to use rather picturesque language to give expression to his assessment of the young naval officer's assessment of the situation. After what to the young naval officer seemed to be an eternity, the admiral asked, "Now what do you think we ought to do, lieutenant?"

"Sir," the young naval officer replied, "I recommend that we ask fleet headquarters whether they want us to continue the mission or break it off."

"Do it," the admiral ordered, having heard what he wanted to hear.

The young naval officer ordered the technician in his division in charge of communications to send a message to fleet headquarters noting the circumstances and inquiring as to whether to continue the mission or terminate it. Within a few minutes, a response from fleet headquarters came back ordering them to break off the mission rather than operate where they had no business operating and risk provoking an international incident.

Though the admiral could have used some improvement in his people skills, he was right and the young naval officer was wrong. The young naval officer was wearing blinders and had a very narrowly defined "orders are orders" understanding of what his job was. When that happens, the stage is set for all sorts of things going wrong, be it in the military, in the business world, or elsewhere.

As we look at what has gone wrong in the business world – and we all know that a good deal has gone wrong – it is easy to attribute it to greed, lust for power, and other forms of pernicious behavior. Behavior of this sort, of course, is not unknown in the business world (or elsewhere). Bernie Madoff is a prime example of this. Greed, lust for power, and other forms of pernicious behavior, however, are only part of the story. Many of the things that have gone wrong are the result of good people doing bad things. It is easy to rail at those who are greedy. It is far more difficult to understand how good people can do bad things.

Part of the answer to this puzzling question is that good people can end up doing bad things when they do not stop to ask the tough questions of themselves and of others and just plunge blindly ahead with a narrowly defined understanding of what their job is. In short, they are like the young naval officer.[2]

Guideline No. 2: It is essential that we increase our awareness of the humanity of other people and that we encourage others to do likewise.

Human nature being what it is, it is far easier to do things harmful to other people when we block from our consciousness awareness of their humanity. As Adam Smith correctly realized when developing his theory of fellow-feeling, we are more inclined to refrain from harming other people when we view them as fellow human beings and gain a sense of the pain they experience. It is for this reason that we argued in Chapter 2 that it is essential that we increase our awareness of the humanity of other people and that we encourage others to do likewise. As noted in Chapter 2, this is particularly challenging in a

---

[2] Daniel E. Lee, one of the coauthors of this book, was that young naval officer.

global economy when the decisions we make and the courses of action we take often have implications for people living in other countries – people we never see face-to-face. Yet increasing our awareness of the humanity of those whose lives intersect with ours, including distant neighbors we never see face-to-face, is something we must make every effort to do. Failure to recognize the humanity of other people, like failure to ask hard questions of ourselves and others, is a reason that good people sometimes do bad things.

Guideline No. 3: It is essential that the corporate culture affirm social responsibility and that the reward system encourage employees to act in an ethical manner.

Yet another reason that good people sometimes do bad things in the business world is that the corporate culture often does little, if anything, to promote social responsibility and encourage employees to act ethically. This, of course, is not universally the case. As noted in previous chapters, Target Corporation and Deere & Co. are two examples of companies that place strong emphasis on social responsibility and high ethical standards. We are naïve, however, if we think that all companies are like Target Corporation and Deere & Co. If such were the case, there would be no need for a book of this sort.

It is easy to say that all employees ought to do what is right even if they are not rewarded for so doing. Should not charity be done for the sake of charity, not for reasons of gaining personal recognition? In an ideal world, absolutely.

We do not live in an ideal world, however. In companies where the corporate culture does not affirm social responsibility and reward ethical conduct, those who wish to maintain high ethical standards often find themselves swimming against the current. There is a limit to how long anyone can swim against the current. Even the strong grow weary after awhile. Thus, it is not surprising that ethical people who find themselves swimming against the current sometimes end up, with various degrees of resignation, going along with policies and practices that harm other people.

An additional observation is here in order. In many companies and other organizations, it is the chief executive officer who sets the tone for the organization and, more than anyone else, defines the corporate culture. It is for this reason that a number of groups encouraging greater social responsibility – groups such as the Committee Encouraging Corporate Philanthropy (CECP)[3] – focus their efforts on CEOs.

In short, challenging people to think about the ethical implications of what they are doing, increasing awareness of the humanity of those whose lives intersect with ours, including distant neighbors we never see face-to-face, and fostering a corporate culture that expects ethical behavior and rewards those who act in an ethical manner can help ensure high ethical standards in business. Moral persuasion, however, is not enough. Justice will not be realized if we simply focus on humankind's capacity for justice while ignoring humankind's inclination to injustice. As Reinhold Niebuhr reminded us,[4] power must be challenged by power. Pressure must be brought to bear on companies inclined to injustice, be it in the form of public pressure of the sort that Oxfam International was able to bring to bear on Starbucks with respect to their business relations with coffee farmers in Ethiopia[5] or pressure in the form of litigation such as that involving Unocal's activities in Burma.[6]

Some cautionary notes, however, are here in order. It is essential that advocacy groups have verifiable facts to back up their allegations and that they be willing to engage in constructive dialogue with company officials. Oxfam International is very good at this and, as a result, is widely respected and viewed as a responsible voice for change, including by many in the business world. Other advocacy groups are not and do little more than succumb to righteous indignation as they vent their anger with little regard for the facts. In contrast, responsible advocacy groups such as Oxfam International contribute significantly to efforts to improve the lot of those adversely affected by globalization.

---

[3] Committee Encouraging Corporate Philanthropy, "About CECP: An Overview" at http://www.corporatephilanthropy.org/membership/ (last accessed September 15, 2008).

[4] Reinhold Niebuhr, *Moral Man and Immoral Society: A Study in Ethics and Politics* (New York: Charles Scribner's Sons, 1932), xiv-xv.

[5] Oxfam International, "Starbucks Signs Historic Agreement with Ethiopia" at http://www.maketradefair.com/en/index.php?file=starbucks_main.html (last accessed March 25, 2008). See also Oxfam America, "Starbucks Agrees to Honor its Commitments to Ethiopian Coffee Farmers" at http://www.oxfamamerica.org/whatwedo/campaigns/coffee/starbucks.

[6] *John Doe I v. Unocal Corporation*, 395 F.3d 932, 940 (9th Cir. 2002).

As in the case of advocacy groups such as Oxfam International that use the power of adverse publicity to bring pressure to bear on companies such as Starbucks, those resorting to litigation to address these issues would be well advised to have verifiable facts to back up their cases and to pursue these matters in a practical and appropriate manner. Righteous indignation, whether expressed in public attacks without the facts to back up the allegations that are made or in frivolous litigation similarly lacking in supporting evidence, accomplishes little, if anything, and often makes the situation worse, rather than better.

In summary, we are cautiously optimistic about what might be accomplished – optimistic because of humankind's capacity for justice but cautious because of humankind's inclination to injustice. It is for this reason that we encourage constructive engagement and dialogue, backed up by whatever constructive pressure can be brought to bear on those inclined to injustice.

Select Bibliography

Amnesty International USA. "Internal Migrants: Discrimination and Abuse" <http://www.amnestyusa.org/document.php?lang=e&id=ENGASA 170082007> (accessed September 23, 2008).

Amnesty International, "People's Republic of China: The Olympics Countdown – Three Years of Human Rights Reform?" (accessed August 5, 2005). <http://web.amnesty.org/library/Index/ENGASA17021205> (accessed September 8, 2006).

Bentham, Jeremy. *Anarchical Fallacies.* <https://www.college.columbia.edu/core/students/cc/settexts/bentanar.pdf> (accessed October 4, 2007).

Black Gold: A Film about Coffee and Trade <http://www.blackgoldmovie.com> (accessed February 13, 2008).

Buelna, Genoveva, and Rumana Riffat. "Preliminary Environmental Monitoring of Water Quality in the Rio Grande in the Laredo–Nuevo Laredo Region." *Journal of Environmental Science and Health,* 42 (2007), 1379–90.

Cañas, Jesús, Thomas M. Fullterton, Jr., and Wm. Doyle Smith. "Maquiladora Employment Dynamics in Nuevo Laredo." *Growth and Change,* 38 (March 2007): 23–38.

Caux Round Table Principles for Business. <http://www.cauxroundtable.org/principles.html> (accessed March 24, 2006).

Chalk, Frank. "The Anatomy of an Investment: Firestone's 1927 Loan to Liberia." *Canadian Journal of African Studies* 1 (March 1967): 13.

China Blue <http://www.pbs.org/independentlens/chinablue/film.html> (accessed September 18, 2008).

Committee Encouraging Corporate Philanthropy. "About CECP: An Overview" <http://www.corporatephilanthropy.org/membership/> (accessed September 15, 2008).

Constitution of the People's Republic of China <http://english.peopledaily.com.cn/constitution/constitution.html> (accessed October 13, 2006).

Cravey, Altha J. *Women and Work in Mexico's Maquiladoras.* Lanham, MD: Rowman & Littlefield Publishers, Inc., 1998.

D'Amato, Anthony. "The Alien Tort Statute and the Founding of the Constitution." *American Journal of International Law* 82 (1988): 62–63.

Davis, Jeffrey. "Human Rights in U.S. Courts: Alien Tort Claims Act Litigation after *Sosa v. Alvarez-Machian.*" *Human Rights Review* (July 2007): 362.

Ethiopian Coffee Network. "About the Trademarking and Licensing Initiative" <http://ethiopiancoffeenetwork.com/about.shtml> (accessed February 14, 2008).

Fair Factories Clearing House. "FFC Home" < http://www.fairfactories.org/> (accessed September 12, 2008).

Fairtrade Labelling Organizations International. "What Is Fair Trade?" <http://www.fairtrade.net/about_fairtrade.html> (accessed September 3, 2008).

Filártiga v. Pena-Irala, 630 F.2d 876 (2nd Cir. 1980).

Flores v. Southern Peru Copper Corporation. 414 F.3d 233, 254 (2nd Cir. 2003).

Friedman, Milton. *Capitalism and Freedom.* Chicago: University of Chicago Press, 1962.

   "The Social Responsibility of Business Is to Increase Its Profits." In Lisa H. Newton and Maureen M. Ford, eds., *Taking Sides: Clashing Views on Controversial Issues in Business Ethics and Society,* 9th ed. Guilford, CT: McGraw-Hill/Dushkin, 2006.

Glendon, Mary Ann. *A World Made New: Eleanor Roosevelt and the Universal Declaration of Human Rights.* New York: Random House, 2001.

   Rights Talk: The Impoverishment of Political Discourse. New York: The Free Press, 1991.

Global Exchange. "Fair Trade Farmers in Ethiopia" <http://www.globalexchange.org/campaigns/fairtrade/coffee/EthiopiaFlyer.pdf> (accessed March 14, 2008).

Global Reporting Initiative. "Reporting Framework" <http://www.global-reporting.org/ReportingFramework/AboutG3/G3GlossaryOfTerms.htm> (accessed December 1, 2006).

Global Sullivan Principles <http://globalsullivanprinciples.org/principles.htm> (accessed March 24, 2006).

Glueck, Sheldon. *The Nuremberg Trial and Aggressive War.* New York: Alfred A. Knopf, 1946.

Greenhalgh, Susan. "Women's Rights and Birth Planning in China: New Spaces of Political Action, New Opportunities for American Engagement" (testimony prepared for the Congressional Executive Commission on China) <http://www.cecc.gov/pages/roundtables/092302/greenhalgh.php> (accessed October 20, 2006).

Grotius, Hugo. *The Rights of War and Peace, Including the Law of Nature and of Nations.* Trans. A.C. Campbell. Washington, DC: M. Walter Dunne, Publisher, 1901.

Hesketh, Therese, and Zhu Wei Xing. "China's One-Child Family Policy (Letter to the Editor: The Authors Reply)." *New England Journal of Medicine* 354 (February 2006), 877.

Hesketh, Therese, Li Lu, and Zhe Wei Xing. "The Effect of China's One-Child Family Policy after 25 Years." *New England Journal of Medicine* 353 (September 2005), 1171–76.

Human Rights Watch. *Defend the Alien Tort Claims Act* <http://www.hrw.org/campaigns/atca/index.htm> (accessed October 21, 2008).

Human Rights Watch. *Mexico's National Human Rights Commission: A Critical Assessment.* <http://hrw.org/reports/2008/mexico0208/1.htm> (accessed September 25, 2008).

Information Office of the State Council of the People's Republic of China. *Human Rights in China* (1991) <http://news.xinhuanet.com/employment/200211/18/content_633179.htm> (accessed September 8, 2006).

International Coffee Organization. *International Coffee Agreement* 2007. <http://dev.ico.org/documents/ica2007e.pdf> (accessed March 25, 2008).

Jackson, Thomas R. "China's One-Child Family Policy (Letter to the Editor)." *New England Journal of Medicine* 354 (February 2006), 877.

Jefferson, Thomas. "Jefferson's 'Original Rough Draught' of the U.S. Declaration of Independence." *The Papers of Thomas Jefferson*, Vol. I. Ed. Julian P. Boyd. Princeton, NJ: Princeton University Press, 1950.

John Doe I v. Unocal Corporation, 395 F.3d 932, 940 (9th Cir. 2002).

Kadic v. Karadzic, 70 F.3d at 242–243 (2nd Cir. 1995).

Kaku, Ryuzaburo . "The Path of *Kyosei.*" *Harvard Business Review* 75 (July–August 1991), 55–63.

Lane, Robert W. "The Great Corporation: Vigorous Competition, Cardinal Virtues, and Value Creation" <http://www.deere.com/en_US/compinfo/speeches/2003/031028augustana.html> (accessed September 23, 2005).

Lewin, Bryan, Daniele Giovannucci, and Panos Varangis, *Coffee Markets: New Paradigms in Global Supply and Demand.* Washington, DC: International Bank for Reconstruction and Development, 2004.

Liebenow, J. Gus. *Liberia: The Quest for Democracy.* Bloomington: Indiana University Press, 1987.

Locke, John. *The Second Treatise of Government.* Ed. Thomas P. Peardon. Indianapolis: Bobbs-Merrill Company, Inc., 1952.

Maquilapolis <http://www.pbs.org/pov/pov2006/maquilapolis/about.html> (accessed September 26, 2008).

National Assembly of France. *Declaration of the Rights of Man.* <http://www.yale.edu/lawweb/avalon/rightsof.htm> (accessed October 4, 2007).

OECD Guidelines for Multinational Enterprises <http://www.oecd.org/dataoecd/12/21/1903291.pdf> (accessed March 24, 2006).

Organization of American States. *Additional Protocol to the American Convention on Human Rights in the Area of Economic, Social and Cultural Rights (1999)*

<http://www1.umn.edu/humanrts/oasinstr/zoas1ope.htm>   (accessed November 21, 2008).

Quintero-Ramírez, Cirila . "The North American Free Trade Agreement and Women." *International Feminist Journal of Politics* 4 (August 2002), 252.

Rainforest Alliance. "Ethiopian Coffee Farmers Lead the Way with First Rainforest Alliance Certification in Africa," <http://www.rainforest-alliance.org/news.cfm?id=africa_certification> (accessed January 23, 2008).

Rinehart, Robert. "Historical Setting." In Harold D. Nelson, ed., *Liberia: A Country Study*. Washington, DC: United States Government, 1985.

Shamir, Ronen. "Between Self-Regulation and the Alien Tort Claims Act: On the Contested Concept of Corporate Social Responsibility." *Law and Society Review* 38 (2004), 635–38.

Sherman, Gordon E. "Jus Gentium and International Law. *American Journal of International Law* 12 (January 1918), 56–63.

Smith, Adam . *The Theory of Moral Sentiments*. Indianapolis: Liberty Classics, 1976.

Sosa v. Alvarez-Machain, 542 U.S. at 714–15 (2004).

Target Corporation. "Corporate Responsibility" <http://sites.target.com/site/en/corporate/page.jsp?contentId=PRD03–004325>   (accessed September 12, 2008).

The Case against the Nazi War Criminals: Opening Statement for the United States of America by Robert H. Jackson and Other Documents. New York: Alfred A. Knopf, 1946.

Twiss, Sumner B. "History, Human Rights and Globalization." *Journal of Religious Ethics* 32 (2004), 39–70.

U.S. Department of State Bureau of Democracy, Human Rights, and Labor. *2008 Human Rights Report: China* (issued February 25, 2009) <http://www.state.gov/g/drl/rls/hrrpt/2008/eap/119037.htm> (accessed April 15, 2009).

U.S. Department of State Bureau of Democracy, Human Rights, and Labor. *Liberia Human Rights Report – 2008* (February 25, 2009) <http://www.state.gov/g/drl/rls/hrrpt/2008/af/119009.htm> (accessed September 21, 2008).

United Nations Global Compact. *Ten Principles* <http://www.unglobalcompact.org/AboutTheGC/TheTenPrinciples/index.html>   (accessed March 24, 2006).

United Nations. *International Covenant on Economic, Social and Cultural Rights* <http://www1.umn.edu/humanrts/instree/b2esc.htm>   (accessed October 15, 2007).

United Nations. *International Covenant on Civil and Political Rights* <http://www1.umn.edu/humanrts/instree/b3ccpr.htm> (accessed October 15, 2007).

United Nations. *Norms on the Responsibilities of Transnational Corporations and Other Business Enterprises with Regard to Human Rights* (2003) <http://www1.

umn.edu/humanrts/links/norms-Aug2003.html> (accessed November 21, 2008).

United Nations. *Preamble of the Charter of the United Nations.* <http://www. un.org/aboutun/charter/> (accessed October 13, 2007).

United Nations. *Universal Declaration of Human Rights.* <http://www.un.org/ Overview/rights.html> (accessed October 13, 2007).

VerSchoor, Curtis C., and Elizabeth A. Murphy. "The Financial Performance of Large U.S. Firms and Those with Global Prominence: How Do the Best Corporate Citizens Rate?" *Business & Society Review* 107 (Fall 2002), 378.

Index

act of state doctrine, 219, 225–26
Acton, John Emerich Edward
  Dalberg (Lord), 203
*African (Banjul) Charter on Human
  and Peoples' Rights*, 239
Aguinda v. Texaco, 224, 231–33
Alien Tort Claims Act (ATCA), xvi,
  34, 137–38, 204, 210–45; and
  grounds for dismissal, 219–27;
  evolution of, 211–12, 214–19,
  241–45; law of nations and,
  212–19; origin of, 210–11
All-China Federation of Trade
  Unions (ACFTU), 95–98
American Airlines, 107
American Chamber of Commerce
  (AmCham), 95–96
American Colonization Society.
  See Liberia, early history
American Federation of State,
  County, and Municipal
  Employees (AFSCME), 171
Amlon Metals, Inc. v. FMC Corp., 204
Amnesty International, 85, 101,
  133–34, 152, 188, 190
Anebo, Tsegaye, 148
Aquinas, Thomas, 5, 23–24n46
Aristotle, 49–51, 69, 77–78
Ashcroft, John, 230

Asia Monitor Resource Centre
  (AMRC), 111–12, 244
Augustine, 23–24n46

Baer v. United States, 27
Baker v. Carr, 226
Barth, Karl, 34
*Beanal v. Freeport-McMoran Copper
  and Gold, Inc.*, 231, 234–35
Beer, William, 177
Beijing, 83, 90–93, 102, 112
Benedict XVI, 203, 247
Bentham, Jeremy, 8–9, 20, 22
*Black Gold: A Film about Coffee and
  Trade*, 39, 43, 157
Blackstone, William 215–16, 218
Bolivia, 222
bona fide occupational
  qualifications (BFOQs),
  65–66, 65–66n14
Bose, 161
Bradford, William, 214–15
Brevard, Dave, 177
Burma (Myanmar), 211, 229–30,
  245, 251
Bush, George H.W., 91, 163, 171
Bush, George W., 90, 93, 102–03,
  230
Butler, Joseph, 9